T0302157

PRAISE FOR THE FIRST EDITION

A unique feature of the book is the HRD Score Card, which has been developed and tested by the author. This Score Card can be used to assess and benchmark the maturity level of the HRD function in organisations and make them business-driven.

Written in a readable and accessible style, this practice-based book includes several cases, examples, illustrations, detailed questionnaires and checklists.

~Business Line

There is a wide recognition that the HR function can be a key factor in business success and improved organizational performance. Yet, in many organizations, the HR function has either not performed up to expectations or has been unaware of its required role. Hence, a thorough evaluation of the HR function is imperative both to rejuvenate it and to make it more business-driven. HRD audit makes such an evaluation possible by examining the adequacy and appropriateness of the existing HRD systems.

~Financial Express

The HR function is the next horizon Indian firms are out to conquer. Rao's four parameters for good HR functions – HR linked to business, systems-driven HR, HR values and employee competencies – are today's catchphrases.

~Businessworld

HRD AUDIT

This book presents the first-ever comprehensive approach to evaluating and redesigning Human Resource Development (HRD) function and intervention to maximise their contribution to business excellence.

The HRD function recognises the significance of competent and committed people in helping organisations achieve excellence. Studies across the globe have indicated that good HR systems and practices go a long way to make firms effective. Competent employees, top management, HR staff and the HRD climate play a critical role. This book examines how users of HRD are partners in any review and evaluation. It uses multiple methods like interviews with stakeholders, observation, questionnaires, analysis of documents and workshops. The book also outlines key HRD audit methodologies to review and rejuvenate HRD and align it with business excellence, including intellectual capital building for the long term.

An incisive and invigorating read, this book would be useful to students, researchers, line managers, CEOs, CXOs and faculty of Human Resource Management, Organisational Behaviour and Applied Psychology. It would also be an invaluable handbook for practising business executives to help them implement performance management and other talent management systems, leading to excellence.

T. V. Rao is currently Chairman of T.V. Rao Learning Systems (started in Ahmedabad and now in Bangalore) and a former Professor at the Indian Institute of Management Ahmedabad. He has also worked as the L&T Professor of HRD at XLRI, Jamshedpur, between 1983 and 1985. Rao is the co-founder and first president of the National HRD Network and the first honorary director of the Academy of HRD, India. He was also President of the Indian Society for Applied Behavioural Science. He worked with

David McClelland of Harvard University (the initiator of the competency movement) and had joint research projects with him in the seventies. Rao was also a visiting faculty at the Indian Business School, Hyderabad, and was on the Boards of IIMA and GIM.

Rao has worked as a short-term consultant for UNESCO, USAID consultant to the Ministry of Health, Indonesia, the National Entrepreneurial Development Association, Malaysia, and the Commonwealth Secretariat, London. Rao has designed and assisted in implementing performance appraisals and other HRD systems for a number of organisations in India and a few other countries. His consulting experience includes designing and implementing performance management and other HR systems for various organisations like SAIL, NTPC, Indian Oil Corporation, HPCL, Bharat Petroleum, NALCO, SBI, Bank of Baroda, Neyveli Lignite, MRL, BEML, Reserve Bank of India, Larsen & Toubro, Voltas, Sundram Fasteners, EID Parry, TI Group, Crompton Greaves, Transpek Industries, BILT, NOCIL, IL&FS, Mahindra and Mahindra, Escorts, Tata Finance, Titan, Taj Group of Hotels, Tata Cummins, KPMG, ICI, Hindustan Levers, Pfizer, Chanrai Group (Nigeria), Indorama (Indonesia), Godfrey Phillips India, Amway, Nestle, Wockhardt, Wyeth, Fulford, Galfar, FAO, Rome, Commercial Bank (Sri Lanka), Hemas Group (Sri Lanka), CHR (Oman), Alexandria Carbon Black, Egypt, etc.

Rao, along with Udai Pareek, is credited with having established the first dedicated department of HRD at L&T in the mid-seventies, much before HRD was widely known. Rao has been working in the HRD field for the last 50 years and has over 60 books to his credit. Dr Rao was awarded HR Professional of the Year 2019 by the Asia Pacific Federation for HR Profession, Ravi Matthai Fellow by the Association of Indian Management Schools and Life time achievement by INDAM, Business World and many other bodies.

HRD AUDIT

Rejuvenating HR Function for Business Excellence

T. V. Rao

Routledge
Taylor & Francis Group

LONDON AND NEW YORK

Designed cover image: © phototechno / Getty Images

First published 2025
by Routledge
4 Park Square, Milton Park, Abingdon, Oxon OX14 4RN

and by Routledge
605 Third Avenue, New York, NY 10158

Routledge is an imprint of the Taylor & Francis Group, an informa business

© 2025 T. V. Rao

British Library Cataloguing-in-Publication Data
A catalogue record for this book is available from the British Library

ISBN: 978-1-032-87026-7 (hbk)
ISBN: 978-1-032-83294-4 (pbk)
ISBN: 978-1-003-53053-4 (ebk)

DOI: 10.4324/9781003530534

Typeset in Sabon
by Deanta Global Publishing Services, Chennai, India

For Jaya, Raju, Nandini and Kritika

CONTENTS

ILLUSTRATIONS

Figure

Tables

FOREWORD

Has the following ever happened to you or your company?

- After months of working on a future vision, mission and values, a dramatic roll-out occurs with video, brochures and employee meetings. Six months later, most employees have not changed their behaviour; the firm faces the same challenges, and senior management loses some credibility about being able to deliver what they promise.
- New technology promises a new business model. But, after acquiring both the hardware and software, many of the anticipated outcomes fail to follow. Technology promises are unfulfilled; information management does not lead to business success.
- A new leader arrives with great hope. Through competitive analysis, a bold new strategy is declared with expected investor and customer results. However, after months into the effort and changing the organisation reporting relationships, results are delayed, then missed and, finally, the strategy is realigned.
- A new performance management system (PMS) is introduced: pay and incentives linked to performance, and committee constituted to ensure equity and distribution of ratings; detailed manuals prepared; key performance areas (KPAs) identified; goal setting done in a transparent way and made accessible on the intranet for all; workshops held and all employees educated; and links with training streamlined and automated. Months after the system is introduced, employee morale due to the new PMS goes down rather than to increase.

Unfortunately, these and similar experiences happen all too often because of three false assumptions. First, competitiveness is not strategy. Building a direction for an organisation does not make it more competitive. Without being able to turn direction into action, strategy statements lack vitality. Competitiveness equals Strategy x Organisation. This equation implies that the strategy espoused must turn into organisational action to deliver results. Aspiring, bold statements of purpose need to become real to employees through organisation processes.

Second, organisation is not structure. Changing an organisation's structure or shape through technology, process reengineering, human resource (HR) systems or reporting relationships matters less than changing the underlying capabilities embedded within a firm. An 'organisation' may be defined as a combination of talent, leadership, and capability. Talent represents the competence and commitment of employees in the firm; leadership refers to the collective individuals who make decisions about the future of the firm; capabilities represent what a company does well (e.g., Marriott manages food and lodging through dedicated people; Southwest Airlines ensures a positive customer experience through discipline for on-time arrival and employee creativity and service). Changing organisation structure, systems, or process without upgrading talent, leadership, and capability will not endure.

Third, because of the first two assumptions, HR does not equal HR. Traditionally, 'human resources' is a function mired in administrative processes, focused on building systems that police employees and restrain managers. Increasingly, HR delivers value to employees (more productivity), customers (higher quality products and services with reduced costs), and investors (more financial success, including share price) through delivering talent, leadership, and capability through innovative, integrated, and aligned HR practices.

If HR professionals are to deliver more value, they must learn how to define their outcomes (talent, leadership, and capability) much more clearly. They must then have the capacity to align their HR investments to those outcomes. Next, they must transform their HR department and themselves as HR professionals to deliver this value. Failing to transform HR into value-adding HR will result in outcomes like the ones mentioned earlier.

The *HRD Audit* offers the discipline that business leaders require to deliver on their goals and ensures that HR professionals know how to deliver more value. The book presents a comprehensive approach to evaluating how well your human resource development (HRD) function and interventions are contributing to business goals through talent, leadership, and capabilities. The book presents a variety of methodologies for evaluating HRD and its impact using observation, questionnaires, interviews, workshops, examination of records, etc.

The book presents a good amount of evidence on the linkages between HRD and business performance and offers a systematic way of enhancing HRD value and impact. Chief executive officers (CEOs), line managers, all corporate employees, and particularly all professional HR Managers will find these ideas extremely useful tools for delivering business results and upgrading the HR function as well as the HR professionals.

The book offers specific insights and tools on how to turn business aspirations into human capital goals (talent, leadership, and capability), and then how to transform the HR department, HR practices, and HR professionals to make this happen.

The ideas for HR audits presented in this book will help line managers take more ownership of HR's contribution to business success. In addition, it will help HR professionals play very different roles. They will become coaches, architects, builders, and facilitators. As coaches, they provide line managers with personal feedback to improve performance. As architects, they create blueprints that turn organisational ideas into choices and actions. As builders, they design and deliver HR systems and practices that enhance talent and implement strategy. As facilitators, they manage the process of change for teams and organisations. These are new roles for HR professionals; they will require HR professionals to review the past and focus on the future.

HRD audit is a useful tool to make a new beginning and let go of the past. It provides a milestone in HR transformation. It needs leadership, courage, and perseverance on the part of the HR directors and their CEOs to evaluate their HR systems, practices, and competencies and enhance their business impact and value addition.

In this direction, this book is a great contribution from Prof. T.V. Rao to enhance the value proposition of HR.

Dave Ulrich
Professor, Ross School of Business, University of Michigan
Partner, the RBL Group
1 March 2014

PREFACE TO THE SECOND EDITION

The second edition of this book is being brought out nearly a decade and a half after the first edition. I am happy that the first edition was received very well and even got translated into other Indian languages (Marathi). HRD audit is perhaps the first book of its kind across the globe. Subsequent to the publication of the first edition of the book, we trained a large number of HR and line managers in India and other countries like Egypt, Malaysia, Sri Lanka, and Thailand. Interest in the HRD Audit is being shown in other countries like South Africa and the Gulf region. Many HR managers want the audit to be converted into measurable indices. We introduced the concept of the HRD Score Card in the first edition itself in 1999. However, we had not offered a point system. Based on our experience before the first edition and subsequent to it, we developed a point system. The point system ensured that the audit resulted in measures of maturity of systems, strategies, competencies, culture and values, and business linkages or business impact of HR. A total of 2500 points were assigned for various dimensions. In the last decade, the concept of human capital and intellectual capital has gained prominence. Accordingly, the HRD Score Card 2500 book took into account all such developments in human capital measurement.

In this edition, I have aligned the chapters with the HRD Score Card 2500. The HRD Score Card 2500 itself was based on the first edition of the HRD Audit and developments thereafter. I am happy to bring this alignment as it now makes a lot more sense to use this book in conjunction with the HRD Score Card 2500. Only marginal modifications were required for this purpose. Styles were taken as a part of the competencies of the line managers and top management. New literature was added on the impact of HR

xvi Preface to the Second Edition

practices on business outcomes. A detailed assessment of the HRD Score Card has been presented and HRD audit as an organisational development (OD) intervention was added. Almost about 30 per cent of new content has been added and 10 per cent has been dropped. Many new references have been added.

I hope this new edition helps HR managers, their unit heads and CEOs to understand what makes HR impactful and how to measure the impact of HR on human and intellectual capital formation, thereby improving their human capital. This book also makes it clear that HR is not the business of HR people alone. It is the business of all employees. We expect all organisations to benefit from this book by gaining insights into the role of human capital in organisational effectiveness and the means of forming and managing such human capital.

Dr Dave Ulrich is one person who has inspired thousands of HR leaders across the globe with his thoughts, books and talks. It is nice to begin this book with his 'Foreword'. I am grateful to Dr Dave Ulrich who has promptly written the Foreword to this book.

T.V. Rao

PREFACE TO THE FIRST EDITION

Human resource development in India has a rich history and has come a long way in the past two decades. Liberalisation of the economy and its movement towards globalisation have brought in new challenges for Indian business in terms of business strategies, technology, quality concerns, cost-effectiveness, management systems, etc. All these, in turn, have brought new challenges for the HR function. If HRD was promoted as a responsibility of CEOs and the top management in the eighties, it has become a business necessity in the nineties. In the eighties, we used to argue that an average employee gives more than 60 per cent of his waking life to the organisation and that the organisation is his first family. We therefore argued that it was the responsibility of the top management to ensure that the employees find their work enjoyable and satisfying. The organisation should ensure that they have good careers, receive rewards, training, feedback, job rotation and other such development opportunities. Although we had adopted a systems approach even in those days, the emphasis was more on HRD as a philosophy, as a value and culture of a corporation. Profits were taken for granted, and the argument was that since the employees contribute so much to the corporation, the corporation should take care of them. When the corporation takes care of its people, they, in turn, will also take care of the corporation. Thus, people were put first in HRD and business goals were taken for granted.

In the post-liberalisation period, with several businesses being threatened by global competition, the focus of HRD has shifted to establishing direct links with business improvement. If the corporation does not survive, there is little it can do to take care of its employees. There will be no careers, no rewards, no job rotations, no training and, in fact, no jobs. Hence, business survival has become a significant and non-negotiable goal, and all HRD efforts have to be redirected towards business goals. HRD systems, relevance and synergy have become more important than before, and the business goals have become sharply focused. It is this shift that has necessitated a relook at the HRD function and its implementation. Another trend that has taken place in India with the multiplication of HRD is the indiscriminate appointment of HRD managers. In the eighties, some of the corporations, in their eagerness to be in tune with the times, renamed their training centres as HRD centres without changing anything else, and a few others re-designated their personnel managers as HRD managers (HRD standing for the human resource department rather than human resource development). This has also created some confusion in the profession, as several corporations had large HRD or HR departments with 'development' missing or very inadequately focused. Even professional bodies like the Indian Society of Training and Development (ISTD) and the National Institute of Personnel Management (NIPM) have unknowingly contributed to this confusion, though with good intentions, by mostly retitling their conferences as HRD conferences. As a result, the attention paid to HRD has got diluted. There are quite a few HR departments today that do not pay adequate attention to development. Yet, in the post-liberalisation era, competence building, commitment building and culture building have become important concerns of corporations. Many CEOs have begun to wonder why competence building is not taking place in spite of their large HR departments. Line managers are also becoming disillusioned with the HRD staff. And while 'human resource development' has got mixed up with 'human resource department', the new HRD manager has often been reduced to becoming a recruitment manager or a compensation manager or, at best, a rewards manager. In all these cases, the old personnel function has once again got back into the driver's seat with limited business concerns.

It is in response to these changes and with the intention to refocus HRD on business goals, business linkages, competence building, commitment building and culture building that we at T.V. Rao Learning Systems (TVRLS) initiated a comprehensive HRD audit programme in the early nineties. Our intention was also to come up with a rating to be given to each corporation on the basis of their HRD status. Initially, we worked with individual corporations to conduct the HRD audit. It was during this period that the HRD audit seemed to have caught the attention of Mr Aditya Vikram Birla, who asked all his companies to get themselves audited by consultants. During this period, we also brought out a comprehensive HRD audit questionnaire and methodology. The questionnaire was made available through the Academy of HRD and HRD Network to a number of consultants and professionals. The first software was developed and marketed by the Academy of HRD through Equinox and later by TVRLS through Software Creations, a Delhi-based software systems company. TVRLS has taken up the task of doing further research work and also promoting the development of internal auditors. The company has started developing internal auditors through HRD audit programmes. Benchmarking data are being collected on the basis of consultancies done by TVRLS as well as through sponsored research. Detailed manuals are being developed to promote and make the audit easier. An HRD Score Card has been proposed, which I have elaborated on in this book. We hope that this HRD Score Card will enable corporations to assess their HRD and eventually even include it in their balance sheets.

Why This Book?

This book is essential to place HRD in the right perspective. Many corporations have invested a great deal in HRD. They have started new HR departments, given top-level positions to HR personnel, created reasonable budgets and expect the HR function to provide a strategic advantage to their corporations. Unfortunately, only a few corporations have experienced success. The failure of HRD in some corporations is indicated by the fact that, for the first time in India, some corporations have asked their HRD chiefs to leave, downsized their HR departments or replaced HR chiefs with line managers who are not as well trained in HRD. By themselves, all these may not be bad decisions. And there are still a large number of corporations that are not able to take such tough decisions and are willing to carry the HR function along.

Recent research and surveys from the West indicate the importance of the human factor in successful corporations. They also indicate the strategic role human resources can play. If this is true, why is it that some corporations fail to use their human resources for their strategic advantage, while others use it to build strong and lasting organisations and institutions? This is where a comprehensive evaluation of the HR function can provide useful insights. An HRD audit, perhaps, is an answer, and that is what this book is about. The book intends to provide a comprehensive evaluation of the HR function in an effort to align it with business goals and strategies. This book presents the need for an HRD audit, gives in detail the various aspects of HRD that should be looked at for a comprehensive evaluation and also presents an in-depth methodology to assess HRD in all its aspects, including its relevance. This book then goes on to propose a new measure called the HRD Score Card to grade organisations with respect to their HRD maturity. It proposes a four-dimensional assessment. The four dimensions include (*i*) the extent of maturity of the corporation in terms of its HRD systems, (*ii*) HRD structure and competencies (of HRD managers, line managers, the top management, and the workmen and their representatives), (*iii*) HRD culture and values and (*iv*) business impact of HRD and its strategies in terms of intellectual capital, talent management and firm's performance. The HRD audit methodology outlined in this book should be able to assist any corporation in internally evaluating its HRD systems. This book also aims to help the concerned HR personnel to become internal auditors who can periodically audit and rejuvenate their HRD function. I hope this book will help managers, HRD professionals, CEOs, consultants, academicians, students and all those involved in HRD to uplift the HR function and utilise its full potential for building competent and lasting organisations.

ACKNOWLEDGEMENTS

In all the work reported here, Dr Udai Pareek was a friend, collaborator and a well-wisher. I wish to acknowledge his continuous support in the past few years of working together on quite a few audits. Dr E. Abraham joined in some of these audits. Dr M.J. Jomon, who worked as an Associate Consultant at TVRLS, has completed his doctoral dissertation to study the impact of HRD audit as an intervention. He followed up the cases of four corporations where I had conducted HRD audits and studied the changes that had taken place in these corporations as a result of the audit. He has made the first audit data available for comparison purposes to me with the permission of these corporations. The results of Jomon's research, giving details of factors relating to the use of the audit, are presented in one of the chapters.

My special thanks to Ms M. Vijayalakshmi, Associate at TVRLS, for going through the manuscript and making a number of editorial suggestions. I also thank Mrs Merlin George, Mr Santosh Kumar, also at TVRLS, who have assisted me from time to time in various HRD audit programmes. Special thanks to the CIPM Sri Lanka and Open University of Malaysia for facilitating various HRD audit programs in both the countries. Dr. Raju Rao, Director and Ms. Nandini Chawla CEO, TVRLS have been part of many audits and programmes. Special thanks to the CIPM Sri Lanka and Open University of Malaysia for facilitating various HRD audit programs in both the countries. Dr. Raju Rao, Director and Ms. Nandini Chawla CEO, TVRLS have been part of many audits and programs.

I thank all the corporations that had the courage to evaluate themselves and the wisdom to see the need for an external evaluation. I hope this book will inspire others to evaluate their own HRD function.

T.V. Rao

LETTER TO CEO/CHRO/CXO

Dear CEO/CHRO/CXO,

Research and experience from several countries, including India, have demonstrated beyond doubt that good HR practices can go a long way in increasing organisational effectiveness, operational efficiency, profits, stakeholder value, customer service, quality, intellectual capital and many more variables of significance. Though the relationship is not simple and is being investigated, evidence is clear that intermediate variables like employee commitment, motivation and engagement, etc., are directly affected by good HR practices. Working in these areas over the past three decades, we have been able to demonstrate that a systematic evaluation of HRD systems (including how well they are structured, communicated and implemented) will help streamline HR practices and develop new ones. Our work also indicates that to make this happen, what is needed is a competent HR department with competent staff, positive attitudes of line managers and workmen to learn and top management who have an empowering and developmental style to create the right culture in their organisation. Research also has shown the importance of organisational culture and values in influencing employee productivity and firm output.

By now, there are well-tested-out and established HRD principles and practices. However, not all corporations are getting the best from this knowledge and making efforts to enhance their HR practices. HRD udit is a means of assessing how mature the current HRD systems are. It also aims at assessing the extent to which they are continuously building the capabilities of HR staff, line managers, workmen and top management to facilitate and manage good HRD, which results in stakeholder value, intellectual capital and even achieving profits and productivity.

There is nothing to be afraid of in an HRD audit. *Audit is a term that is used to create a base for renewal and enhance the internal efficiency and effectiveness of HR practices.* In recent times, we have come across HR professionals who are hesitant to get their HRD audited for fear of criticism. Without assessment, we don't know where we stand, and without knowing where we stand and then undertaking development activities, improvements are unlikely. An HRD Audit is not a criticism of the past, or of individuals or the HR departments. It aims at finding opportunities and gaps for creating an enabling future and strengthening the systems and capabilities of corporations. CEOs, CHROs and even the CXOs should get their HRD audited as explained in this book. Such an audit could be carried out by well-trained internal facilitators. An internal audit of HR once every three to five years can go a long way in building sustainable corporations that do well in this competitive world.

I hope you will read at least the first chapter of this book to see how HR practices influence organisational outcomes and impact. If convinced, you will use internal teams and train them to be internal auditors to do the audit for your corporation. Post-pandemic, the last few years have seen significant developments in HR. The significance of "People" in any business activity has enormously increased and has been recognised in all sectors of life. So is the significance of the HR profession. This edition rightly focuses on "Rejuvenating the HR Profession". In helping your HR systems and practices to rejuvenate, all CEOs and CXOs are enhancing the effectiveness of their own organization or function as no one can perform well without "People".

T.V. Rao

ABOUT THE AUTHOR

T.V. Rao is Chairman of T.V. Rao Learning Systems Pvt. Ltd, Ahmedabad, a company devoted to behaviour systems and HR research and consultancy. He worked as a Professor at the Indian Institute of Management, Ahmedabad between 1973 and 1994 and subsequently as a Visiting Professor until 2014. He started the Centre for HRD at XLRI, Jamshedpur in 1983 and founded the National HRD Network in 1985. He also served as Larsen & Toubro Professor of HRD at XLRI, Jamshedpur, and as a Visiting Research Associate at Harvard University in the early part of his career, where he worked with the late David C. McClelland.

A pioneer in the field of HRD in India, Dr Rao was associated with setting up the first HRD department in the Indian corporate sector in Larsen & Toubro and also worked as General Manager, HRD at Bharat Earth Movers Ltd. He has been a consultant to many organisations in India and abroad. He has authored, co-authored and co-edited over 50 books in the areas of HRD, organisational behaviour and performance management. Among them are *Human Resources Development: Experiences, Interventions, Strategies* (SAGE, 1996); *Organisation Development: Interventions and Strategies* (co-editor, SAGE Response, 1998); *HRD Score Card 2500* (SAGE Response, 2008); *The Power of 360 Degree Feedback* (SAGE, 2005); and *Performance Appraisal and Management for Global Competitiveness* (SAGE Response, 2005). Dr Rao has personally supervised and conducted HRD audits for several organisations in India and abroad and trained auditors in India and Malaysia through his company TVRLS in recent years.

SECTION 1

Introduction

Good HRD practices can influence financial and other performance indicators of corporations by generating employee satisfaction and commitment, which in turn can influence customer satisfaction. Recent studies across the world confirm this. Most successful corporations believe that it is their people who provide them with a competitive advantage. The mission statements, annual reports, value outlines, vision statements and training calendars of these corporations reflect the great value that they attach to their employees. Yet many organisations have been unable to cash in on such top management commitment and translate it to build credibility for the HR profession. Even nearly 40 years after the first HRD department was established in the Indian corporate sector, HR professionals in many corporations seem not adequately concerned about what good HR practices are and how one can link them with business.

What are good HR practices? How can one rate the status of a corporation's HRD? On what dimensions can such a business-driven HRD be assessed? How can one go about making such an assessment? These are some basic questions that this book seeks to answer in Section One, consisting of the first three chapters. This section also briefly introduces the concept of the HRD Score Card, a concept that is referred to throughout this book as a measure of good HR practices. This section reviews the research studies and other evidence available from the West as well as from India to show that good HR practices do have an impact on the business performance of corporations. Such research, demonstrating the linkages between good HR practices and achieving business goals, is on the increase globally.

DOI: 10.4324/9781003530534-1

With increased research evidence of the linkages between HR practices and business development, corporations are getting more interested in establishing good HR practices. The elements of such HR practices are described in the second chapter of this section. The third chapter introduces the concept of HRD audit and also spells out why some corporations undertake an HRD audit.

1

GOOD HR PRACTICES CAN MAKE A DIFFERENCE

There is little doubt that good HR practice has a tremendous influence on business outcomes. There is ample research and experimental data to suggest this. While data from the West comes from systematic researches, the Indian experience is documented in case studies of successful corporations and reports. This chapter presents research studies from the West as well as some Indian case studies to conclusively show that good HR practices do indeed make a difference in terms of business effectiveness.

What Constitutes Good HR Practices?

Any practice that deals with enhancing competencies, commitment and culture building can be considered an HR practice. The practice can take the form of a system, a process, an activity, a norm, a rule, an accepted or expected habit, or just a way of doing things. HRD has been defined as essentially consisting of these three Cs: Competencies, Commitment and Culture. All three are needed to make an organisation function well. Without competencies, many tasks of the organisation may not be completed cost-effectively or with optimal efficiency. Without commitment, they may not be done at all or are done at such a slow pace that they lose relevance. Without an appropriate culture, organisations cannot last long. Culture provides the sustaining force and spirit for organisations to live. It provides the oxygen needed for them to survive. Its utility comes to the fore especially when organisations are in trouble.

Competencies are not merely related to a single individual. They can also relate to pairs of individuals, for example, the boss and his or her subordinate, two departmental heads, two managers or any two people who

DOI: 10.4324/9781003530534-2

transact organisation-related activities. When a particular boss–subordinate meet, they could have such a high mutually empowering attitude and style that they end up doing many more things and more effectively than other pairs in the same organisation. Similarly, two departmental heads may have a high degree of conflict–resolution capability so that their transactions are extremely smooth even when their tasks may require them to pull in seemingly two different directions (e.g., cost reduction versus stocking inventory to take care of unexpected raw material shortages). Competencies may also relate to a team or a group of individuals. This includes departments, task forces, teams and other formal or informal groups and/or teams that may come into existence from time to time on a temporary, permanent or semi-permanent basis. Competencies may also be related to the organisation as a whole. They may also deal with various areas and functions: technology, organisation and management, behavioural, conceptual, etc. They may include a variety of skills and abilities ranging from simple awareness, knowledge and information to highly sophisticated and complex ones. Attitudes, values and habits also become competencies though they more often deal with patterns of working. Developing commitment has a lot to do with motivation and work habits. Commitment is indicated by work effort, zeal, involvement and enjoyment of the work or the job. Commitment building and its management are very much an HR function. Management of commitment should go beyond incentives and rewards. Commitment should be continuous and become part of life. Commitment building should be at the level of individuals, dyads, teams, the work unit and the entire organisation. Various HR systems, processes and activities contribute to developing commitment among employees. At the more visible level, rewards, recognition and similar interventions can lead to greater commitment and motivation. At the less visible level, managerial style, work culture, the behaviour of seniors towards their juniors, etc., influence commitment. Unlike competencies that once developed are difficult to lose, it is easy to lose commitment, though it can be as easily gained. For instance, a particular personnel policy may demotivate some employees to the extent that they stop giving their best. At the same time, a particular reward system or practice may have a high motivational value. Often, an individual does not respond to all interventions in the same way in terms of commitment. Thus, salary increases may have a high motivational value at one time, whereas even higher compensation increases may not cut much ice on another occasion. It is the job of an HR manager to be in constant touch with the employees and be aware of the HR systems, tools and interventions that can keep their motivation and commitment levels high.

A strong culture can have a lasting effect and provide sustenance to an organisation. It gives a sense of pride and identity to individuals and teams. It enhances predictability, reduces transactional costs and also contributes to commitment. However, the culture and values associated with an organisation need to be appropriate and well articulated. The instruments of culture building include organisational climate surveys, total quality management (TQM) interventions, value-clarification exercises, vision–mission workshops, organisational renewal exercises and various other OD interventions.

Good HR practices are those that contribute to one or more of the three Cs – Competencies, Commitment and Culture – described previously. They need to be identified and implemented cost-effectively, reviewing and revising them from time to time to enhance their effectiveness and appropriateness.

Research evidence Relating Good HR Practices to Business improvement

Recent researches worldwide have shown that good HR practices and policies can go a long way in influencing business growth and development. The researches indicate the following HR practices that effective firms adopt (Pfeffer, 1994):

- Financial incentives for excellent performance
- Work organisation practices that motivate employee effort and capture the benefits of know-how and skill
- Rigorous selection and selectivity in recruiting
- Higher-than-average wages
- Employee share-ownership plans
- Extensive information sharing
- Decentralisation of decision making and empowerment
- Work organisation based on self-managing teams
- High investment in training and skill development
- Having people do multiple jobs and job rotation
- Elimination of status symbols
- A more compressed distribution of salaries across and within levels
- Promotion from within
- A long-term perspective
- Measurement of HR practices and policy implementation
- A coherent view of employment relations

Yeung and Berman (1997) point out that HR practices can play three major roles. These are as follows:

1. Building critical organisational capabilities
2. Enhancing employee satisfaction
3. Improving customer and shareholder satisfaction

The following studies summarised by Yeung and Berman (1997: 323–324) can help us understand the linkages.

Macduffie and Krafcik (1992) studied 70 automotive assembly plants representing 24 companies and 17 countries worldwide. This study indicated that manufacturing facilities with 'lean production systems' are much higher in terms of both quality and productivity than those with 'mass production systems'. For example, those with lean systems took 22 hours to produce a car and with a quality benchmark of 0.5 defects, whereas those with mass systems took 30 hours and 0.8 defects for 100 vehicles. The HR strategy of a mass production system was to create a highly specialised and de-skilled workforce to support a large-scale production process, while that of the lean system was to create a skilled, motivated and flexible workforce that could continuously solve problems. The study concluded that the success of the lean production system depended on high commitment of employees, decentralisation of production responsibilities, broad job classification, multi-skilling practices, profit/gain sharing, a reciprocal psychological commitment between firm and employees, employment security and a reduction of status barriers.

Ostroff (1995) developed an overall HR Quality Index based on the aggregate ratings of all HR activities of a firm. On the basis of this index, firms were grouped into four categories. The firms that scored higher on the HR Quality Index consistently outperformed than those with a lower index on four financial measures: market/book value ratio, productivity ratio (i.e., sale/employees), market value and sales. Pfeffer (1998) has more recently reviewed considerable evidence on the effectiveness of good HR practices on business performance. Some of it is summarised below.

Macduffie (1995, cited by Pfeffer, 1998: 32) observed from his studies that innovative HR practices are likely to contribute to improved economic performance only when

1. Employees possess knowledge and skills managers lack
2. Employees are motivated to apply this skill and knowledge through discretionary effort
3. Employees contribute to such an effort

Huselid (1995) used two scales – one to measure employee skills and organisational structure and the second to measure employee motivation. The first scale included a broad range of practices intended to enhance employee knowledge, skills, and abilities (KSAs) and provide mechanisms to use those for performing the roles. The second scale measured how well designed the appraisal systems were and how well they were linked to compensation and merit decisions in the corporation.

Huselid (1995) found that in a sample of 3,452 firms representing all kinds of industries, one standard deviation increase in management practices was associated with increases in sales, market value and prof- its. A subsequent study by Huselid and Becker (1997) found that a one standard deviation improvement in HR system index was associated with an increase in shareholder wealth of US\$41,000 per employee.

Similar results were found in Germany by Bilmes et al. (1997). This study found a strong link between investing in employees and the stock market performance of the corporation. Companies that placed workers at the core of their strategies produced higher long-term returns than those who did not.

Welbourne and Andrews (1996) studied the survival rate of 136 non-financial companies that initiated public offerings in the US stock market in 1988. The firms studied were drawn from various industries ranging from food service retailing to biotechnology and varied in size from less than 110 people (about 50 per cent of them) to 700 or more (about 20 per cent of them). They developed and used a scale to measure the value the firm placed on human resources. This scale used five items:

1. Whether the company's strategy and mission statement cited employees as constituting a competitive advantage
2. Whether the company's initial publicity material mentioned employee training programmes
3. Whether a company's official was charged with the responsibility for human resource management (HRM)
4. The degree to which the company used full-time employees rather than temporary or contract workers
5. The company's self-rating on office–employee relations.

A second scale measured how the organisation rewarded its people, that is, whether through stock options, gain sharing, profit sharing, etc. The study indicated that with the other factors, such as the size, nature of industry and profits controlled, the HR scale and the rewards scale were significantly related to the probability of survival.

In a 1989 study by Macduffie (1995) covering 70 automobile plants representing 24 companies from 17 different countries, the traditional mass production system with a control-oriented approach to managing people was contrasted with a flexible production system that placed emphasis on people and their participation. In the traditional systems of management practice the emphasis was on the control-oriented approach to manage people, building inventories to maintain production volumes against uncertainties and inspection and control to ensure quality. In contrast, in the flexible system, the emphasis was on teams, employee involvement and reduction of inventories to highlight production problems that could be remedied. The results revealed that quality and productivity were much higher in the flexible rather than in the mass production system and the two systems differed substantially on how they managed their people – in terms of emphasis on training, use of teams, reduction of status differences and the use of contingent performance-related compensation.

Arthur (1994) studied the impact of two different management approaches on the productivity of steel mills. His study of 30 of the 44 existing steel mills in the US at that time differentiated the 'control' approach to HRM from that of the 'commitment' approach. In the control approach the goal of HRM is to reduce labour costs or improve efficiency by enforcing employee compliance with specified rules and procedures and basing employee rewards on some measurable output criteria. In the commitment approach the HR systems are intended to shape desired employee behaviours by forging psychological links between organisational goals and employee goals. The focus is on developing committed employees. After statistically controlling for age, size, union status and business strategy of the mills, the results showed that using a commitment strategy was significantly related to improved performance in terms of labour hours and scrap rate. Mini-mills using the commitment approach required 34 per cent fewer labour hours to produce a ton of steel and showed a 63 per cent better scrap rate.

'A number of studies spanning different organisations operating in various service industries provide evidence for a positive relationship between employee attitudes, customer service and satisfaction and profits' (Pfeffer, 1998: 55). Schneider and Bowen (1985) reported in a study of bank branches that when the branches had sufficient numbers and quality of people to perform its tasks (called the service imperative) customers reported receiving higher levels of service. In another study Schneider (1991) found that customer perceptions and attitudes were affected by what employees experienced. Organisational practices that are both service related and human resources related seem to provide cues to customers to evaluate a bank's service.

A study by Johnson et al. (1994) at the Ford Motor Credit revealed that attitudes concerning workload, teamwork, training and development, satisfaction with the job and satisfaction with the company were all related to customer satisfaction. Schmit and Allscheid (1995) found that customer satisfaction and perceptions of service quality were significantly related to measures of employee attitudes about the fairness of pay, whether management was concerned about employee welfare and treated people fairly and whether supervisors encouraged an open and participative work environment. Employee attitudes are in turn related to profits. For example, in a study of an eye care company a significant relationship was found between employee attitudes and profit (Moeller and Schneider, 1986).

Pfeffer, after examining evidence from a large number of studies linking strategy with HR strategy, concludes:

I have come to believe that the strategic fit argument is sometimes mus- tered by managers and organisations that don't want to acknowledge that the way they manage their people is less than optimal and that they should change. They find it easier to say "Even though we aren't doing what some firms have found to be effective, that's all right because we are pursuing a different strategy." This rationalisation should be chal- lenged by asking a simple question: Wouldn't our existing strategy, whatever it is be better implemented if our people were more involved, committed, and better skilled?

(Pfeffer, 1998: 59)

Delery and Doty (1996) in a study of nearly 200 banks found that differ- ences in HR practices accounted for large differences in financial perfor- mance. Huselid concluded that 'prior empirical work has consistently found that use of effective human resource management practices enhances firm performance' (Huselid, 1995: 640).

Pfeffer (1998) presents the following rationale to explain this relationship:

- Performance increases because people work harder
- People put in effort and show greater commitment if they have greater control over their environment; see their effort as related to compensa- tion and pressure activated from self-managed teams
- Training, job rotation and such other practices help people to work smarter also. High commitment to work also saves direct and indirect costs of labour
- Trained, multi-skilled, self-managed and motivated employees save on a variety of administrative costs, including the cost of management, thus reflecting in profits

In spite of all this research evidence, as Pfeffer (1998) observes, even in coun- tries like the US and the UK, the spread of the practices is not as rapid as one might expect. Research by Ichniowski (1992) has indicated that only 16 per cent of the uS businesses have at least one innovative practice in each of the four major HRM policy areas: flexible job design, worker training, pay-for- performance compensation, and employment security.

Pfeffer (1998) has identified the following seven practices of successful organisations on the basis of his review of various research studies, related literature and his own personal observations and experience. These seven dimensions seem to characterise most if not all of the system-producing prof- its through people. These dimensions are as follows:

- Employment security
- Selective hiring of new personnel

- Self-managed teams and decentralisation of decision-making as the basic principles of organisational design
- Comparatively high compensation contingent on organisational performance
- Extensive training
- Reduced status distinctions and barriers, including dress, language, office arrangements and wage differences across levels
- Extensive sharing of financial and performance information throughout the organisation

Impact of HR Practices on Employee Productivity and Organisational Effectiveness: An Update

Research evidence collected in the last one decade has further confirmed that good HR practices have an impact on employee performance and organisational effectiveness. The researches on this theme are spread over several countries, including New Zealand, Pakistan, Bangladesh, Greece, Vietnam, China and South Africa.

Guthrie (2001) surveyed corporations in New Zealand and found that their HR practices were related to turnover and profitability. This vein of research has been summarised by Huselid and Becker, who stated, 'Based on four national surveys and observations on more than 2,000 firms, our judgment is that the effect of a one standard deviation change in the HR system is 10–20% of a firm's market value' (Huselid and Becker, 2000: 851).

Certainly, the existing research suggests a positive relationship between HR and performance. However, contrary to Huselid and Becker's (2000) claim, this body of work tends to lack sufficient methodological rigour to demonstrate that the relationship is actually causal in the sense that HR practices, when instituted, lead to higher performance. Little, if any, research has utilised rigorous designs to test the hypothesis that employing progressive HRM systems actually results in higher organisational performance in a causal sense.

Wright et al. (2003) examined the impact of HR practices and organisational commitment on the operating performance and profitability of 50 business units. Using a predictive design with a sample of 50 autonomous business units within the same corporation, the study revealed that both organisational commitment and HR practices are significantly related to operational measures of performance as well as operating expenses and pre-tax profits. It was concluded that good HR practices influence employee commitment, which in turn impacts organisational performance.

In another study using data from 45 business units, Wright et al. (2005) examined how measures of HR practices correlate with past, concurrent and future operational performance measures. The results indicated that correlations with past, concurrent and future performance measures were both high and invariant and that controlling for past or concurrent performance virtually eliminated the correlation of HR practices with future performance.

Wright et al. examined about 68 research studies between 1994 and 2003 on the relationship between multiple HR practices and performance and concluded the following.

They included only studies that reported empirical relationships between a system of HR practices (excluded studies examining a single practice) and organisation-level performance measures. All of the published studies have reported at least one significant relationship between HR practices and performance. They also concluded that the relationships have some research design flaws indicating that HR practices measured are often current and performance is largely that of the past. However, in spite of methodological limitations most studies report an association between HR practices and firm performance. They conclude from their survey the following:

> So, in summary, the literature on the HR performance relationship has (a) universally reported significant relationships between HR and performance, (b) almost exclusively used designs that do not logically allow one to draw causal conclusions, and (c) very seldom actually tested for a reverse causal order.
>
> *(Wright et al., 2005: 416)*

From their own study while they found evidence of relationship between HR practices and subsequent performance, they also found a relationship with current HR practices and past performance, raising doubts on causality of HR practices.

Guthrie (2001) found that in New Zealand HR practices had an impact on turnover, and that the relationship between retention and productivity was positive when firms implemented high-involvement HR practices, but negative when they did not. The results of this study on 50 units revealed that HR practices were strongly related to organisational commitment. Both HR practices and employee commitment were strongly and significantly related to operating expenses and profitability.

Koys (2001) examined the relationship between the HR outcomes of employee satisfaction, employee turnover, citizenship behaviour, organisational outcomes of profits and customer satisfaction among 28 branches of a restaurant chain. He found that the HR outcomes in one year more strongly predicted the organisational outcomes in the following year than the organisational outcomes in one year predicted the HR outcomes in the following year (as quoted by Wright et al., 2005: 417).

Teclemichael Tessema and Soeters (2006) collected data from studies covering civil servants in Eritrea, Africa's youngest and poorest country. Although the results generally are in line with previous studies using Western data, their implications in this particular country may be different. Therefore, the challenges and prospects of HR practices in Eritrean civil service organisations are critically analysed and discussed. In the authors' opinion, the Eritrean economic and political environment within which HR practices operate has not been conducive in maximising the impact of HR practices on performance. These findings highlight the situation of most developing countries. In this article, the authors examine how, when and to what extent HR practices affect performance at the employee level. As performance is a multi-faceted and complicated concept, HRM outcomes were used as mediating factors between HR practices and employee performance. Tzafrir (2006) investigated whether there is any difference in the relationship between HRM practices (HRMPs) and organisational performance across time (stable or not). This study was conducted in two phases using 1996 data where the questionnaires were completed by 102 of the 230 companies. In 2000, using an identical sampling methodology and a similar questionnaire, data was collected from 104 usable responses of the 275 firms. In general, results for both periods of time indicated that several HRMPs contribute to enhanced organisational performance. Firms exhibited higher organisational performance when they treated their employees as assets and invested in their abilities, enhanced their power in the decision-making process and used them as the main source for new employment. The author concludes that researchers and HR managers have to take into account the cultural context in each country when they try to export successful HRMPs from one country to another.

Katou and Budhwar (2007) investigated if HRM policies have an impact on organisational performance in the Greek manufacturing context. The research was based on a sample of 178 firms. The results showed a strong support for the model, indicating that the HRM policies of recruitment, training, promotion, incentives, benefits, involvement, and health and safety are positively related with organisational performance.

Katou and Budhwar (2010) indicated in their study of 178 organisations operating in the Greek manufacturing sector that in terms of the ability to perform (resourcing and development), motivation to perform (compensation and incentives) and opportunity to perform (involvement and job design), HRM policy domains are moderated by business strategies (cost, quality, innovation), and in addition, the motivation to perform is further moderated by managerial style and organisational culture. Further, the results indicate that the impact of HRM policies on organisational performance is fully mediated by employee skills, attitudes and behaviour. They concluded that although the motivation-to-perform HRM policy domain causes organisational performance, through employee attitudes, it may be supported that organisational performance positively moderates the effectiveness of this HRM policy domain, raising thus the question of reverse causality. Thang and Quang (2007) used data from 66 studies conducted between 1991 and 2007. The research results show that training has a positive and significant impact on firm performance. The second study used data from the Vietnam Employer Survey Instrument (VESI), which was designed to measure the impact of training programmes on firm performance. The findings indicate that manufacturing companies that increased training in 2006 achieved significant increases in sales and productivity. However, the study found that training had no statistically significant effect on sales and productivity of non-manufacturing companies. Results of the hierarchical regression from the VESI 2007 showed that quality strategy moderated the relationship between training and firm's sales and productivity. No significant moderating effects were found on cost strategy and flexibility strategy on the training–firm performance relationship. The research results show that training has a positive and significant impact on firm performance and reveal some convergences of HR training that have occurred in both Vietnam and China.

Tahir Masood (2010) from Pakistan surveyed 274 HRM professionals from 129 companies using questionnaires. HR professionals working in different companies of five industries – banking, insurance, leasing, Modaraba and investment – were selected for data collection. Secondary data was collected from the published financial reports of the companies listed with Karachi Stock Exchange (KSE) for a period of five years starting from 2004 to 2008. This study indicated that organisations using HRMPs (i.e., recruitment and selection, training and development, performance appraisal, career planning system, employee participation and compensation system) effectively on a wider scale generate higher performance (Perceived Organisational Performance (POP) and Organisational Financial Performance). To survive and sustain for the future, it is important that the financial sector companies should implement HRMPs to boost employee performance and the organisational performance index (OPI).

Mohamad et al. (2009) have examined HR practices and the impact of incentives on manufacturing companies in the Malaysian context. Three types of HR practices, namely, performance appraisal, training and information technology, have been chosen as the focus of this research with the presence of incentives as the moderator on organisational performance. They studied 85 firms in Sarawak, Malaysia. The results indicated that training and information technology had direct impact on organisational performance. It was found that incentive is positively related to organisational performance but did not moderate the relationship between HR practices and organisational performance. Chadwick et al. (2012) from a study of 1,579 private sector establishments, demonstrated that HR practices are significantly associated with differences in relative firm-level efficiency. They employed 10 HR practice variables in their analysis: pay policy, incentive pay, benefits breadth, pay for skill, quality improvement meetings, job rotation, flexitime, job sharing, selection/recruiting breadth and training breadth. As a group, these 10 HRM variables reflected the kinds of practices that have been utilised in the previous research on HRM and firm performance, which has emphasised areas such as compensation (pay policy, incentive pay, benefits, pay for skill), participatory management (quality improvement meetings), flexible work organisation (job rotation), employment flexibility (flexitime, job sharing), selection (selection/recruiting breadth) and training (training breadth). Overall, the results from their analysis supported the argument that estimating HR practices' relationships with relative firm-level efficiency is a useful way to evaluate firm-level labour productivity. Their analysis demonstrates that HR practices significantly influenced differences in relative firm-level efficiency in their sample. Some HR practices were associated with greater firm-level relative efficiency; other HR practices had the opposite relationship, and a number of the HR practices did not have significant relationships with relative firm-level efficiency. They noted that a great many differences in relative firm-level efficiency with respect to HRM are firm specific.

Colakoglu et al. (2006) have argued that strategic HRM research has mostly gravitated towards financial measures of performance in order to assess the effectiveness of HRM initiatives. They argued that focusing on organisational performance mainly from financial stakeholders' perspective is no longer sufficient. They suggest that in the light of globalisation, changing nature of work and the need to satisfy multiple stakeholders the effectiveness of HRM systems needs to be measured differently. They point out, for example, shareholders want to have larger profits, customers look for high-quality products and services with low price tags and employees desire a meaningful job in which their earnings are in line with their perceived contribu- tion, while the society expects corporations to be socially responsible by considering the needs of the local communities in which they operate. They pointed out that when researchers focus exclusively on financial or market performance, they tend to ignore how the bigger picture may look like and whether high financial performance is being achieved at the cost of other stakeholders. For example, they argue, that efficiency and cost-cutting measures may prove to be beneficial for shareholders and customers (if the low cost is reflected in the price of goods and services), but it is not as appealing to employees who may have to pay health insurance from their own pockets. Organisations that score high on financial performance metrics may not be doing equally well on other types of metrics that focus on other stakeholders. The measurement of intellectual capital parameters suggested for HR impact in this book takes into consideration this multiple stakeholder point of view and, hence, the relevance of this argument.

Buller and McEvoy (2012), after reviewing the literature on the role of human resources in creating competitive advantage, present a multi-level model illustrating how HRMPs can effectively align organisational, group and individual factors with the organisation's strategy. We then present a multi-level model illustrating how HRMPs can effectively align organisa- tional, group and individual factors with the organisation's strategy. They redefine line of sight (LOS) as the alignment of organisational capabilities and culture, group competencies and norms, and individual KSAs, motiva- tion and opportunity with one another and with the organisation's strategy. The assumption underlying the LOS concept is that employees' knowledge and behaviour, aligned with strategic priorities, are keys to achieving posi- tive organisational outcomes. Further, HRM activities are critical to the extent that they motivate employees' interests and actions in line with the firm's strategic objectives. They further proposed that such alignment con- tributes to the creation of human capital and social capital, both of which are necessary to achieve and sustain superior performance.

Guest and Conway (2011) in their study adopted a stakeholder perspective, hypothesising that the ratings of HR effectiveness of senior line managers will be more strongly associated with the outcomes than those of HR man- agers. Furthermore, building on Bowen and Ostroff's concept of consensus as part of a 'strong' HR system, they hypothesised that shared perceptions of (high) effectiveness will be associated with higher performance. This study was based on a sample of 237 matched pairs of senior line managers and HR managers and measured a range of subjective and objective outcomes. The analysis confirmed the association between more HR practices and higher HR effectiveness and a range of performance outcomes. There were low lev- els of agreement between HR and line managers about HR effectiveness, and where agreement existed it was not associated with superior outcomes. The HR managers' ratings of effectiveness of HR practices were more strongly associated with the 'objective' measures of labour turnover and profit per employee. This study, therefore, confirmed the importance of HR effective- ness but failed to support any impact of consensus. They concluded that there are three elements in a logical model of HR effectiveness. HR practices must be present, they must be effective and they must be effectively imple- mented. The HRD Score Card 2500 adopts this model (see Rao, 2008b).

Good HR Practices and Business Excellence: An Update

There is more evidence from across the world on the positive relationship between HRM practices and organizational performance: some of the stud- ies in recent times are presented below:

Sudan: A study by Arab and Mahdi (2018) on a random sample of 245 employees found that there is a statistically significant effect of the dimensions of HRM practices on various dimensions of organisational excellence in Sudanese public organisations.

USA: Delery and Gupta (2016) used a large-scale cross-sectional survey design. In a sample of US motor carriers, questionnaires completed by senior HRM department staff were used as the primary data. The data were supplemented by organisational effectiveness data reported by motor carriers to the US Government. The results support the general hypothesis that HRM practices enhance organisational effectiveness, provide some evidence that HRM practices can enhance each other's effectiveness, and underscore the value of theory-driven methodological approaches. Specifically, the authors found that an HRM system comprising practices that ensure selectivity in staffing, performance-based pay, and enhanced employee opportunity through participation in decision-making results in higher levels of organisational effectiveness. Additionally, the effects of other combinations of these practices varied.

Romania: In a study of 441 Romanian employees in the healthcare industry, (Rotea et al., 2023) showed that HRM practices directly impact organisational performance and have a mediated impact through the organisational change process. Additionally, the direct and mediating effects are consistent, and healthcare employers consider appropriate HRM practices and effective management of the organisational change process as essential drivers to achieve superior performance. The empirical findings provide valuable insights for government policymakers, stakeholders, and health managers on how suitable HRM practices can influence organisational performance.

Caliskan (2010) conducted an extensive literature review on human resource management as a competitive advantage, the strategic role of human resource management, and then how strategic human resource management impacts organisational performance.

Talukdar (2016) recently reviewed a number of studies from across the globe establishing the positive relationship between HR practices and various dimensions of firm performance. The following is a summary from these reviews:

Malaysia: Abdullah et al. (2009) found that training and development, team work, HR planning and performance appraisal have a positive and significant influence on business performance in Malaysian private businesses.

Nigeria: Khan (2010) measured recruitment and selection, training and development, performance appraisal, compensation and reward, employee relations to see their impact on performance optimisation of the oil and gas industry in Nigeria. A positive and statistically significant association of these practices with performance optimisation is established. Qureshi et al. (2010) studied HRM practices in selection, training, performance appraisal systems, compensation, employee participation and their impact on the financial performance of banks in Nigeria. All variables had a positive relationship and impact on the financial performance of banks. The performance appraisal system was the least contributor to the performance of banks.

Pakistan: Khalid and Rehman (2010) investigated the impact of human resource management practices on performance optimisation of two telecommunication companies. Training, employee participation, job definition, compensation and selections are positively associated with overall performance optimisation. Mukhtar et al. (2011) investigated the role of HRM in managing organisational conflict in public sector universities of Pakistan. The study indicated that HRM practices (namely recruitment and selection, training and development, performance appraisal and role of unions) can transform dysfunctional conflict into functional conflict and have a significant relationship with organisational effectiveness. Shabbir (2014) studied through questionnaire from pharmaceutical companies located in Islamabad and Rawalpindi cities of Pakistan. He studied the impact of human resource practices on employee-perceived performance, using correlations and multiple regressions. The results showed a significant relationship between human resource practices and employee-perceived performance. Multiple regressions presented substantial variance in perceived employees' performance due to these human resource practices. The study recommended that the pharmaceutical companies may pay special attention to these three practices in order to ensure employees' performance.

Jordan: Rawashdeh and Al Adwan (2012) studied the impact of human resource practices on the corporate performance of Jordanian commercial banks. The results showed a positive and significant positive relationship between recruitment and selection, compensation and reward with corporate performance and a negative association between training and development and corporate performance.

Nairobi: Agusioma (2014) critically analysed the HRM practices' effect on organisational performance of public universities in Kenya with a focus on Nairobi. The study found that recruitment and selection, training and development, reward management, and employee relations affect organisational performance.

Kim (2010) in her study addressed the question of whether public sector can increase productivity through competition in spite of inherent limitations by examining the impact of four factors (rewards for merit such as salary and benefits, opportunities, organisational rules, and the capacity to deal with risks as perceived by employees) that contribute to employees' expectations regarding competitive work environments on organisational performance in terms of overall quality of work and client satisfaction. It was found that salary and benefits were positively related to employees' perception of organisational performance. Moreover, employees' perceptions of organisational performance tended to increase when they felt that organisational rules were oriented toward performance and organizational members and top leaders exhibited greater risk-taking behaviours.

This update makes it clear that there is an overwhelming evidence of the association between HR practices and organisational performance and there are a number of other variables that seem to have mediating effects, and hence, the need to look at other variables like competencies, culture, HR strategies, and the like. Recent studies that have gone into depth of this matter have issues with the methodology and raise doubts about causative relationships but confirm the association between HR and firm productivity.

Impact of Good HR Practices: The Indian Experience

A lot of evidence linking organisational effectiveness with good HR practices comes from case studies of HR practices and organisational performance. The National HRD Network and the Confederation of Indian Industry (CII) have been giving HRD awards for organisations that have had outstanding HRD practices or at least distinguished themselves in this regard. To confirm the linkages between organisational performance and HR practices, a search can be undertaken into these organisations in terms of how well they have done financially as well as on other parameters like growth and their capability to withstand competition after liberalisation. An ideal design is to compare them on various performance parameters (financial, market share, growth, customer satisfaction, etc.) with another control group. Such comparisons can be extended to the HR practices. Unfortunately, no such study is available as yet. However, with the available data it is possible to come to some conclusions. For example, if the organisations have done well in spite of many odds, including the turbulent environment in India prevailing in the last few years, one can say with some degree of confidence that HRD practices did matter. An analysis of the HRD award-winning organisations does indicate that excellent performers in the Indian corporate sector do seem to have excellent HR practices. In order to draw attention to some of the emerging areas and issues relating to HRM effectiveness I undertook an analysis of the HRD award-winning companies and individuals in the last two decades to see whether their HR strategies continued to be effective (Rao, 1996). See Box 1.1 for HRD award-winning companies with an updated list up to 2010. This list includes the award-winning companies of the National HRD Network and also those shortlisted for SAIL (Steel Authority of India) award for their outstanding work in HRD. Of the 43 organisations that were considered for awards about half of them qualified for the same. Details of these organisations are available from the National HRD Network website and from the book titled *HR Best Practices* by Nisha Nair and team (Nair et al., 2010).

Current Status of Award-Winning HRD Companies

About 90 per cent of these companies have continued to grow and expand in spite of having to face a turbulent environment in the recent past.

BOX 1.1 HRD AWARD-WINNING COMPANIES OF THE NATIONAL HRD NETWORK IN THE LAST FEW YEARS

L&T (ECC Construction Group) (1989)
SAIL (1989)
Crompton Greaves (1989)
Sundaram Fasteners (1989)
Canara Bank (1990)
TISCO (1990)
Petrofils Co-operative (1990)
Eicher (1990)
C-DOT (1990)
Indian Oil (1991)
Marico Industries (1994)
Widia India (1994)
Power Grid Corporation Limited (1998), Bharat Petroleum Corporation (2000) and ICICI (2000)
IGNOU (2000)
Infosys Technologies (2000), Satyam Computer Services (2000), IFFCO (2002)
Sasken Communication Technologies (2002), Wipro Spectramind Services (2004), Management Development Institute (2006) and Tata Chemicals (2006)
Zensar Technologies (2006) Indian School of Business (2008)
Maruti Suzuki India Limited (2010)
Thermax (1991)
TELCO (1989)
EID Parry (1991)
Indian Hotels (1991)

CMC Limited (1992)
Modi Xerox (1992)
ITC (1992)
Widia India (1993)
Marico Industries (1993)
Vijaya Wires (1993)
NIIT 1998 (not included in the study by Rao, 1996)

SAIL HR Award-Winning Companies

Honey Well Jindal Steel
Philips Electronics India Schneider Electric Moser Baer
Tata Motors ITW Signode Castrol India HPCL
NTPC
Jindal Steel and Power

They have shown that they have the wherewithal to withstand all kinds of turbulence, including the onslaught of globalisation after having been in a protected environment for several years. They seem to be doing as well as the 'In Search of Excellence' companies of Peters and Waterman fame in the US. Most of them exhibit the following other characteristics.

They seem to have the capability to cope well with leadership and techno-logical changes.

In at least 50 per cent of these companies there have been leadership changes in the last few years, but the companies continue to progress. This evidence leads us to hypothesise that an HRD company is likely to build a large amount of internal talent and competencies and have sustaining capability. Good examples of these are SAIL, Indian Oil, Larsen & Toubro (L&T), Tata Steel, Telco (which is now Tata Motors), ITC, Bharat Petroleum, Infosys, IFFCO, Tata Chemicals, etc.

They seem to have coped well with changes due to liberalisation and have even exploited the opportunities to their advantage.

Almost all the companies have grown from their previous stage and expanded and/or improved their profits as well as asset base. There are a few exceptions as such companies may have gone astray due to unanticipated value erosion.

All the companies seem to have attempted to meet the challenges of liber-alisation by becoming customer-oriented and quality conscious.

A number of them have developed mission statements and declared their vision for the future. An HRD orientation seems to have helped them to articulate these and their core values. Most of them have gone in for ISO certification and TQM. Some of them have restructured themselves. A few of them have reduced their layers and also revised their salary structures.

Most of these organisations seem to demonstrate that they are changing and are learning organisations.

The organisations have been reviewing their salary structure, performance appraisal practices, personnel policies, etc., from time to time. They have been getting their organisational culture and employee satisfaction surveyed periodically and using the data to bring about improvements. A few of them also have begun to benchmark their systems and select management practices.

Most of them have very effectively used their personnel or HRD departments to initiate and manage changes.

Some of the organisations gave their HR managers charge of strategic planning, quality programmes, customer-orientation programmes, restructuring exercises, etc. In a few of these organisations, HR managers were even given line responsibilities or helped to head separate outfits. Eicher, SAIL, L&T, Modi Xerox and Sundaram Fasteners are some illustrations of this.

These organisations have also invested heavily in training and some of them have even established new training centres.

Their budgets for employee training seem to have gone up considerably. They have continued to sponsor their executives to external programmes to keep them abreast with new technologies and practices. They have become quite liberal in terms of sending their employees for training abroad to keep them in touch with global changes. Some of them like Infosys and L&T have set up their leadership institutes or academies. Nair et al. (2010) indicated the following on SAIL award companies:

> The investments on people development reflected through training ranges from ₹0.8% to ₹2.14%. Which means for every 100 rupees earned 80 paisa to two rupees are spent exclusively on training? The training investments as a percentage of annual turnover figures indicate that Castrol India spends 2.1%, ITW Signode 0.8%, Honeywell India 2.16%, Moser Baer 0.5%, Tata Motors 2.14%, HPCL 1.66%, and Jindal Steel and Power spends 1.35% on training investments respectively.
>
> *(Nair et al., 2010: 7)*

They have integrated well the personnel and the HRD functions.

As a matter of fact, quite a few of these organisations have personnel departments rather than HRD departments. In most cases there has been a movement from the personnel function to HRD departments. This change has been positive. The number of HR staff employed in SAIL award companies seems to range from one HR professional for every 50 employees to one person for every 250 employees (Nair et al., 2010).

The chiefs of these departments, however, act and behave as business-minded HRD managers integrating themselves totally with the business. They have used the HRD systems to their advantage and constantly integrated personnel and HRD functions.

They have well-formulated vision and mission statements.

Most award-winning organisations seem to have a well-articulated vision or mission of its people management. The vision statements of most award-winning organisations seem to have a well-articulated vision or mission of its people management. The vision statements of a few organisations are given below:

Moser Baer: 'To provide pride of association to our associates by having meaningful professional life and joy of association through work-life balance'

Tata Motors: 'To be a world-class corporate constantly furthering the interests of all its stakeholders'

HPCL: 'Excellence in harnessing the full potential of all employees for becoming a global energy company'

Castrol: 'To nurture human capability and invest to ensure that the right technology, skills, behaviours and intellectual property are available for the pursuit of the broad goals; to treat employees fairly and with respect and dignity, to make clear the expectations the group has of each employee in line with the group's general principles of delegation'

Jindal Steel and Power Limited: 'To create competitive advantage for all stakeholders through effective people management'

Honeywell India: 'We as Human Resource function are committed to provide quality services in a professional, caring and consistent manner; we shall strategically work with the business to its changing needs. We are dedicated to clear communication, progressive thinking, and resourceful solutions in meeting our organisational goals'

Their departments are well staffed.

The number of HR staff employed in these companies seems to range from one HR professional for every 50 employees to one person for every 250 employees. In Castrol India and ITW Signode there is one HR professional staff for every 50 employees and in Jindal Steel and Power Limited it works out to be one professional HR staff for every 70 employees. In Honeywell India for every 80 employee there is one HR staff. Moser Baer and Tata Motors have one HR staff per every 100 employees. HPCL has one

HR staff for every 250 employees. In all companies a large majority of the staff is professionally qualified. In most large organisations law graduates also form an integral part of the HR fraternity (Nair et al., 2010).

They are getting designated by different names indicating the new thrust of HR Function.

The HR department, in most cases is the main functionary for managing people management practices. The HR department and its chief are known by different names, such as HR Head Business Excellence at ABB, Country Talent Manager at Philips, Head Talent Management at SKF India and ITW Signode, Matrix Manager at Honeywell, Managing Executive Officer at Maruti Suzuki and different names for various HR functions such as Head HR Performance Management, Head HR Training, Head HR Recruitment, etc., as practised in HPCL. These designations indicate a high degree of alignment with business. No other function has undergone such change as HR in India.

These companies spend a good deal on their people practices and HR departments.

SAIL award-winning companies survey by Nair et al. (2010) have indicated their spending on people management (i.e., people's cost as a percentage of annual turnover) ranges from 0.84 per cent in HPCL to 11.1 per cent in Moser Baer and 9.2 per cent in ITW Signode. HPCL being a petroleum and process-driven industry like NTPC may need to have different norms from hardcore product companies such as Moser Baer or Tata Motors. The next lowest is Jindal Steel and Power with 2.67 per cent followed by Castrol with spending on people management at 4.8 per cent of its annual turnover. For ITW Signode it is 9.2 per cent, Honeywell India 5.8 per cent, Moser Baer 11.1 per cent, and for Tata Motors it is 5.4 per cent. These data also indicate that in HR wise companies, out of every rupee earned 5 to 10 paisa are spent on its people. ITW Signode spends nearly 5 per cent of its people costs on HR function. Moser Baer spends 3 per cent and Tata Motors spends 3.44 per cent of their employee costs on HR function. Jindal Steel and Power spends 3.4 per cent, HPCL spends 1.66 per cent, Honeywell India spends 5.19 per cent and Castrol India spends 7.1 per cent of its people costs on the HR function, respectively (Nair et al., 2010: 7–8).

Although the above generalisations are based on impressionistic data, a scientific study may not reveal too different a picture. The only scientific study in this direction has been made by Abraham (1989) who surveyed the HRD practices of 68 Indian organisations. He measured various elements of the HRD profile of these organisations, including performance management practices, training, career planning, promotions, rewards, etc., and the HRD climate (openness, collaboration, trust, authenticity, pro-action, autonomy, confrontation). Abraham also constructed an index of growth of the company profitability as a measure of organisational performance. He was able to use this index only in 14 of the 68 companies. He found that while the HRD profile did not correlate with company performance, the HRD climate did. He found that the perception of the HRD climate of the company was more important than the HRD practice itself. This study also indicates that HRD culture is a powerful intervening variable in translating HRD practices into profit. The HRD manager matters a lot in this regard along with line managers and top management. Some indirect evidence to this effect is also provided by Khandwalla, who, after a review of several case studies and experiences in India, concluded, 'Western and Third World studies of organisational excellence indicate five major keys to organisational excellence: mission, vision of excellence, core values; style of management; goals, policies and choices of domain; management systems and structure; and organisational renewal processes' (Khandwalla, 1992: 69).

In a study of 54 organisations post-liberalisation in India, Som (2002) found that professionalised HRD comes as a key differentiator of performance. People focus has emerged as a source of sustainable competitive advantage. Capabilities to build strategic competence and effectiveness seem to be facilitated by professionalised HR.

Singh (2004) studied the relationship between HRMPs and firm-level performance. The study conducted on 82 Indian firms indicated that there is a significant relationship between thebetween two human resources practices, namely, training and compensation, and perceived organisational and market performance of the firm.

Chand and Katou (2007) conducted a study to investigate whether some HRM systems affect organisational performance in the hotel industry in India. A total of 439 hotels, ranging from three-star to five-star deluxe, responded to a self-administered questionnaire that measured 27 HRMPs, 5 organisational performance variables and 10 demographic variables. Correlation analysis was used to test the relationship between HRM systems and organisational performance. The results indicate that hotel performance is positively related to the HRM systems of recruitment and selection, manpower planning, job design, training and development, quality circle and pay systems. From their study they conclude that if hotels are to achieve higher performance levels, they should preferably belong to a chain and increase their category, and management should focus on 'best' HRMPs indicated in the study.

This evidence is sufficient to indicate that good HR practices do matter. However, the relationship between good HR practices and organisational effectiveness is not so simple. It is not that all one has to do is to have good HR practices and everything else will automatically follow; however, good HR practices can ensure a number of things. They can lend competitive advantage to a corporation if other things are equal. There are other intervening variables. For example, one cannot make good HR practices work wonders if the organisation is not located in a strategic place or it started with or already invested in bad technology or it is in a low-margin business or if the economic policies of the country of its location get changed to its detriment, etc. Even within HR there are a number of variables to be understood and differentiated. Abraham's study provides some insights into this and shows that it is a good HRD climate rather than HRD practices by themselves that are responsible for organisational performance. This is not to deny the importance of good HR practices. One can create an appropriate HRD climate only through good HRD practices and processes.

HRD and Organisational Effectiveness: Some Concluding Remarks

From the above review of studies it may be concluded that good HRD practices do make a difference on many counts. They enhance internal capabilities of an organisation to deal with current or future challenges to be faced by an organisation. Good HR practices also energise people. The commitment and motivation built through good HR practices can lead to hard work and can have a multiplier effect on the conversion of human capital to organisational capital. The culture so built can help to create a sustainable and lasting capability of the organisation to manage itself and not only cope with the external turbulence but even cash in on the opportunities offered by the changing environment. However, such a linkage cannot be taken as automatic and direct and there are many intervening forces affecting it.

I had presented (Rao, 1990) a model to explain the linkages between HRD instruments (put in operation they become practices), processes, outcomes and organisational effectiveness. In this model, schematically presented in Figure 1.1, the HRD instruments include various tools of HRD that corporations are likely to use for competence, commitment, and culture building in their respective organisations. These tools include the various subsystems, such as the performance appraisal system, feedback and counselling sessions and potential development exercises like assessment centres, training, job rotation policies, etc. A feature of this model is that the HRD department is also included as an instrument of HRD, implying that while organisations always have the choice of establishing HRD departments, they could carry on HRD activities even without an HRD department.

The HRD tools if effectively used can create a conducive HRD culture and HRD learning processes. HRD processes are intermediate variables and affect the HRD outcomes. They are less easily observable and are softer dimensions that indicate the effectiveness of HRD tools. HRD process variables include role clarity on a continuous basis, work planning, awareness of competencies and a more directed effort to build them, better

HRD Mechanisms or Subsystems of Instruments	HRD Processes and HRD Climate Variables	HRD Outcomes Variables	Organisational Effectiveness Dimensions
• HRD department • Performance appraisal • Review discussions, feedback counselling sessions • Role analysis exercises • Potential development exercises • Training • Communication policies • Job rotations • OD exercises • Rewards • Job-enrichment programmes • Other mechanisms	• Role clarity • Planning of development by every employee • Awareness of competencies required for job-performance • Proactive orientation • More trust • Collaboration and teamwork • Authenticity • Openness • Risk taking • Value generation • Clarification of norms and standards • Increased com munication • More objective rewards • Generation of objective data on employees, etc.	• More competent people • Better developed roles • Higher work commitment and job involvement • More problem solving • Better utilisation of human resources • Higher job-satisfaction and work motivation • Better generation of internal resources • Better organisational health • More teamwork, synergy and respect for cach other	• Higher productivity • Growth and diversification • Cost reduction • More profits • Better image

Other Factors
Environment, technology, resource availability, history, nature of business, etc.

Other Factors
Personnel policies, top management styles, investments in HRD, top management commitments, history, previous culture, line manager's interest, etc.

FIGURE 1.1 A Schematic Presentation of Linkages between HRD Instruments, Processes, Outcomes and Organisational Effectiveness

communication and the practice of HRD values like openness, collaboration, trust, pro-action, authenticity, autonomy, confrontation, etc. Such HRD culture and processes can result in more observable and quantifiable outcomes.

The HRD outcomes may include a higher level of competencies of the employees (technological, managerial, human relations and conceptual), better utilisation of human resources through better developed roles, higher work commitment, work motivation, greater teamwork and synergy, etc. The HRD outcomes can influence the organisation's business goals, which may be in terms of higher productivity, cost reduction, more profits, better image and more satisfied customers and stakeholders.

Thus, the essential components implied in this model are as follows:

- Aligning HRD with business by linking HRD strategies with corporate strategies
- Instituting appropriate HRD structures to translate these strategies into action
- Hiring competent HR staff and developing HR competencies among other employees
- Having appropriate HRD tools or instruments (systems and practices)
- Generating the right HRD climate and processes through HRD tools and styles
- Enhancing the satisfaction and motivational levels of employees through the above
- Having more satisfied customers and getting better business results

The model gives scope for other factors and their influence on the linkage between HRD variables and organisational effectiveness. For example, it is understood that HRD cannot by itself contribute to profits. Strategies, technology, finances, markets, etc., also need to be in place. HRD alone cannot make all these variables happen. However, good HR practices may build the competencies and commitment of employees to such an extent that they make sure that the other variables are taken care of to a great extent. Thus, it is people who can provide competitive advantage to corporations. And it is the main task of the HRD function and HRD agents (HR managers or facilitators or HRD role holders) to enable employees to deliver competitive advantage.

Some questions that every corporation needs to address are as follows: How well are HR practices (systems, processes and activities) linked to business goals? Do they flow from strategies or are they aligned with the strategies? Do corporations have appropriate HRD structures to translate HRD strategies into actionable goals with short- and long-term perspectives?

Are the HRD structures manned by competent individuals who know their job and are well prepared to do it effectively? What are the HRD competency levels of all other stakeholders (line managers, top management, union leaders, workers, etc.)? Are they at an adequate level for effective HRD?

Are good HR practices and HRD systems and processes being designed? Are these systems internally sound, consistent and relevant? How well are they being implemented?

Is there a good HRD climate being developed as a result of the HRD practices or otherwise? Is the leadership behaviour of managers and the supervisory class tuned to create or promote learning and empowering culture?

Are the HRD systems and processes being orchestrated to lead to organisational performance? Are good HR practices leading to employee and customer satisfaction, and translating the same into organisational performance parameters?

Is the HRD function appropriately placed and being managed to ensure its positive effect on organisational performance?

These questions need to be answered not once but on a continuous basis, and hence, the need for HRD audit. HRD audit is the methodology of evaluating various elements of HRD and providing a balance sheet of the strengths and weaknesses of the HRD practices for a given organisation. The subsequent sections in this book define the various elements of HRD and provide insights into the methods of evaluating them. Chapter 2 gives an outline of the various elements of HRD and makes a case for undertaking HRD audit. Simultaneously, I have also assessed the current situation of the HR function in India, using my HRD audit experiences. Then follows a brief review of some approaches to evaluate HRD and the HR function. Chapter 4 presents in detail the concept of HRD audit. The second section details the methodologies used in HRD audit and proposes the use of an HRD Score Card as a tool to document and summarise the outcomes of HRD audit. The third section concludes with a few case studies of HRD audit.

HRD and HR

A point needs to be mentioned here about HRD and HR. The former stands for human resource development while the latter stands for human resource function. The HR function is all-encompassing and includes HRD and more. It goes far beyond the traditional personnel function. It is more proactive and change-orientated and requiring competencies of a different nature from what the traditional personnel function requires. The traditional personnel function had been more of a maintenance function with very little growth focus. The modern HR function has HRD at its core. HRD is its soul, as Udai Pareek once put it in a talk at the NIPM convention in 1978 on 'Personnel Management in Search of a Soul'. The HR function, as it has evolved in India, consists of three main sub-functions: HRD, Industrial Relations and Worker Affairs and Human Resource Administration. All three can be combined to form HRM. However, due to the restricted connotation of the term management, and in order not to lose focus of the proactive and growth orientation of HRM, I would rather call it the HR function rather than HRM. At the same time, all aspects of the HR function are not covered in using the term HR. For example, all areas dealing with industrial relations, labour laws, legal aspects, administration, etc., are ignored or underplayed in the use of the term HR. The HRD audit does not include these aspects. HRD includes all aspects of competence, commitment and culture building. As some aspects of the HR function that are traditionally not included as a part of HRD also matter in commitment building and culture building, and these are taken to be included as contextual factors of HRD. Thus, in the traditional HRD function, manpower planning, recruitment and placement have a limited place. However, as contextual factors influencing HRD they are significant. Thus, HRD cannot be dealt with in isolation of HR and HR cannot be dealt with without HRD in the current global business scenario. As a result, HRD and HR can be treated very close to each other. An extended definition of HRD includes a number of elements of the HR function, whereas a focused and narrowed-down definition of the HR function can mean HRD. Thus, HRD is treated as the soul of the HR function and both terms are used somewhat interchangeably. The reader must note this deliberate interchangeability of the terms. However, to communicate appropriately to the reader and to give the respect due to the all-encompassing HR function, the book focuses on HRD audit and not on HR audit. HR audit may require a lot more areas to be covered. In the changing scenario, I believe, like many other professionals that HRD should be the focal point of study, assessment, application and renewal. HRD audit does not include any evaluation of HR function like industrial relations, worker welfare and management, legal and statutory aspects of HR, compensation management, facilities management and administrative functions like transportation, housing, estates and security services, etc. HRD audit focuses on evaluating growth functions of people.

2

ELEMENTS OF GOOD HRD

Need for Realignment

HRD has been defined as

> a process by which the employees of an organisation are helped, in a
> continuous, planned way, to: acquire or sharpen capabilities required
> to perform various functions associated with their present or expected
> future roles; develop their general capabilities as individuals and discover
> and exploit their own inner potential for their own and/or organisa-
> tional development purposes; develop an organisational culture in which
> the supervisor–subordinate relationships, teamwork, and collaboration
> among subunits are strong and contribute to the professional well-being,
> motivation and pride of employees.
>
> *(Rao, 1985)*

Put simply, HRD also means competence building, commitment building
and culture building (Rao, 1990).

In the past, HRD definitions have also differentiated the HRD instru-
ments/subsystems/mechanisms (e.g., HRD departments, appraisal systems,
job rotation and training) from the HRD processes and culture (e.g., role
clarity, trust, openness, pro-action, collaboration, etc.), HRD outcomes
(e.g., more competent people, better developed roles, better organisational
health and more teamwork) and organisational outcomes (profits, diversification, image productivity, etc.; Rao, 1990). Starting with six subsystems in
the mid-seventies, HRD came to include several other components as newer
subsystems were discovered and brought to significance. For example, job
rotation, quality circles, shop floor committees, task forces, communication
systems, meetings, mentoring systems, worker development programmes,

DOI: 10.4324/9781003530534-3

etc., came to be considered as HRD mechanisms. The HRD department or the function has sometimes been treated as an HRD instrument as it is essentially a facilitator of development. However, given the significance of the HRD department in producing good employees, the HRD department can be treated as a separate element for good HRD.

Elements of Good HRD

The elements of good HRD are as follows:

- Corporate strategy- and business-linked HRD
- Systems-engineered and systems-driven HRD
- Appropriately structured and competently handled HRD
- Appropriately rooted (in terms of culture and values) and sustainability focused HRD

Corporate Strategy- and Business-Linked HRD

HRD and HR practices should be linked to business goals and corporate strategy. As indicated by Pfeffer (1998), irrespective of the business strategy, human resources should be continuously aligned with it. Such an alignment is in the interest of the organisation. The organisation may use a variety of strategies. Some of these include the following:

- Change in technologies or introduction of new technologies
- Change in markets
- Acquisitions and mergers
- Internationalisation of business
- Addition of new products and services
- Cost reduction efforts
- Quality enhancement programmes
- Reorganisation or rationalisation of organisational structure, including downsizing or upsizing
- Change in equity, financial structures, etc.
- Joint ventures, etc.

An important dimension that has emerged in recent times is the intellectual capital-building and talent-managing HRD. Talent management has become the new imperative of business. With the right talent, a lot can be achieved by corporations.

All these have an impact on the employees or human resources in the organisation. If these strategies have to succeed, the people who are required to implement them should have a high degree of commitment. They should also develop new competencies. For example, all expansion programmes require a stretch in competencies or the use of new competencies. No technological change can be brought about without a proper HRD effort, as all technological changes require readjustment of people in relation to the new technology. Acquisitions and mergers put demands on the culture-building and culture-integration exercises. Even cost reduction exercises require HR interventions or can, at least, be greatly facilitated by HR departments by getting employee involvement and commitment. PMS can be redesigned to promote cost reduction. Quality enhancement programmes can be facilitated by redesigning the PMS. Training plays a role all the time in most of these interventions as a direct competence-building tool. Cultural integration can be achieved through mission–vision workshops and redesigning various HR systems.

In an earlier research of 14 Indian organisations, it has been found that good companies use the following strategies. Sometimes organisations may start HR activities for short-term goal considerations. If they do not soon graduate by ensuring that the activities are linked to corporate strategy, they may move into the wrong direction. Hence, it is important to ensure the linkage between HRD and corporate strategy. All assessment of HRD should start with the business goals and business considerations. Any assessment of HRD should examine the extent to which such linkages exist. A number of such approaches have come into existence in recent years. One of these is the Balanced Score Card approach, described later in this chapter, which focuses on business and HR linkages.

Systems-Engineered and Systems-Driven HRD

HRD cannot be a series of ad hoc decisions and practices. It has to be based on a set of predictable practices and measures. HRD literature identifies a number of systems and subsystems. On the basis of the past 20 years of work in this area, Pareek and Rao (1992a, 1992b) have developed the following systems framework of HRD that is useful for an in-depth understanding of HRD.

Component systems of hRd (Pareek and Rao's framework)

An earlier approach presented by Pareek and Rao envisaged the following classification of various HRD systems.

Career system. Attracting and retaining the right kind of people can be ensured through manpower planning, recruitment, continuous potential appraisal and career planning and development activities. These constitute career subsystems of the HRD system. This requires a good competency mapping or role analysis.

Work-planning system. Employees will effectively contribute to organisational goals if they are helped to understand organisational needs, plan their work to meet these needs and review their work and make improvements. These activities can be grouped under the work-planning subsystem. This system deals with human resource utilisation. This is largely taken care by performance-planning and management systems, including appraisal.

Development system. That the required competencies are available continuously for the present as well as the future can be ensured through training, counselling and other development mechanisms. These constitute the development subsystem. This includes training, including induction, on the job coaching, job rotation for development and also career development initiatives like the 360 Degree Feedback and Development centres.

Self-renewal system. That the organisation as a whole and its subunits are constantly kept dynamic, responsive as well as proactive can be ensured through role efficacy, team building, survey feedback, research and other related activities. These, and other activities, constitute the self-renewal system. These may again get covered in some organisations through OD interventions and in some others through training and related systems.

Culture subsystem. A climate that sets norms, values and culture and ensures a high level of motivation for employees constitutes culture-building subsystems. Sometimes these are covered as employee engagement surveys, etc.

As mentioned earlier, there are various systems in HRD literature. The systems approach to HRD is inevitable. It is only a systems approach that can institutionalise HRD and facilitate its contributions. There are a number of systems. Some of these are linked with one another. It is not necessary to use all the systems at the same time. For example, it is not necessary to have job rotation as a system in all organisations. Some organisations by virtue of their size, nature of work and specialisation may not be amenable to job rotation. Similarly, organisations with flat structures may not be amenable to career planning and potential appraisal.

Factors like periodic evaluation of how these systems are working, whether they are working as systems, whether there is oversystemisation and whether the most appropriate and potential systems are being used can go a long way in reengineering HRD as well as realigning HRD to the organisation's business needs.

Appropriately Structured and Competently Handled HRD

HRD has a critical role to play in the achievement of organisational goals and helping the organisation to achieve and maintain excellence. Good people and good culture make good organisations. 'Good people' means competent, committed, learning and team-oriented people. HRD has the role of getting the right kind of people, creating a culture that nurtures and retains talent, providing avenues for competence development at all levels, ensuring utilisation of talent and aiding in renewal of various productive human processes. While the HRD department facilitates the achievement of these goals, every senior employee becomes a facilitator of the development of both herself or himself and those who work with her or him.

HRD needs to be appropriately structured and competently handled. Since the time HRD has emerged as a new profession in many countries including India and since the time the first HRD department was set up, HRD has come a long way in India (see Box 2.1 on the history of HRD in India). However, post-liberalisation requirements and challenges have shown that a lot can be improved in terms of the structuring of the HR function as well as of the professional preparation of HRD managers.

BOX 2.1 HRD IN INDIA

The first HRD department in the Indian corporate sector was started in 1975 in L&T, after recommendations by two consultants, Udai Pareek and T.V. Rao, from the Indian Institute of Management, Ahmedabad (Pareek and Rao, 1975). In the next year, State Bank of India and its associate banks, influenced by the conceptual underpinnings of HRD, decided to establish HRD departments. State Bank of India was one of the earliest organisations in India to try sensitivity training-based interventions in the sixties. Two years later, Bharat Earth Movers Limited, Bangalore, one of the large public sector companies in India, established its HRD department. All these companies followed the basis provided by Pareek and Rao.

Pareek and Rao's model for L&T was also disseminated to other organisations. The model envisaged the HRD function as consisting of six subsystems: (*i*) development-oriented performance appraisals, (*ii*) potential appraisal, (*iii*) training, (*iv*) feedback and counselling, (*v*) career planning and development and (*vi*) OD. These subsystems are linked to one another and are conceived as a part of the HR system (Pareek and Rao, 1975).

Up to the late seventies, there were hardly a dozen organisations with HRD departments, and by the eighties many had started establishing them. One of the early OD works was done by the HRD departments of the associate banks of State Bank of India using the survey feedback methodology. The importance of HRD had grown so much by the mid-eighties that almost every second organisation in India had established an HRD department. By the nineties, almost every organisation had an HRD department with the function being fully institutionalised. A new professional body called the National HRD Network took birth in 1985 and is comparable to the OD Network in the US. This body has even established a national-level research institution called the Academy of HRD.

Thus, the HRD movement in India has its own unique history. Today, OD is very much institutionalised in India through the HRD departments.

As Ulrich (1997b) argues, human resource professionals need to have highly specialised skills to realign HRD. A competent HR manager is required to be a specialist in HR systems, facilitator of HRD processes, diagnostician, change manager, skilled craftsman and a leader. There are many other qualities required to be a good HR manager. Today, many organisations have large-sized HR departments. Do corporations need such large-sized HRD departments? More important than the size is to see which roles of the HRD department add value to the organisation. What are the competencies required by HR professionals to orchestrate human resources and realign them with business goals? This calls for a different kind of evaluation. An evaluation of HR competencies may begin with the HR managers and HR professionals, and then extend to the HR orientations of line managers, top management, union leaders and all other categories of stakeholders. It may also deal with the competency of the HR department as a whole and examine the professional profiles and competencies of the HR staff. While it is necessary to gauge the efficacy of the HRD department, it is also necessary to examine its structure. Some organisations have set up HRD departments with faith in them and do not really know what to expect from them. Some have set them up as they do not want to miss out by not having an HR department. In mid-eighties there was a big rush for setting up HR departments as a fashion. Many CEOs just started HR departments and cells with whatever talent they could get. With high demand for HR professionals there was a shortage of adequately trained HR professionals. HRD appeared to be anyone's territory as there was an insufficient body of knowledge. It was felt that anyone could acquire these soft skills. In the absence of any clear-cut expectations from the top management many HRD managers did only what they felt comfortable with and hired whatever employees they could get hold of, irrespective of the organisational needs. Thus, HRD was fashion driven rather than organisation driven. Another thing some HRD managers did was to expand their empires. A manager needs a deputy manager, the deputy manager needs an assistant manager and the assistant manager needs a couple of assistants. Thus, HRD departments have grown and continue to make do with whatever is available in the market. In the recent past, organisations have realised that they are saddled with HRD structures that are not as responsive to company needs as they are to their own growth needs.

The time has come to re-examine the appropriateness of HRD structures. Thus, along with the competencies of the HRD staff the appropriateness of the HRD structures needs to be examined. This examination has become a new imperative post-pandemic as the role of HRD has become more critical than before.

Appropriately Rooted HRD

The culture of an organisation plays an important role in ensuring the capability of an organisation to achieve excellence. To gain competitive advantage through people, it is necessary to have human processes and value systems that enable the organisation to be customer focused, cost conscious, quality driven, innovative, proactive, leading in technology, etc. Udai Pareek and T.V. Rao, at the time of setting up the first HRD department in India in 1975, identified the following principles (only some are listed here) to design the HR system (Pareek and Rao, 1998).

1. Enhance the enabling capabilities of people
2. Integrate the development of people with that of the organisation
3. Maximise individual growth and autonomy with increased responsibility
4. Decentralise through delegation and shared responsibility
5. Encourage participative decision-making
6. Balance adaptability to change and changing the organisational culture
7. Balance differentiation with integration
8. Balance specialisation with diffusion of the function
9. Build feedback and reinforcement mechanisms
10. Ensure continuous review and renewal

These principles are the roots of organisational culture.

It is necessary to ensure that all HR practices do not have only short-term objectives; they should also build long-term enablers. Enablers are the cultural dimensions. They are norms, values, attitudes and other expected and valued patterns of behaviour that maximise the impact of people in organisations. These values and norms should not merely be the enablers of individuals but also of the other units of work (dyads, teams and the organisation as a unit). Besides cultural dimensions, enablers also imply the styles of the seniors and the top-level managers who also influence the motivation of employees. Thus, it is important to address the following issues. What is the kind of culture that the organisation is able to create? Is it a learning-oriented and enabling culture? Does it empower individuals, teams and the organisation, or is it a burden on the organisation? What effect do the working styles of seniors have on the juniors and the entire organisation? Is it enabling or crippling?

Approaches to Evaluate the HR Function and Its Impact

It is now clear that there is a need to evaluate and align or realign HRD for organisational effectiveness on a continuous basis. Without such realignment the HR function loses its credibility and place in the organisation. Such an alignment should be multidimensional. It should start with business linkages, look at the systems requirements, examine the competencies of the HR people and the appropriateness of the HR structures and, finally, examine the quality of culture created by HR practices as well as by the styles and behaviour of seniors. Thus, alignment has to be examined in terms of strategy, systems, structure, competencies, styles and culture. This approach is discussed in detail in this book.

There are a few approaches, which are of recent origin and available in management literature, that come close to the above approach. Some of these, for example, the Balanced Score Card approach, have a focus on business goals rather than on human resources. These have been included in the book for illustrative purposes and also to signal that the measurement of the effectiveness of the HR function has to be done in the business context, like for all other tools.

The Balanced Score Card Approach

Popularised by Kaplan and Norton (1992, 1993), the Balanced Score Card approach assumes that for a business to succeed in the long run, the expectations of three stakeholders – employees, customers and shareholders – must be satisfied (see Box 2.2). The model also assumes that all the three stakeholders are interrelated: employee attitudes and behaviour influence customer satisfaction and retention and, in turn, influence shareholder satisfaction and investments. Furthermore, shareholder satisfaction affects employee satisfaction through bonuses, stock options and further investments on employees. If even one of the components breaks down, the chain does not work, leading to drops in performance. The HR function has a significant role to play in ensuring that all three stakeholders remain satisfied.

The Balanced Score Card approach of Kaplan and Norton (1992), later published in their book entitled *The Balanced Score Card Approach*, attempts to measure organisational performance from four distinct perspectives: (*i*) financial, (*ii*) customer, (*iii*) internal and (*iv*) innovation and learning.

BOX 2.2 EXAMPLES OF THE BALANCED SCORE CARD APPLICATIONS IN SOME COMPANIES

Company	shareholders	Customers	employees
Sears	Compelling place to invest	Compelling place to shop	Compelling place to work
Eastman Kodak	Shareholder satisfaction	Customer satisfaction	Employee satisfaction
AT&T	Economic value addition	Customer value addition	People value addition
American Express	Shareholder outcomes	Customer outcomes	Employee outcomes

The financial measures of performance indicate whether a company's strategy, implementation and execution contribute to improvements in the bottom line. Financial measures relate to profitability and can include operating income, return on capital employed, etc. Sales growth and generation of cash flow are the other alternate measures of financial performance. The internal business process measures focus on the internal processes that will have the greatest impact on customer satisfaction and achieve an organisation's financial objectives. Measures of quality, response time, cost and cycle time and new product introductions are some examples. On customer perspective, the measures include customer satisfaction, customer retention, new customer acquisition, customer profitability and market and accounted share in targeted segments. The fourth perspective of learning and growth focuses on the infrastructure the organisation should build to create long-term growth and improvement – people, systems and organisational procedures. Employee-based measures include employee satisfaction, retention, training and skills. Information system capabilities are measured by the real-time availability of accurate and critical customer and internal process information to employees who are on the frontline making decisions and taking action. Organisational procedures examine alignment of employee incentives with overall organisational success factors and measured rates of improvement in critical customer-based and internal processes.

The name Balanced Score Card reflects the balance provided between short- and long-term objectives, between financial and non-financial measures, between lagging and leading indicators and between internal and external perspectives.

Kaplan and Norton (1996) report that innovative companies use the Balanced Score Card as a strategic management system. It is also used as a management tool. It is used to clarify and translate vision and strategy; communicate and link strategic objectives and measures; plan, target and align strategic initiatives; and enhance strategic feedback and learning curves.

The Strategic HR Framework

The strategic HR framework (Ulrich and Lake, 1990) aims to leverage and/or align HR practices to build critical organisational capabilities that enable an organisation to achieve its goals. While the Balanced Score Card approach defines what a business should focus on, the strategic HR framework offers specific tools and paths to identify how a firm can leverage its HR practices. The sample questions asked for each of the three components in aligning business strategy with HR practices are given below:

1. *Business strategy.* What is the business strategy of our company? How do we win in the marketplace with regard to customer-buying criteria, competition, government regulations, supplier situation, etc.?
2. *Organisational capabilities.* In order to implement the business strategy, what are the critical organisational capabilities we need to develop? (These can include speed, a competitive mind-set, innovation and quality.)
3. *HR practices.* How should HR practices be designed and delivered to build these organisational capabilities? How do we motivate and build our leadership capabilities and also empower people to contribute towards the development of organisational capabilities?

The Integrative Framework

The integrative framework has been offered recently by Yeung and Berman (1997) and builds on earlier approaches. This framework identifies three paths through which HR practices can contribute to business performance:

1. By building organisational capabilities
2. By improving employee satisfaction
3. By shaping customer and shareholder satisfaction

This is called the first linkage chain. In the second linkage chain, organisational capabilities become key drivers that implement business strategy, impact customer satisfaction and eventually contribute to shareholder satisfaction.

Dynamic changes in HR measures are urgently required to refocus the priorities and resources of the HR function. Instead of being HR driven (what makes sense to HR professionals), the next generation of HR measures need to be business-driven (how HR can impact business success). Instead of being activity-oriented (what and how much we do), new HR measures should be impact-oriented (how much we improve business results). Instead of looking backward (what has happened), innovative HR measures should be forward looking, allowing the managers to assess and diagnose the processes and people capabilities that can predict the future success of corporations (Kaplan and Norton, 1992). Finally, instead of focusing on individual HR practices (the performance of staffing practices, training and development practices, etc.) future HR measures should focus on the entire HR system taking into account the synergy existing among all HR practices.

(Yeung and Berman, 1997: 330)

The integrative framework proposes three sets of measures:

1. *Internal operational measures dealing with how well HR practices are designed and delivered*
   Some examples of these are measuring the efficiency, quality and speed of delivering HR practices and managing the HR function as a whole. These measures include process measures, such as cycle time, quality and cost of HR practices, and result measures such as offer/accept ratios, different levels of training evaluation and business impact. Some other examples of internal operational measures are the ratio of HR professionals to employee population, the ratio of HR expenses to operating expenses and results of client satisfaction surveys. These measures are, however, inadequate to assess the performance of new HR roles and activities.
2. *Internal strategic measures dealing with how effectively HR practices build desired organisational capabilities and how effectively they increase employee satisfaction*
   Eastman Kodak has identified three critical organisational capabilities:
   1. Leadership effectiveness (measured by 360-degree assessment)
   2. Workforce competencies (measured by percentage of employees with documented development plans; number of hours devoted to development; results of development actions, such as planned action; reaction; learning; on-the-job behaviour; and business results)
   3. Performance-based culture (measured through surveys and by performance tracking)

Motorola developed an index, Individual Dignity Entitlement, based on six questions:

1. Do you have a substantive, meaningful job that contributes to the success of Motorola?
2. Do you have on-the-job behaviours and the knowledge base to be successful?
3. Has training been identified and made available to continuously upgrade your skills?
4. Do you have a career plan and is it exciting, achievable and being acted on?
5. Have you received candid, positive or negative feedback within the last 30 days, which has helped in improving your performance or achieving your career plan?
6. Is adequate sensitivity shown by the company towards your personal circumstances, gender and culture?

By tracking these six questions Motorola ensures that its HR practices add value through a more committed and content workforce.

3. *External strategic measures dealing with how well HR practices increase customer and shareholder satisfaction*
The measures include customer satisfaction enhancement programmes, executive education programmes to provide customer satisfaction, incentive compensation plans, etc.

Arthur Anderson's Human Capital Appraisal Approach

Friedman et al. (1998), on the basis of their consulting work at Arthur Anderson, have outlined an approach to assess the human capital in any corporation. They describe, specifically, how managers can evaluate the current effectiveness of a firm's human capital strategies and also the efficiency of its current HR programmes. The authors describe a five-stage framework to measure, manage and leverage the corporation's investment in people.

The approach is based on the belief that there are five stages in the management of human capital. Furthermore, there are five areas of human capital management. These five stages and five areas constitute a 5 × 5 matrix, and an assessment of how well the human capital is managed can be made by asking a number of questions that fall into the five areas.

The five stages are as follows:

1. *The clarification stage.* The firm identifies and confirms the overall business direction. An appraisal of this stage focuses on the business

goals of the company, its culture and values and its management philosophy and its impact on human capital.

2. *The assessment stage.* The firm calculates the cost of investment on the human capital and the value placed by employees on this investment.
3. *The design stage.* The firm creates programmes that can yield better returns on human capital.
4. *The implementation stage.* The firm puts the proposed changes into practice.
5. *The monitoring stage.* The firm checks the new system against strategy.

The five areas of human capital are as follows:

1. Recruitment, retention and retirement
2. Rewards and performance management
3. Career development, succession planning and training
4. Organisational structure
5. Human capital enablers

As mentioned above, for each stage a number of assessment questions are generated in relation to each human capital area. For example, in the clarification stage, managers examine their human capital programmes to ensure that they fit the organisation's overall culture and strategy. It is possible that the company may have a change plan but still expects the HR director to continue with his or her old HR policies on compensation and reward, even if they clash. Similarly, the HR director may initiate a change that may clash with the company strategy. Thus, a good fit requires clarification and good communication of business strategies and human resources elements. For example, on recruitment, clarification is sought on issues such as current system of recruitment, its adequacy or inadequacy, openings expected in the next five years and strategies for finding new talent. Similarly, performance management and rewards, career development, succession planning and training, organisational structure and HR enablers need to be clarified in relation to future strategies and plans.

HRD Score Card: A Proposed Model

This book proposes an HRD Score Card to measure the HRD maturity level of an organisation. The HRD maturity level depends on the following four factors:

1. HRD systems maturity and HRD strategies and appropriateness of HRD Structures and strategies
2. HRD competencies of the employees, including the line managers, top management, workmen and the HR department

3. HRD culture and values
4. Business impact and alignment of HRD in terms of intellectual capital building and talent management along with financial impact

The proposed model for the HRD Score Card draws heavily from the conceptualisation of HRD stated earlier (Pareek and Rao, 1992a) and also takes into consideration the research understanding gained in the past few years.

The model is based on the following assumptions:

- Competent and motivated employees are needed to provide quality products and services at competitive rates and in ways that enhance customer satisfaction
- Competencies and commitment can be developed through appropriate HRD mechanisms. In an HRD-mature organisation, there will be well-developed HRD systems, and the maturity of HRD systems can be measured through HRD audit (HRD Systems Maturity Score [SMS])
- HRD competencies of the HRD department and the line managers play a significant role in implementing the systems and processes in ways that can ensure employee satisfaction, competence building and customer satisfaction linkages. The competencies of the HRD staff and other employees can be measured in terms of an index (HRD Competence Score [CYS])
- The HRD culture, values and processes, created by the HRD tools, and the HRD staff and their styles also play a crucial role in building sustainable competencies in the organisation. These need to be measured and monitored. It is possible in some corporations, for example, small corporations, to have less of HR systems and yet have a high level of HR competencies and HR culture. Traditional, family-owned organisations, in the years when there were no systems approaches, used to have a good degree of HRD culture, which has resulted in effective functioning and business. The HRD culture can be measured and valued (HRD Culture and Values Score [CVS])
- HRD systems, competencies, values and culture should ensure achievement of business goals both short term and long term. Short-term business gaols can be measured in terms of talent management variables like employee utilisation, commitment, retention and development. Long-term measures include intellectual capital building. Business linkages of HRD are a very crucial component of HRD effectiveness. HRD systems, competencies and culture must be aligned with the business goals (short- and long-term goals, including intellectual capital generation) of the corporation. The alignment can be ensured through the direct linkages with customer satisfaction and employee motivation indices (Business Impact and Alignment Score [BLS])

These four indices mentioned above are the four pillars of HRD effectiveness. All the four dimensions are assessed using a 10-point rating system.

The 10-point rating scale is represented as follows:

A*	Highest score and highest maturity level
A	Very high maturity level
B*	High maturity level
B	Moderately high maturity level
C*	Moderate maturity level
C	Moderately low maturity level
D*	Low maturity level
D	Very low maturity level
F	Not at all present
U	Ungraded

The rationale of the scoring is explained in the subsequent sections.

The score card may read as follows:

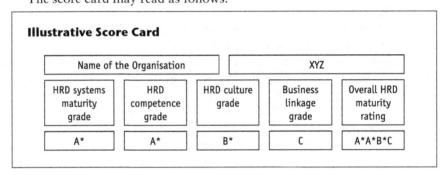

Illustrative Score Card

Name of the Organisation			XYZ	
HRD systems maturity grade	HRD competence grade	HRD culture grade	Business linkage grade	Overall HRD maturity rating
A*	A*	B*	C	A*A*B*C

HRD Audit and the HRD Score Card

The assigning of HRD scores can be done on the basis of HRD audit. The HRD audit described in the subsequent sections of this book helps in assessing each of the dimensions discussed above. The process of arriving at the HRD Score Card is described at the end of the book, after a detailed description of HRD audit. HRD audit is more than just assessing HRD maturity and assigning scores.

Detailed points and assessment methods are presented in a separate book *HRD Score Card 2500* (Rao, 2008b).

Conclusion

HRD, an organisation science dealing with competence building, commitment building and culture building, has undergone a major metamorphosis over the past three decades. The Rao and Pareek model consists of the linkages between HRD instruments, processes, outcomes and organisational effectiveness. The essential components of this model are as follows:

- HRD tools or instruments
- HRD climate and processes
  - Competent and well-structured HRD department to manage the above, resulting insatisfied and motivated employees,
  - more satisfied customers and better business results

An HRD Score Card approach is proposed to measure the HRD maturity level of an organisation. This is based on four indices, namely, HRD competencies of the employees, HRD strategies and systems maturity, HRD culture and values and HRD influence on short- and long-term business goals and talent management variables. HRD audit is a methodology to arrive at the HRD Score Card. HRD audit and the resulting HRD Score Card provide the necessary information required to realign HRD and build competitive advantage in terms of people and people processes.

3

HRD AUDIT

Basic Concepts and Components

Need For HRD Audit

In the last three decades a large number of corporations have established HRD departments, introduced new systems of HRD and made structural changes in terms of differentiating the HRD function and integrating it with the HR function. A good number of CEOs saw hope in HRD for most of their problems, issues and challenges. It is estimated that on an average, establishing a new HRD department with a small size of about five professionally trained staff costs about three to four million rupees per annum in terms of salaries, another 10 million in terms of budget (e.g., training budget, travel, etc.) and probably about 5 to 10 times the amount in terms of managerial time costs and opportunity costs. This is because HR systems are people intensive and require a lot of managerial time.

In spite of these investments in a number of corporations, there is a widespread feeling that HRD has not lived up to the expectations of either the top management or the line managers. There are also examples of corporations where HRD has taken the driver's seat and has given a lot of benefits. In today's competitive world, 'people' or employees can give a good degree of competitive advantage to the company. To get the best out of the HR function, there should be a good alignment of the function – its strategies, structure systems and styles – with business goals (e.g., financial and customer parameters). It should be aligned both with short-term goals and long-term strategies. If it is not aligned, the HR function can become a big liability to corporations and they will have no alternative but to close their HR departments. Besides this alignment, the skills and styles of the HR staff, line managers and top management should be in synergy with the HR

DOI: 10.4324/9781003530534-4

goals and strategies. HRD audit is an attempt to assess these alignments and ensure that they take place.

HRD audit is a comprehensive evaluation of the current HRD strategies, structure, systems, styles and skills in the context of short- and long-term business plans of a company. It attempts to find out the future HRD needs of the company after assessing the current HRD activities and inputs.

In the last few years the author along with his colleague Udai Pareek pioneered, in India, a methodology for auditing the HRD function called HRD audit and implemented it in many companies. This chapter describes the basic concept behind HRD audit.

Concepts of HRD Audit HRD Audit Is Comprehensive

HRD audit starts with an understanding of the future business plans and corporate strategies. Although HRD audit can be done even in organisations that lack well-formulated future plans and strategies, it is most effective as a tool when the organisation already has such long-term plans. The HRD audit starts with the following questions:

Where does the company want to be 5–10 years from now, three years from now and one year from now? (Answers to this question contribute to the HRD business linkages score of the HRD Score Card.)

The top management needs to provide the answer to this question. If there are any long-term plan documents they are also reviewed. On the basis of the answers, the consultants finalise the subsequent audit strategies and methodology. They identify the nature of the core competencies the organisation needs to develop in order to achieve its long-term, 5- to 10-year plans. The consultants also identify skills to be developed at various levels (e.g., workmen, supervisors, junior management, middle management, top management) and with respect to various functions (e.g., finance, production, marketing, etc.). Listing all these core competencies and skills for the future is the starting point of HRD audit. HRD audit normally attempts to assess the existing skills and competency gaps in order to achieve the long-term business goals and short-term results. The competencies may deal with technical aspects, managerial aspects, people or conceptual aspects. They may cover the knowledge base, attitudes, values and skills.

What is the current skill base of the employees in the company in relation to the various roles and role requirements? (Answers to this question contribute to the competency score on the HRD Score Card.)

This is assessed through an examination of the qualifications of employees, job descriptions, training programmes attended, etc. Besides this, interviews are conducted to identify the skill gap in the organisation. Training needs and performance appraisal forms provide further insights. Departmental heads and other employees provide insights into the competency and other skill requirements.

What are the HRD subsystems available today to help the organisation build its competency base for the present, immediate future and long-term goals? (Answers to this question contribute to the HRD SMS of the HRD Score Card.)

The auditors identify various HRD subsystems that are available to ensure the availability, utilisation and development of skills and other competencies in the company. The framework for evaluating these HRD subsystems has been presented earlier in Chapter 2 where all the component HRD systems have been presented. These systems and other HRD tools that an organisation may be using are studied in detail for arriving at the SMS.

What is the current level of effectiveness of these systems in developing people and ensuring that human competencies are available in adequate levels in the company? (Answers to this question contribute to the HRD SMS on the HRD Score Card.)

The consultants assess the effectiveness of each system. For example, the effectiveness of performance appraisal system is assessed by discussing with employees, individually and in groups, about the efficacy of the system. The auditors look at the appraisal forms, at the linkages between appraisal and training, conduct questionnaire surveys to assess the extent to which coaching and other components of other appraisals are being utilised and also conduct workshops, if necessary, to assess the effectiveness of these systems. Similarly, in relation to induction training, the consultants make it a point to meet those who have been through the induction training recently or those who are in the process of being inducted into the company and take their views to improve the induction training methodology and so on.

Is the HRD structure existing in the company adequate enough to manage the HRD in the company? (Answers to these questions contribute to the HRD competencies score of the HRD Score Card.)

In this stage, the auditors or consultants examine whether the current HRD structure can handle the pressing and future HRD needs of the company. They examine the existing skill base of the HRD staff, their professional preparation, attitudes, values, developmental needs, the line managers' perceptions regarding them and so on. In addition to the full-time staff, the consultants also assess the HRD structure in terms of the use of task forces and other mechanisms. Special attention should be paid to the role played by HRD staff and other employees in "people management attitudes and service" at times of emergency like the Covid 19.

Are the top management and senior manager styles of managing people in tune with the learning culture? (Answers to these questions contribute to the HRD culture score of the HRD Score Card.)

Here the consultants examine the senior managers' leadership styles, human relations skills and so on. The extent to which their styles facilitate the creation of a learning environment are examined.

HRD Audit Examines Linkages with Other Systems

HRD audit also examines the linkages between HRD and other systems like TQM, personnel policies, strategic planning, etc.

The consultants make suggestions on the basis of evaluation about the future HRD strategies required by the company, the structure the company needs to develop new competencies, the systems that need to be strengthened and the styles and culture that have compatibility with the HRD process.

HRD Audit Is Business Driven

HRD audit always keeps business goals in focus. At the same time, it attempts to bring in professionalism in HRD. In keeping the business focus at the centre, HRD audit attempts to evaluate HRD strategy, structure, system, staff, skill and style and their appropriateness.

Why Do Most Companies Want HRD audit?

There are various reasons why companies want to undertake HRD audit, some of which have been stated as follows:

To Make HR Function Business Driven

HRD audit is undertaken by most organisations to make HR systems and processes more relevant to business goals. Over a period of time, business changes may have taken place for a variety of reasons, including environmental changes. Organisational restructuring (financial, technological, marketing, manufacturing, engineering, etc.) may have necessitated meeting the changing environmental demands and opportunities. Such changes should be accompanied by appropriate changes in the HR function (its goals, emphasis, strategies, systems and processes). Some companies go in for HRD audit to examine and make changes in the HR function to accompany organisational changes. Some organisations that have undertaken business process reengineering have conducted HRD audit to ensure that the HR function is aligned with business goals and strategies.

To Take Stock of Things and to Improve HRD for Expanding, Diversifying and Entering into a Fast-growth Phase

Many good organisations in India, after liberalisation, have entered a competitive phase. These are those organisations that saw a lot of opportunities, both within the country and abroad. In light of these new opportunities, some of these felt that they had not paid adequate attention to their human resources due to constraints of the past. They used to recruit employees at low salaries and on the basis of contacts rather than competence. As a result, the organisations ended up having very heterogeneous categories of employees. Moreover, organisations suddenly discovered that what was valued in the past – employees with average competence and high loyalty – had become a weakness in the present. In order to compete for the future, they had to change their profiles. Thus, companies felt the need to take stock and see the direction in which they should move.

Some of these companies have borrowed many HRD practices from professionally managed companies, but without adequate preparation. They are not sure if they are going in the right direction. Thus, to know in which direction their HRD should move, they have gone in for HRD audit.

For Promoting Professionalism among Employees and to Switch Over to Professional Management

With the world becoming a global village, some companies started realising the importance of skill development and professionalism among the employees. In order to inculcate professionalism they wanted to take stock of their HRD and therefore undertook an HRD audit.

Multinationals Want to Know the Reasons for Lower Labour Productivity and for Improving Their HRD Strategies in the Indian Context

Some multinationals who have been operating in the country found from their experience that though they pay low salaries in India as compared to other plants they have in their countries, the labour productivity is poor. After a careful examination of a number of good practices they had introduced, they discovered that they had some unique problems with the Indian people. Some of these included high designation consciousness, low level of teamwork, tendencies to unionise, lack of trust on the management, low energy levels and preference for a paternalistic treatment. Some of these companies relied heavily on their HRD departments to change the situation. Their experiences were not as positive as they desired. Therefore, they decided to undertake an HRD audit. They perceived HRD audit more as a renewal exercise.

For Growth and Diversification

A few organisations after their initial success and building core competencies in certain areas wanted to diversify and expand into new areas. They even undertook the initial steps of using their existing staff to handle new projects. They were not very sure whether this was likely to work out. They also wanted to know the direction in which they should move. Therefore, they decided to undertake HRD audit.

Dissatisfaction with a Particular Component

A few organisations undertook HRD audit more as a necessary, comprehensive review to assess their needs given from their dissatisfaction with one or two subsystems of HRD. For example, in one company, I saw HRD audit as a means to improve communications. In another company, appraisal was the starting point, but they decided that since appraisal is linked to many HRD subsystems they should get a comprehensive examination of HRD done. A third company used HRD audit for developing a training plan as their main interest was training. In all these cases the influencing factor for initiating and using HRD audit has been some visionary either at the top level or at the board level who has a more holistic view of the organisation.

Change of Leadership

Some organisations undertook HRD audit as their HRD manager was leaving and they needed to recruit a new HRD manager and reorient the entire HRD department. Sometimes a change in the CEOs and other top management members may also prompt HRD audit.

Thus, there can be various reasons for initiating HRD audit.

For Effective Talent Utilisation, Retention and Development and Intellectual Capital Building

In the recent times, the intellectual capital building and stakeholder value creation are largely driven by the need to enhance the market value of an organisation, which is the total value of its net tangible assets and the value of its intangible assets. The *tangible assets* include the book value of all assets, shares, land and buildings, machinery and all that can be seen and accounted for, whereas the *intellectual capital* of the company includes the image of the company; its internal strengths in terms of talent, people, management systems and practices; its customers, brands, patents and everything else that comprises its market value. HRD practices are expected to contribute to such intangible asset creation. Audit examines the visible and less visible contributions being made by HRD to procuring competent people (talent) and using them to achieve organisational goals and results and build other forms of capital like the structural capital, customer base, innovations, new products, customer loyalty, cost-effectiveness, etc. HRD audit is also useful to examine the agility of people leadership and care provided by the top management and HR functionaries during pandemics like Covid 19.

Role of HRD Audit in Business Improvement

The experiences of the companies discussed previously indicate that HRD audit can give many insights into a company's affairs. HRD audit is also cost-effective. In India it costs as low as US$10,000–25,000. The auditors normally camp in the organisation for one to two weeks, make their observations and give their report in a month's time. They normally make a preliminary presentation at the end of their visit.

The auditors bring with them their experience of HRD with a large number of companies and provide a good degree of qualitative data. Thus, the returns on such low-cost audit can be substantial.

The following are some of the favourable consequences of HRD audit that have been observed:

It Can Get The Top Management to Think in Terms of Strategic and Long-term Business Plans

Ironically, it may seem that HRD audit should begin with such strategic plans, but in some cases it has propelled the top management to formulate such plans. Another aspect in this regard is that people cannot participate in the HRD audit without some sharing of these plans. The audit, therefore, has forced the top management to share their plans across the organisation, resulting in increased involvement and commitment of employees. In a few cases, a new system of annual planning and sharing of the business plans with management staff, to enable them to plan their own activities and competency development programmes, has been initiated.

Changes in the Styles of the Top Management

Any successful HRD company has an excellent learning environment. Thus, one of the objectives of HRD is to create a learning organisation. A learning culture can be created only if the top managers of the company exhibit an HRD orientation. Such a style requires an empowering attitude, participative style of management and the ability to convert and use mistakes, conflicts and problems as learning opportunities and so on. Some top-level managers in India have been found to block the motivation and learning of employees through coercive, autocratic and even paternalistic styles of management. HRD audit highlights such detrimental styles of management, thereby pointing out the difficulties in developing and preparing the employees for the future. This has helped in providing subtle feedback to the top management and initiating a change process.

Role Clarity of HRD Department and the Role of Line Managers in HRD

In almost all cases, the HRD audit has been found to draw the attention of employees at various levels to the important role of the HRD department: current as well as the future. Better role clarity of the HRD department and the HRD function, resulting in increased understanding of line managers about their HRD role are the uniform results of HRD audit. While the degree may vary from organisation to organisation depending on various factors, this exercise has a favourable impact on employee productivity.

Improvements in HRD Systems

HRD audit has helped most organisations in measuring the effectiveness of their HRD systems and in designing or redesigning HRD systems. The most frequently changed or renewed systems include performance appraisal, induction training, job rotation, career planning and promotion policies, mentoring, communication and training. A number of organisations have changed or strengthened one or more of their HRD subsystems as a result of HRD audit.

Increased Focus on Human Resources and Human Competencies

One of the results of HRD audit is to focus on new knowledge, attitudes and skills required by the employees. Comments are made about the technical, managerial, human and conceptual competencies of staff at various levels. This differentiation has been found to help organisations in identifying and focusing sharply on the competency requirements and gaps. The audit establishes a system of role clarity and fixing of accountability. This may take place through separate role clarity exercises or through the development of an appropriate performance appraisal system. In any case, the attention of the organisation gets focused on developing the competency base of the organisation. More sensitivities are developed towards missing aspects of competencies. For example, one organisation was found to neglect the human relations competencies of their staff, which led to quite a few problems and wastage of time. With HRD audit, many of these were streamlined. The various HRD policies also got strengthened.

Better Recruitment Policies and More Professional Staff

HRD audit proposes the competence base required by the organisation. It gives direction for competency requirements of employees at various levels, thus providing a base for recruitment policies and procedures. As a result, in some companies, new recruitment and retention strategies have been worked out. In other companies, the audit has led to strengthening of recruitment policies and procedures.

More Planning and More Cost-Effective Training

HRD audit has been found to assist in assessing the returns on training. One of the aspects emphasised in the HRD audit is to calculate the investments made in training and ask questions about the returns. The process of identifying training needs and utilisation of training inputs and learning for organisation growth and development are assessed. As direct investments are made in training, any cost–benefit analysis draws the attention of the top management and HRD managers to review the training function with relative ease. For example, one organisation has strengthened its training function by introducing a new system of post-training follow-up and dissemination of knowledge to others through seminars and action plans. Many organisations have developed training policies and systematised their training function. Training needs assessment also has become more scientific in these organisations.

Strengthening Accountability through Appraisal Systems and Other Mechanisms

HRD audit can give significant inputs about the existing state of accountability of employees. This can be assessed through performance appraisal as well as through the work culture and other cultural dimensions. A number of organisations have introduced systems of performance planning, sharing of expectations and documenting the accountability of staff. HRD audit has led to the changing of appraisal systems.

Streamlining of Other Management Practices

Most often HRD audit points out the strengths and weaknesses in some of the management systems existing in the organisation. It also indicates the absence of systems that enhance both human productivity and utilisation of the existing competency base, for example, MIS, rules and procedures, etc., which may have an effect on the functioning of employees. In a few cases HRD audit has helped the management to look at some subsystems and work procedures. Preparation of a manual for delegation of powers, clarification of roles and responsibilities, developing or streamlining the manuals of financial and accounting procedures and systems, strengthening the information systems and sharing the information are some of the resultant activities.

TQM Interventions

Quality improvements and establishing TQM systems require a high degree of involvement of employees. In a number of cases HRD audit has pointed out to the linkages between TQM and other quality programmes and helped in strengthening the same.

Due to improvements in the training system, enhancement of the quality of group work and strengthening of the appraisal systems, TQM programmes also get improved. In a few organisations performance appraisals have been changed to integrate quality aspects and internal customer satisfaction into the appraisal system. Thus, HRD audit leads to the strengthening of quality systems.

It Can Enhance the Return on Investment (ROI) of the HR Function

In addition to all the aforesaid points, HRD audit aligns the HR function and activities with business goals. In the process it eliminates non-value-adding HR systems, activities and processes and enhances the value-adding activities and processes. It reduces non-productive assets of the HR department (e.g., underutilised training centres, ill-implemented appraisal systems, etc.) and sharpens the focus of the HR function to get better results. The main contribution of HRD audit is to focus on value-adding HRD.

Methodology of HRD Audit: An Overview

HRD audit requires the use of a number of methods for HRD audit. The methods are presented as follows. These methods are used in combination, and a good audit requires the use of all these methods.

Individual Interviews

The auditors normally make it a point to interview the top-level management and senior managers individually. Such individual interviews are a must for capturing their thinking about the future plans and opportunities available for the company. Also, by virtue of occupying strategic positions, the top management has the required perspective for a good HRD audit. Thus, a good HRD audit begins with individual interviews of the top management.

Individual interviews are also essential when sensitive information has to be obtained. Such information pertains to working styles and culture. Union leaders, departmental heads, some strategic clients and informal leaders are all interviewed individually. In addition, if the organisation is small and is largely manned by professionals, the coverage can be enlarged to include interviews with randomly selected representative sample of employees from different levels and functions.

Group Interviews

Normally, in an audit of companies having thousands of employees, it is not feasible to meet everyone individually. It is my experience that group discussions and interviews serve as a good mechanism for collecting information about the effectiveness of existing systems. Group interviews are conducted normally for groups of four to eight individuals. It is preferable to have employees drawn from same or similar levels. This is because in Asian cultures there is likely to be some inhibition on the part of junior employees to freely express their views in the presence of their seniors. However, it is quite common to give cross-functional representation of employees in the same group. If the organisation is large, an attempt is made to conduct group interviews for each function separately to keep the levels homogeneous.

In both individual and group interviews for HRD audit, the following open-ended questions are normally asked.

1. What do you see as the future growth opportunities and business directions of the company?
2. What skills and competencies does the company have that you are proud of?
3. What skills and competencies do you need to run your business, or to perform your role, more effectively at present?
4. What are the strengths of your HRD function?
5. What are the areas where your HRD function can do better?
6. What is good about your HRD subsystems, such as performance appraisal, career planning, job rotation, training, quality circles, induction training, recruitment policies, performance counselling, worker development programmes and HRD departments?
7. What is weak about them? What can be improved?
8. What changes do you suggest to strengthen HRD in your company?
9. What do you think are the ways in which line managers can perform more development roles?

Workshops

In some cases individual and group interviews are substituted by large-scale interactive process (LSIP) workshops (see Box 3.1). In such workshops, a large number of participants ranging from 30 to 300 can be gathered in a room and asked to do the HRD audit. Normally, the participants work in small groups, either around various subsystems or around different dimensions of HRD, do a SWOT (strengths, weaknesses, opportunities and threats) analysis and make a presentation. The workshops also can be used to focus specifically on individual HRD systems like performance appraisal. The workshop outcomes have been found to be very good.

BOX 3.1 LSIP WORKSHOP METHODOLOGY APPLIED TO HRD AUDIT

In one company, the author used an LSIP methodology in which a large number of executives from the organisation participated in conducting the HRD audit. The methodology required the large group to be divided into the maximum number of mixed groups (designation, age and function). They were all seated in a large hall in groups of six to seven members around each table. During the day they were taken through a series of diagnostic exercises through questions such as the following:

1.   What are the three good things in your performance appraisal system?
2.   What is the one thing you would like to change in your performance appraisal system?
3.   How would you critically evaluate the job rotation in your company?
4.   What are the strengths and weaknesses of your training policies and practices?
5.   What three adjectives would you use to describe the promotion policies as they exist in your company?

The results were compiled by a group of research assistants and fed into the computer and the analysis was fed back to the group. By the end of the day, the group knew the results of the audit and the recommendations the consultants would give to the top management. Some of the top management team members participating in the exercise also got more motivated to improve the state of affairs. Thus, in conducting HRD audit through participative methods, the consultants were able to diagnose and start the change process. The HRD audit itself became an OD intervention.

HRD audit, if conducted through participatory methods, may itself initiate the change process. Even if it does not, it is a potential diagnostic tool and can provide a lot of information to the top management on employee-related processes and help them plan further interventions.

Questionnaire Method

A comprehensive questionnaire, which Dr Udai Pareek and I jointly developed (Rao and Pareek, 1994, 1998) is administered to company executives.

This questionnaire has over 250 items and requires about 90 minutes to complete. The questionnaire can be administered individually or in a group. I have found it useful to call groups of respondents, selected randomly, to a room and explain the objectives and the process of HRD audit and administer the questionnaire then and there itself. This ensures uninterrupted answering of the questionnaire and provides scope for getting more credible data due to the personal explanations given by the auditors.

A number of other questionnaires have been developed since the time this first comprehensive HRD audit questionnaire was prepared by us. These are explained in detail in subsequent chapters. These questionnaires attempt to assess various dimensions of HRD, including the competency base of HRD staff, styles of line managers, implementation of various HRD systems, etc.

The most significant use of the questionnaire method is that it helps in benchmarking.

Observation

In addition to the aforesaid methods, the auditors should physically visit the workplace, including the plant, machinery room, canteen, toilets, training rooms, hostels, hospital, school, living colony, etc. These visits and observations are meant to assess the extent to which a congenial and supportive human welfare-orientated climate exists in the company. This is essential because employees are not likely to give their best if they do not live in good surroundings, their health and education are not taken care of, they do not have good communication and other facilities and their work conditions are poor. The observations can be made using a checklist of questions.

Analysis of Secondary Data

Analysis of secondary data and HR analytics can give a lot of insights into the HRD assets and liabilities of the company. For example, in a company that had about 50 HR people, only two had the required technical training in HRD. When an analysis of the training programmes attended by others was carried out, it was found that a large number of them did not attend any HRD programme in the last five years. Such analysis of secondary data can give many insights. Analyses of age profiles of the employees, trainings attended, minutes of the meetings held, etc., help in determining the assets and liabilities. Such an analysis should also pay attention to the costs incurred by the company in terms of maintaining the HRD infrastructure.

Analysis of Reports, Records, Manuals and Other Published Literature

Published literature of the company, such as annual reports, marked hand-outs, training calendar, personnel manual and various circulars issued from time to time are also likely to help in assessing the strengths and weaknesses of HRD.

Limitations of HRD Audit

The audit itself is rarely a failure. However, when HRD audit is conducted as a fashion or as a requirement of someone else and the CEO has no way of refusing such an HRD audit, it can have some negative results. For example, in one organisation where HRD audit was conducted at the instance of the headquarters located in a different place, the CEO was very cooperative but later became very defensive and started justifying everything that was going on in his unit. The message went fast down the line and the employees formed themselves into groups – those who were in favour of the CEO and those who were against him. As a result, the auditors had a difficult time finding the truth and it became more of a political game than a genuine effort for improvement. However, such cases are rare.

Most HRD audit failures are due to failures of implementation. Some CEOs are simply curious. They are restless until they know the results of the audit, but once they know the audit results, they feel reassured that they are above average and therefore forget about the audit. Sometimes HRD audit can also be used against the HRD department. It can be used to get rid of some staff in the department. Such a decision can have an adverse effect on the overall HRD of the company subsequently, unless it is made carefully and after adequate time and scope is given to develop the competencies of the employees concerned. Although HRD audit does point out to the competency gaps in the HRD department and also indicates the mismatch, if any, between the organisational needs and the employee competencies, normally an attempt is made to suggest development strategies rather than retrenchment strategies. HRD audit does not give evaluation of individuals but focuses on units and systems. The consultants may, however, give their informal feedback, if any, to the person concerned.

Conclusion

HRD audit is a comprehensive evaluation of the current HRD strategies, structure, systems, styles and skills in the context of short- and long-term business plans of a company. It provides inputs required to assess all aspects of HRD and assign the HRD score for the company on a number of dimensions. Its main objective is to align the HR function (structure, systems and processes) with business goals or to create a business-driven HR function. Since it is comprehensive, it uses a variety of methods, including interviews, observation, secondary data analysis, workshops, etc. It has to be business driven and comprehensive. There are numerous reasons why companies go for HRD audit, the main ones being growth and diversification, promoting professionalism, improving HRD strategies and enhancing the direct contribution of HRD to business. Experience has shown HRD audit to have a tremendous impact on different areas of business, including strategic planning, role clarity, streamlining practices, creation of better polices, top management styles, improvement in HRD systems, focus on competence and TQM interventions. However, proper implementation and top management support are crucial for the success of HRD audit.

The subsequent chapters explore various components of HRD audit. They present in detail how various components of strategies, structure, systems, styles and skills are audited. The methodology is presented in Section Three and some case studies and issues are presented in Section 4.

SECTION 2

HRD and HR Audit

HRD audit starts with an evaluation of HRD strategies. HRD strategies should flow from corporate strategies or at least be aligned with them. For this to happen, the first requirement is that there should be clearly defined business strategies. In the absence of such business strategies HRD becomes directionless and only routine and personnel administration or maintenance activities take the driver's seat. Corporations with reactive HR functions that take care of routine HR requirements cannot provide leadership and may not be able to gain any long-term competitive edge. The first chapter in this section (Chapter 4) outlines the business challenges faced by the corporate sector today and the strategies they tend to follow. The HR strategies needed to meet these challenges are illustrated, followed by an outline of the HRD strategies. The chapter then presents a list of questions to be answered for HRD strategy audit. An assessment of HRD strategies provides inputs for linking or aligning the HR function with business development. These linkages form an important dimension of the HRD Score Card. Methods of deriving the HRD score from the strategy audit are described in Chapter 12.

The best of HR strategies may not enhance company performance if the leadership and managerial styles of the top management and senior executives are not aligned with the HR philosophy and requirements. The best of strategies may fail if some top-level managers get on the wrong side of their employees by being insensitive to their needs. For example, a critical and autocratic style can create morale problems and get the worst out of employees than their best. Therefore, styles should take into consideration the needs of the corporation and the maturity and adaptability levels of people. Chapter 5 highlights the significance of HRD culture and values

DOI: 10.4324/9781003530534-5

in determining organisational performance. HRD culture is a result of the top management's beliefs and behaviour as well as of the successful implementation of appropriate HRD practices. Culture and values have a lasting effect on the behaviour of employees. They provide the milieu for their work and stay. The HRD culture, which can be described as facilitating business development, is presented in this chapter. The values and organisational culture put together provide inputs for another significant dimension of the HRD Score Card. Chapter 5 deals with this significant aspect of the HRD Score Card.

With strategies and styles in place, the structuring of the HR function becomes a significant dimension of HRD audit. When strategies are aligned, and when styles are being developed or modified, an appropriately structured HR department can facilitate the development and implementation of HR systems and processes that can help achieve business goals. In the past, HR departments had grown out of proportion. Some of them have now multiplied to perpetuate systems without appropriate links to organisational goals. The appropriateness of the current structures needs to be examined. Therefore, HRD audit focuses on the structure of the function. Chapter 6 discusses, first, some considerations for structuring or restructuring the HR function. It then goes on to describe the issues or questions that are answered in HRD audit. The assessment from this flows into the competencies section of the HRD Score Card.

If the HR function is appropriately structured, its primary task is to identify HR systems and to achieve appropriate short-term business goals and long-term strategies of the corporation. The HR systems should be in place. These systems can include recruitment and manpower planning, career development, training and performance management. These should flow from immediate needs as well as long-term interests of the organisation. They should be of world-class quality and benefit from benchmarking with others. Some of the most critical HR systems are described in this chapter. The systems framework used in HR audits is presented in Chapter 7, followed by a list of questions. Chapter 8 presents a detailed description of the skills and competencies needed to effectively implement HR strategies systems and processes. The HR competencies needed by the HR staff are different from those needed by line managers and other groups. Both are equally important. While HR function is facilitated by HR people, it has to be owned by every manager as it is an integral part of every employee. The HR skills or competencies audit attempts to assess the extent to which these competencies are existing in the HR staff as well as in line managers. Chapter 8 discusses in detail the competency requirements of the HR staff as well as of the line managers. In discussing these competencies evidence is drawn from successful HR managers. The chapter then goes on to present competency requirements of HR roles and their audit. The chapter also presents a framework for assessing the styles and goes on to suggest some methods of assessment. This is followed by a list of frequently asked questions for auditing HRD styles. Over a period of time, it is the styles and leadership that create a culture. HRD culture plays an important role in ensuring a lasting impact of HRD.

Thus, this section with five chapters covers the auditing of the four pillars of the HR function – business linkages through strategy, styles and culture, structure and competencies, and systems. The next section focuses on the methodology of HRD audit.

4

HRD STRATEGIES

A strategy is a course of action chosen with a view to achieve certain objectives. HR strategies may deal with many aspects of the HR function, including how people should be recruited, placed, trained,
    treated, retained, motivated, empowered and rotated. HR strategies should flow both from the short-term goals of the organisation and the long-term business strategies. Even if they are not derived from them, they should at least be aligned with them. Otherwise, the purpose will not be achieved. Business goals as well as strategies need to be prepared to create new opportunities as well as to make use of the opportunities available. The economic and other aspects of the environment play an important role in strategy formulation and goal setting. As the world moves towards becoming a global village, the environmental changes seem to influence all business activities. All corporations are required to be sensitive to these changes and challenges. These challenges provide the context for HRD. As they influence all HR activities, we discuss these first, followed by the meaning and role of HRD strategy audit.

Globalisation: Challenges for Building World-Class Organisations

Globalisation has brought in a lot of opportunities and challenges for the corporate sector. Most corporations are required to operate in global markets and are therefore required to be of world class in their products, services and approach. Even if a corporation decides to operate in local markets, it has to face global competition due to opening-up of markets and, hence, cannot remain a passive local player. The corporation has to think globally in order to survive competition. All HR strategies should flow from

DOI: 10.4324/9781003530534-6

corporate business strategies and plans. No matter what the specific strategy of an organisation is, in a global economy organisations cannot escape the reality of addressing the following challenges and issues as a part of their strategy:

Quality challenge: World-class organisations are quality-driven organisations. Their products are of high quality and services excellent. Everyone in the organisation is quality conscious and constantly strives to meet high standards. To produce quality products and services at competitive prices is a major challenge for all corporations today. The business goals of any company cannot escape quality emphasis.

People challenge: World-class organisations are manned by employees who are professional, systematic and trustworthy. They can be relied on fully to meet their commitments in terms of delivering services on time and at promised standards. They do not need to be followed up. They are competent, innovative, proactive, change oriented, systems driven and entrepreneurial. How does one recruit, develop and retain such world-class employees? This is a strategy challenge.

Technology: World-class organisations spend on technology. If they are not using the most modern technology, it is for valid reasons, and their product quality does not suffer for want of technology. Getting world-class technology, absorbing it, adapting it and continuously improving on it for strategic advantage is another challenge faced by modern corporates.

Culture: World-class organisations have well laid-out systems and procedures. These systems are not meant to be bureaucratic controls but to increase predictability of actions and output and to ensure reliability of services and actions. They are meant to provide continuous feedback to various categories of employees and ensure coordination among them. They may have fewer systems, but these are appropriate systems and the organisations meticulously implement them. Building a professional, systems-driven and commitment-promoting organisational culture is another major challenge for these corporations.

Speed: World-class organisations distinguish themselves by their speed and response time. These are high-speed organisations. Once a decision is taken, implementation is fast. Their service speed is high. Their response time is small.

Sleek: They are sleek. With fewer people and the aid of modern technologies, world-class organisations are able to accomplish a lot. Managing business with fewer people, small overheads and sleek organisational structures is another business challenge.

Invest on people: To remain continuously competitive, organisations must invest on people and believe in building competencies. They use a variety of methods to develop their people. They use training, mentoring, coaching, 360-degree feedback, rotation, task forces, OD interventions, survey feedback, assessment centre – mechanisms to continuously build people. They may not use all these, but whatever they use they use them well and with seriousness. They are good at implementation. Investing in people in such a way that it adds to strategic advantage is another challenge.

Flat and non-hierarchical structures: World-class organisations tend to have flat structures and decision-making is well structured. There is little bureaucracy and systems are well laid out. They are not hierarchy conscious but are commitment and responsibility conscious. They are goal driven and not procedure driven. Decisions are not made on the basis of levels and positions but on the basis of roles, responsibilities, needs and systems. Employees at all levels are respected and their work is valued. Breaking the existing business to build flat and non-hierarchical organisations is another major challenge for modern corporations.

Social responsibility and high commitment to country: World-class organisations are good corporate citizens. They realise that their own survival is at stake without proper investments in society. They also perceive such investments as having economic value. For example, investing in rural development can be seen as creating new markets in rural areas by enhancing the purchasing power of the people. World-class organisations exhibit high concern for society. They have a high sense of civic responsibility and a sense of duty towards their own country, their host country and to humanity in general. This is reflected in their contribution to the neighbourhood and the country where they are located, their environment consciousness, etc. They have a sense of value, and their concern for people and services override their concern for profits, though they are profit conscious, cost conscious and customer centred. They contribute liberally to social causes.

Learning organisations: World-class organisations constantly experiment and learn from themselves and others. They learn from their successes and failures. They are innovative. They invest in research and development. Their employees are learning oriented. They are networking organisations and have networking skills. They use these networks to influence others as well as to develop themselves. They maintain their competitive edge through benchmarking, comparing themselves with the best using their networks. They use consultants and other external agents to learn and improve. They are reflective organisations. They are change prone and adoption prone. Creating a learning organisation is another major challenge for them.

Some impediments to building world-class organisations are presented in Box 4.1. Most of these impediments pose challenges for the HRD function.

BOX 4.1 INDIA AND WORLD-CLASS ORGANISATIONS: A CRITIQUE

Most Indian organisations have a long way to go in becoming world-class organisations. Only a few have succeeded in some fields, particularly in the software industry, which has had a number of success stories. There are several impediments in India to create world-class organisations. Indian organisations need leadership, vision, commitment (time and effort), perseverance, professionalism and a world view to become world class. They are weak in all these areas though they may have tremendous potential. The following are the other weaknesses to building world-class organisations:

1. *Poor in packaging products.*
2. *Excessive profit orientation with low customer orientation.* Most often Indian organisations sacrifice long-term rewards and accomplishments for trivial short-term benefits.
3. *Low self-respect and low respect for local products, expertise and services.* Indians generally prefer foreign brands and even consultants when there are equally good Indian products and consultants. If Indian products do not sell in the country and Indian organisations do not recognise and popularise their own strong points, how can the rest of the world notice Indian products? See how Indian products shine when they are packaged abroad.
4. *Lack of professionalism and planning.* As a nation India cannot plan beyond five years. Further, the plans made are not implemented properly. With regard to Indian organisations, they do not plan beyond one year though they claim to have strategic plans.
5. *Lack of process sensitivity.* Indian organisations waste a lot of time focusing on procedures instead of on results. They are hierarchy oriented, status conscious, position and designation conscious and not task focused and goal oriented. Individuals are more right conscious and not responsibility centred.
6. *Lack of cost consciousness.* People are not as cost conscious in organisations as they are in their personal lives. They do not mind wasting the organisation's resources. They do not easily identify themselves with their organisation and country. They identify themselves more with their unions, communities and groups that protect them for mundane things and sacrifice their organisational and even national interests for the sake of short-term achievements like minor salary hikes and benefits.
7. *Low or poor degree of quality consciousness.* Indians have a high tolerance for poor-quality products and services and also end up offering the same.
8. *High relationship orientation resulting in a tendency to make promises to please others even if the promise cannot be delivered.* Promises are made but

not kept. There is little respect for time. As a result, a climate of low trust is created. All this leads to more monitoring and more overheads.

9. *Poor infrastructure.* Organisations have a long way to go in terms of technology. Services are extremely poor and unprofessional. They invest very little in research and development.

10. *A tendency to pull down each other and play win–lose or lose–lose games rather than win–win games.* If an organisation has two competent and well-qualified managers in the same department, they spend most of the time fighting with each other to establish their supremacy rather than work together to benefit the organisation. There is a tendency towards jealousy and taking criticism badly. Rather than learning from mistakes, mistakes of others are highlighted to justify one's mistakes and poor quality of services. Organisations benchmark not with better companies but with poorer ones to get away with the current performance.

11. *A predominantly classificatory, divisive, individualistic and dependent culture.* This works against creating a synergy between resources and talent. It adds to the overheads of the organisation and the country. Indian organisations are dependent on the government and its subsidies, and sometimes the government makes those who can be independent to also become dependent through controls.

Prahalad (1999) identifies five Indian realities (failures) that are impediments to progress: stagnation, lack of aspiration to be world class, a sense of collective paralysis, lack of vision and looking to the West all the time for validation.

Organisations should formulate appropriate strategies to build their business to be world class.

How to Create a World-Class Organisation?

India has a large number of people with talent and high potential and can beat any country in various spheres of activity. Indian people are intelligent and emotional. Their emotional intelligence gives them dynamism and energy that is unparalleled. They also have a tremendous capability to learn.

Prahalad (1999) suggests the following steps to make use of the tremendous opportunities in India:

1. Imagination – one has to think outside the box. Strategy is about imagination.
2. Companies need to build their own business models. The business models that work in India are indigenously developed.
3. Strong leadership – knowledge, leadership, belief and commitment.

4. Entrepreneurship is alive among the poorest and needs to be exploited.
5. Technology and adaptations of technology.
6. New organisational models need to be developed and used.
7. Accountability and transparency in performance.
8. Recognition of resistance to change and managing the same.
9. Commercial outlook in all transactions.
10. An optimism to be world class.

It is to meet these challenges the HR function becomes very critical. Unfortunately, the HR function in India suffers many disadvantages.

In a survey conducted at IIMA as part of a programme organised by Khandwalla (1994), a number of chief executives were asked to specifically mention the learning challenges they were facing in the liberalised economy. The following were listed as the significant learning challenges:

1. Learning challenges pertaining to the learning environmentCoping with the market changes and competitiveness
   • Coping with enhanced customer expectations
   • Coping with changing government policies
2. Learning challenges pertaining to the internal environmentImplementing HRD
   • Generating teamwork
   • Technology upgradation
   • Enhancing quality
   • Developing market orientation
   • Improving productivity

Some of the less frequently mentioned challenges included the following:

• Implementing computerisation programmes
• Budgeting and control
• Improving vertical and horizontal communication
• Generating and disseminating knowledge of the competitive situation within the organisation
• Enhancing professionalism
• Diversification
• Getting employee commitment to organisational goals

Organisations also seem to face difficulties and blocks in changing. In the survey, the most frequently mentioned difficulties in coping with the changed situation included the following:

- Slow perception of changes in the environment due to lack of effective information systems
- Lack of employee commitment to learning
- Resistance to change due to perceptual gaps
- Lack of long-term perspective in solving problems or making plans
- Lack of investments in developing employee competencies and motivation
- Prevalence of sectarian viewpoints and absence of group ethos
- Absence of forums and learning mechanisms

Human Resource Strategies at the Corporate Level

Normally when we talk of HR strategy, we deal with strategies of attracting, retaining, developing, motivating and utilising employees and their competencies for effective organisational functioning and growth. Organisations are doing a good deal on these four dimensions to meet their short-term goals and objectives but are not doing enough for meeting long-term goals.

The aforesaid challenges suggest that the following focus is needed in future HRD efforts. These focal points can be taken as strategic focal points. These strategic focal points can vary from organisation to organisation and are only illustrative.

Communication Strategy

Continuous communication with employees, their families, and other stakeholders like the investors, and policy makers, the community is a critical factor. Making employees, at all levels, understand the need for change through information sharing about global changes, and country's standing in the global scene, the standing of the particular organisation or business group in the global scene, the mission, etc., helps in getting them committed to change. Such information sharing should find its place in schoolbooks and lay the foundation for the future. Business groups should not insulate themselves from their surroundings anymore. They need to integrate and develop the communities and the country in which they live. Integration with the family and the society as a strategy is included. It has a lot of binding effect on the individual employee and also deals with corporate social responsibility. It also builds a company brand. It is not public relations but a communication strategy to integrate the individual with the organisation through his or her family and the society.

Employee Engagement Leading to Accountability, Ownership and Commitment

In a competitive world, employee commitment to work, the ability to take ownership and a high sense of responsibility are very critical. Committed and satisfied employees increase the chances of high productivity and high customer satisfaction. HR strategies should aim at enhancing accountability and ownership. Various HR systems and processes can be used in combination. Performance management processes, rewards and recognition, career planning and work culture, etc., contribute to these. Some HRD systems can be used as a part of the strategies to enhance accountability, ownership and commitment. There is clear and mounting evidence that high levels of employee engagement correlates to individual, group and corporate performance in areas such as retention, turnover, productivity, customer service and loyalty. And this is not just by small margins. While differences varied from study to study, highly engaged employees outperform their disengaged counterparts by a whopping 20 to 28 percentage points! Companies are responding to this challenge – by flattening their chains of command, providing training for first-line managers and with better internal communications (Rao, 2008b).

The questions asked in HRD audit for this purpose include the following: What promotes employee engagement? What strategies are being used by the corporation for the same? What are the issues relating to accountability, ownership and commitment? Is the HR function aligned to address these? Are appropriate systems being used to address these issues?

Quality strategies

Globalisation has brought into focus the need for quality products and services. Today's world is quality driven and customer driven. HR strategies, therefore, should aim at total quality and highest customer satisfaction. Ensuring quality products and services requires quality consciousness in every employee. Quality should be promoted in everything and should become a way of life. HRD systems, processes, etc., should aim at achieving this. The appropriateness of HR strategies to meet this business goal can be evaluated through HRD audit. HRD audit examines, first, the existence of quality concerns, its need and then the HR practices and how well they are contributing currently and the ways to improve them.

Customer Orientation Throughout the Company

Companies should continuously ensure the availability of good quality products and services throughout the company, through increased feedback, reviews, surveys, discussions and other forms that facilitate an understanding of the external and internal customers as well as suppliers. Satisfied customers enhance company image and contribute to company profits. Hence, customer satisfaction becomes an important goal and strategy for organisations. Satisfied employees tend to create satisfied customers. HR strategies to link employee satisfaction with customer satisfaction need examination. Customer satisfaction surveys may help. HRD audit examines the adequacies or inadequacies of these strategies. The customer satisfaction also may get extended to all stakeholders.

Efficiency and Cost Management

Operational efficiency and service efficiency are two of the most critical variables that add to profitability. Balanced Score Card approach has come to be understood and effectively used by most corporations. Cost-reduction strategies and internal efficiency-enhancing activities have begun to play a significant role in the current corporate world. Control of costs become very critical when competition goes up and there are price wars. Cost-reduction activities affect most employees and can be demotivating if not properly managed. As every employee is likely to get affected and every employee can contribute to savings and efficiency improvements, HR strategies achieve significance. HRD audit evaluates the need for HRD, strategies used, their appropriateness, etc. The audit can also suggest ways of reducing costs and enhancing operational efficiencies through total employee involvement. It can also be linked to appraisals, rewards, etc.

Developing an Entrepreneurial Spirit among All Employees

This effort should aim at enabling employees at all levels to take charge of their tasks with full autonomy, accountability, cost-effectiveness and service orientation. This may require changing appraisal systems, continuous training, use of small groups and other OD interventions. Training could be undertaken to enhance achievement motivation and entrepreneurial and intrapreneurial spirit.

Culture-Building Exercises

Culture and values have been found to contribute to sustainable organisational success. Studies have indicated that organisations with strong values and culture sustain longer. Culture building as a strategy is used by many successful corporations. Ulrich and team have recently added this as the most important competency for global success. Culture-building and value-enhancing exercises should aim at upholding the dignity of the human being and increasing organisational effectiveness and promoting a global view. Culture should be characterised by values like openness, collaborative attitudes, trust, authenticity, proaction, autonomy, confrontation of issues and problems, and experimentation (OCTAPACE).

Talent Management Strategies

Anything in short supply becomes a strategic variable. In the last two decades, as demographics of the world are changing, there is increased shortage of talent. Talented employees are in short supply and have become expensive. All corporations are working to get leaders. In spite of every effort being made to get leaders to lead and manage corporations, there is an increasing need to build and retain leadership talent. Talent management hence becomes a crucial strategic variable in HR strategies. Old methods of getting, retaining and developing talent have become obsolete. New methods, including 360-degree feedback, survey research and assessment and development centres, have become inevitable strategies for talent management. Corporations are required to innovate and initiate new methods and strategies of talent management.

HR policies should be reframed or reformulated to address these goals. HRD becomes the core of such policies. A round table conference organised in 1994 in Delhi, jointly by the Academy of HRD and the Delhi Management Association, pointed out in detail some of the HRD implications. The observations and recommendations of the round table were illustrative of the directions for change in HR strategies.

HRD Strategies in the Services Sector

Economic liberalisation and globalisation have put pressures on Indian industry, particularly on the service sector, to offer quality products and services at low costs and with high speed. Organisations have to compete with unequal partners from abroad. It is well recognised that developing countries like India are already behind other countries technologically, in many areas, although some of them, particularly India, boast of huge scientific and technical manpower. In addition to this if an entrepreneur or industrialist has to spend a lot of his or her time, money and energy in dealing with unpredictable services and in negotiating with the local bureaucracy, it can have a significant dampening effect on business.

In a survey conducted at Bangalore by Professor Samuel Paul (formerly Director, IIMA, and a World Bank Consultant) with the help of C.K. Sharma and Deenu Basha of Marketing and Business Associates (a summary of this study was presented at the National HRD Network Conference) it was estimated that the residents of Bangalore city may have spent as much as ₹10,000 million in terms of investments in a variety of assets that are directly linked to the inefficient and uncertain water and electricity services. Professor Paul observes that the annual interest on this amount is about seven times the property tax collected in Bangalore city. This is in addition to the direct costs incurred by the public in terms of fee, and another estimated ₹100 million per year in terms of 'Speed money' (bribes) paid (Sharma and Basha, 1994).

Further, 25 per cent of the citizens of Bangalore have excess billing problems with three major agencies (electricity, water and telephones). Poor training, indifferent practices of workers and defects in measuring instruments seem to be the causes.

Nearly 60 per cent of people visit public utility offices two or more times to sort out a simple problem or service. Three-fourths of the cases involved simple problems. A major reason for multiple visits is the lack of information and guidance from agencies. People end up meeting several officials, including supervisors, simply because information and norms about when and how services or approvals can be obtained are not readily available to them.

Professionals who work on industrial and commercial and industrial projects confirmed that cumbersome regulations, lack of coordination and overlapping jurisdictions characterise the public agencies involved in the facilitation of the new projects. The potential of the economic reforms under way will not be fully realised when the productivity of entrepreneurs and of the public at large is hurt by the delays and inefficiencies of public agencies.

The Need for HRD in the Services Sector

Professor Paul's study has significant implications for HRD. There is an urgent need to improve the efficiency and effectiveness of these agencies. The problems are at the operating levels. While the senior officers manning these organisations have a lot of opportunities to train themselves, development of the lower-level staff is grossly neglected. For instance, with the amount spent on sponsoring a senior executive for a training programme at a management institute, a group of 30 field staff can be trained to improve their knowledge or skill base or a small customer education programme can be launched. Most of these service agencies have no HRD departments, budgets or activities. It is high time that HRD is given its due attention in the services sector. This is not to say that HRD will solve all the problems. Many other things need to improve, but without a change in the mind-set nothing is likely to improve.

Jon Quah of the National University of Singapore, in a recent paper prepared for the Commonwealth Secretariat, analysed the experiences of four Asian countries – South Korea, Taiwan, Japan and Singapore. All these countries have increased their gross national product (GNP) between 1962 and 1990 by several times (Quah, 1993). South Korea increased its per capita GNP by 49 times, Taiwan by 47 times, Japan by 42 times and Singapore by 23 times. In all these countries the following phenomena may be noticed: they have invested heavily and continuously on education and training minimised corruption and improved public personnel management by realistic recruitment, effective utilisation of human resources (managing talented people), providing competitive compensation packages (Singapore probably has the highest paid civil services in the world) and minimising over-staffing. From his analysis, Quah draws the following lessons for all developing countries:

1. The government must be committed to economic development
2. The government must be committed to minimising corruption
3. The government must invest in education and training
4. The government must introduce comprehensive reforms in public personnel management

Despite many liberalisation measures very little attention has so far been paid to ensure that liberalisation is supported at lower levels by improving services. Both Quah's and Paul's studies point out the directions to move into. Infrastructural services need to be improved fast to provide the necessary support base. Heavy investment in training lower-level civic staff is an urgent need. This is an HRD challenge. It may be worthwhile for municipal corporations, electricity boards and other service agencies to appoint special task forces to improve the efficiency and effectiveness of these services.

These task forces should focus on HRD for the staff. The industrial sector in each city has a good number of well-trained HRD managers and staff. They should help the civic authorities in examining their systems and procedures and developing the skill base of the staff. Local management associations and professional bodies should carry out this service by donating some time to help civic services improve.

Auditing HRD Strategies

Ulrich and team (Ulrich et al., 2013a) have identified eight strategic variables that bring competitive differentiation in the modern world. These include the following:

1. Managing risks
2. Global positioning
3. Leveraging Information
4. Managing globally diverse work force
5. Adapting or changing
6. Building corporate social responsibility
7. Collaborating or partnering across boundaries
8. Focusing on simplifying

Some of these are stated in different terms in the earlier edition of the book. Others may get added as is relevant to the context. An auditor should be sensitive to the changing strategies that business may adopt and ensure HRD strategy alignment with the same.

HRD audit starts with an understanding of the business goals and strategies of the organisation – both for the short term and long term. HRD audit takes the business strategies and goals as given. The auditors do not question the business strategies or plans. What they attempt, however, is to understand if enough thought has been given to the HR strategies to achieve the business goals. They audit the extent to which the HR strategies are aligned with the business strategies of the organisation. The source of this information is the top management. As sharing business plans and strategies can be very confidential and sensitive matters for some of the organisations, the auditors have to maintain high ethics and only get the information that has implications for HR strategies. However, sometimes it is difficult to differentiate what is useful from that which is not useful. It is the experience and wisdom of the auditor that matters most in such situations.

The following are some helpful questions that may be asked during interviews with the top management and the HR chief.

- What are the competencies required to meet the future business requirements of the organisation?
- What are the business challenges the organisation is likely to face?
- What are the immediate and future business opportunities perceived by the company?
- What competencies are required by the organisation to meet these challenges and opportunities?
- What are the competencies required to meet these challenges or utilise the opportunities at the top, senior and middle levels, supervisory level and at the field level or grass-root level?
- What are the levels of competencies existing at the corporation at the time of the audit?
- What are the competencies in terms of technology management systems, attitude, behaviour, etc.?
- What are the gaps and how are they being planned to be filled? Through recruitment, outsourcing, development? And what is the time frame to be used?
- Are the plans aligned properly with the needs? Are they realistic? Are there obvious gaps in the alignment of the HR strategies and plans with the business goals?

- What can be the most important HRD tools for aligning the business goals and the HR strategies?
- How are various HRD tools being used to ensure that the business goals are understood and commitment is built in employees for the good of the organisation and its business?
- Are the communications, PMS, training systems, job rotation, attachments, recruitments, TQM and other interventions, organisational restructuring, business process reengineering, new management systems, experiments, etc., aligned with the business plans?
- Are they based on an adequate understanding of variables such as human nature, human behaviour, organisational culture, competitive environment, etc.? Or are they being taken up as fashions without proper alignment?
- Are the task forces, committees, working groups, etc., being used tactfully and appropriately for achieving these goals?
- What is being done to ensure continuous linkages and integration between employee development and business development and between employee satisfaction and customer satisfaction? Are there adequate feedback mechanisms? Are there adequate monitoring mechanisms to ensure that the human process variables are enablers for achieving business goals?
- What are the bottlenecks in aligning business goals with HRD practices?

Linking HRD Strategy Audit with the HRD Score Card

The strategy audit should lead to an assessment of the business linkages of the HR function. Two issues become important: first, the extent to which the current HR strategies, systems, practices, activities, processes, etc., are derived from the business needs or organisational goals of the company or the agency; second, the extent to which there are internal processes to ensure that the HRD plans, systems, processes and investments are sensitive to the changing needs of the organisation. Both these need to be assessed.

It is useful to list all the important business needs or organisational requirements on the basis of the organisational mission, vision, strategic plan, current concern, etc. An exhaustive list can be made (e.g., the list could run like this – cost reduction, productivity improvements, quality orientation, market change, new product introductions and emphasis on research and development). The auditors should pick up item by item and look for HRD systems that can address these. Possible systems and practices that can be used to address these needs can also be generated. Depending on the extent to which these issues have been addressed, a score could be assigned to the dimension of business linkages of HRD.

Similarly, to answer the second issue, one needs to look at the existing structural and process mechanisms. For example, the participation of the HR director in strategic planning exercises, the role played by the HR department in policy formulation, the extent to which the HR staff and the director are made members of various committees and task forces are all indicators of the internal processes that ensure business linkages of the HR function.

Conclusion

Globalisation has resulted in new business concerns that focus on customer satisfaction, quality, cost-consciousness, restructuring, etc. All these challenges impact HR strategies. HRD audit examines the sensitivity of HR strategies towards business goals and challenges. Evaluating HRD strategies through an HRD audit is increasingly gaining importance in the services sector. A number of dimensions need to be covered while examining the HR strategies and their linkages with business development. Business needs or organisational needs and plans are the starting points for HRD audit. As HRD needs to be aligned with the business goals, HRD audit should be aligned with both the HRD needs and the strategies of the company.

5

HRD CULTURE AND VALUES

The organisational culture plays a significant role in making organisations get the best out of themselves. Abraham's (1989) study has established clearly the linkage between the HRD climate and organisational performance in financial terms. Even if the climate does not show any direct linkages at a given point of time, logically it makes sense to have a good HRD climate for the benefit of the organisation. Most professional organisations, multinationals and well-run organisations by business families like the Tatas and the Birlas are known for their culture. They have a capability to sustain themselves against many difficulties and challenges due to their culture. Companies like L&T, Hindustan Levers, Crompton Greaves, Sundaram Fasteners, Maruti Udyog, Tata Steel, TELCO, Aditya Vikram Birla Group, etc., are known for their strong culture. In recent times, organisations like Infosys, Mahindra & Mahindra, Wipro, Dr Reddy's Laboratories, Themrax, HCL Technologies, etc., in the private sector and NTPC, SAIL, BPCL, HPCL, etc., in the public sector have come to be known for their culture. The culture provides the energy needed to function well by ensuring as if it were a proper circulation of the blood through all the organs. The culture also acts as oxygen in the case of emergency. The HRD culture is one that results from the beliefs of the top management initially and subsequently from the HRD systems and practices. It deserves to be studied and assessed independently for its importance and independent standing as demonstrated by Abraham's research. Hence it is treated as a separate element in HRD audit. Owing to their closeness, the two soft dimensions of the HR function – HRD culture and HRD styles – are combined for the purposes of the audit.

DOI: 10.4324/9781003530534-7

Octapace Values and Culture

HRD deals with competence building, culture building and commitment building. Competence and commitment can be built on a continuous basis in a certain type of culture. If the milieu is good, a number of things can happen. Hence, creating a culture becomes important in any organisation. The HRD culture should have the following characteristics:

- It should be a learning culture
- It should facilitate the identification of new competencies of people (individuals, dyads and teams) on a continuous basis
- It should facilitate bringing out the hidden potential and new talents of people
- It should help in developing new competencies
- It should have in-built motivational value. In other words, it should have a self-sustaining motivational quality. People are committed to what they do and they need not be told to act. They act
- It should enable people to take initiative and experiment. Initiative and experimentation are the cornerstones of development. They enable individuals, teams and organisations to discover new potential in them
- It should bring joy and satisfaction in work. Work should not become drudgery. It is made enjoyable by a good work culture. Relationships matter and have an enabling capability
- It should enhance creativity and problem-solving capabilities of people
- It should create team spirit and morale
- It should enhance the action orientation of individuals, dyads and teams

Such a culture has been termed as OCTAPACE, which we have seen earlier in the book is an acronym for openness, collaboration, trust and trustworthiness, authenticity, proaction, autonomy, confrontation and experimentation.

Openness is there where people (individuals, dyads, teams and all in the organisation) feel free to express their ideas, opinions and feelings to each other irrespective of their level, designation, etc. There are no barriers to such expressions. They are encouraged to express and are heard. Their views are taken seriously. Such expression provides an opportunity for individuals to explore their own talents. The organisation handles these expressions for discovering new ways of doing things, discovering new potential and taking actions based on the real internal talent of the organisation. There are only some views that can get finally accepted and tested or put to action. That does not disappoint those whose views are not put into action. They continue to contribute as such contribution is a way of life.

Collaboration is the culture where people (individuals, dyads, teams and the organisation as a whole) are eager to help each other. There is a spirit of sacrifice for the sake of each other and larger goals. Personal power is played down and people are governed by larger goals like the goals of the organisation, country and humanity. People are willing to go to any extent to help each other to make sure that the larger organisational goals do not suffer. Particularly, the organisational goals govern the decision making and people do not have narrow departmental or team loyalties. There are fewer overheads in resolving interdepartmental conflicts. The *We* feeling is of the highest order. Team spirit is high. Intradepartmental loyalties do not come in the way of interdepartmental collaboration. Cohesiveness of small groups has an enabling and empowering effect on building organisational identity and cohesiveness.

Trust and trustworthiness deal with a culture of people believing each other and acting on the basis of verbal messages and instructions without having to wait for written instructions or explanations. There is no need for monitoring and controls. There are no overheads to check if people mean what they say. The word given by individuals, dyads or teams is relied on. In such a culture, both trust and trustworthiness are of the highest order. To create a culture of mutual trust, a culture of trustworthiness is essential. If every individual becomes trustworthy, trust automatically follows. Trust puts the onus on the person who is the recipient of the promise or word given. Trustworthiness puts the onus on the person who makes the promise or gives his or her word. Both aspects are equally important and they are two sides of the same coin. To build one the other is required.

Authenticity is speaking the truth fearlessly and keeping up the promises made. It is indicated by the extent to which people mean what they say and do what they say. In a way, it is of a higher order than trust and trustworthiness. Individuals, dyads and teams can be counted on not to make false promises. They never promise or commit to things just to please others. They also make full efforts to implement their promises. They do not need any follow-up, and if they fail to deliver, it is understood that it is due to some extraordinary circumstances beyond their control.

A *proactive* culture promotes initiative and exploration on the part of all employees. A proactive culture encourages everyone to take initiative and make things happen. New activities and new ways of doing things are encouraged. Such proaction can be in any area, including role making (giving new interpretations to one's role for achieving organisational or team goals), role taking (taking new initiatives, initiating new activities, changing the old methods of work), work methodology, cost reduction, quality improvements, culture building, HRM, etc.

Autonomy is present if every role holder in the organisation, irrespective of his or her level, has some scope to use discretion in his or her job. The discretion may be in terms of work methods, decision making, communication or any such area. There should be scope to choose one's activities and role. It can be 10 per cent of the time or 20 per cent. The greater the freedom to choose what one wants to do or the way one wants to do it, the higher the autonomy. Autonomy has been found to characterise most academic and research institutions. This is very critical for bringing out academic excellence. Knowledge workers, the IT industry and R&D departments thrive as a result of this.

Confrontation is the culture of facing issues squarely. People discuss issues with very little fear of hurting each other. Even if one may have to hurt the other, the issue is handled and not put under the carpet. People can be relied on to treat issues not as a personal assault but as focus areas needing improvement. This culture enhances the problem-solving ability.

Experimentation is the orientation on the part of the employees to try out new ways of doing things and take new decisions. It characterises a risk-taking culture in the organisation. Without risk, there is no growth. Without experimentation, there is very little scope for renewal, rejuvenation and simplification of life.

Openness and confrontation go together. Autonomy and collaboration go together. Trust and authenticity go together. Proaction and experimentation go together. Thus, these four pairs are the four cornerstones of HRD culture.

When these values are practised in an organisation, they become a part of life and are likely to get the best out of people. Human potential gets developed to the maximum extent and people competencies are utilised to the maximum.

Organisational Culture

In addition to these values, there are other parameters that have gained significance in the last two decades across the world as constituting an enabling organisational culture. These variables include the following (reproduced from Rao, 2008b):

1. **Empowering leadership climate:** Where the leaders manage the mistakes of juniors, manage their conflicts, provide resources and support juniors and respond to their failures
2. **Motivation through participation:** There are mechanisms to motivate employees, the employees are encouraged to talk about one's responsibilities with enthusiasm and regard, there is a high commitment to work and there is inspiration to work
3. **Communication:** Where the communication mechanisms are good and meet the needs of employees, and there are adequate upward and downward communications, formal and informal communications and verbal and written communications to meet employee needs and make them feel a part of the organisation

4. **Decision making:** Where the decision making is participative, logical and analytical, objective and timely and ensures the interests of the organisation

5. **Goals:** Where goal setting is objective and follows norms and rules based on dialogues and SMART

6. **Control:** Where there is adequate direction and supervision of work, systems are used to ensure checks and there are internal controls

7. **Shared values:** Where there are well-articulated values of the organisation, they are shared across the organisation and transmitted to new recruits, and employees across various levels and departments share the values

8. **Quality orientation:** Where there is quality consciousness across the organisation and quality systems are used

9. **Rewards and recognition:** Where there are adequate mechanisms to recognise and reward desired behaviour and efficacy or effectiveness, and rewards and recognition systems are administered with objectivity

10. **Information:** Where information is shared across various levels and departments of the organisation, and people maintain confidentiality where necessary and there are systems and mechanisms for sharing information

11. **Empowerment:** Where there are efforts made to empower employees to act with authority, and delegation and autonomy are provided adequately

12. **Learning orientation:** Where there is support to learning from the top management, organisational efforts are made to stimulate learning and employees have positive attitude towards learning

13. **Openness to change:** Where the top management and senior managers are open and receptive to change, they are aware of the need to change, are open to change and have formal mechanisms and facilitators to manage change

14. **Corporate social responsibility:** Employees are sensitive to their environment and surroundings and exhibit a high degree of social responsibility and citizenship that extend beyond their organisation to the local community and the country where the organisation is located

15. **Health:** Our climate emphasises health and promotes a healthy living. Employees here are health conscious

16. **Safety:** Employees are attuned to ensure the safety and security of themselves and each other. The culture here is attuned to ensure safety, and physical and mental security of employees

17. **Work satisfaction and motivation:** Employees are satisfied and are motivated to work

Auditing HRD Culture and Values

The extent to which an OCTAPACE culture exists in an organisation can be studied using simple HRD climate questionnaires and surveys. This can also be assessed during interviews. The following questions can be asked for auditing HRD culture.

Openness

- To what extent do people (employees) feel free to express their views and opinions?
- Are they encouraged to do so?
- Is the organisation known to cash on the ideas, views and opinions of employees?
- Do people feel that they are contributing their best by open expression of ideas?

Collaboration

- Is there a culture of collaboration and teamwork?
- Is there a 'we' feeling among different teams?
- Is there a culture of synergy in the organisation?
- Do people try to help each other?

Trust and Trustworthiness

- What is the extent to which people honour their commitments?
- Do people trust each other?
- Is there a lot of supervision and monitoring?
- Is there a culture where people can be counted on to carry out what they say?
- Do people carry out what they say?

Authenticity

- Do people say what they mean?
- Are people authentic in their approach?

Proaction

- Are employees encouraged to take the initiative?
- What is the extent to which proaction takes place?
- Can the culture be characterised as a proactive culture?

Autonomy

- To what extent do people, at all levels, have the scope to take decisions on their own?
- Is there some freedom available at each level to undertake new activities?
- Is there freedom at each level to use one's discretion?
- Is there freedom at each level for exercising some amount of autonomy and creating one's own role?

Confrontation

- Does the culture encourage open discussion of issues and problems?
- Are people habituated to discuss and resolve issues openly?
- Is there a problem-solving culture or approach?

Experimentation

- What is the extent to which employees are encouraged to experiment with new ideas?
- Do employees take risks?
- Is the organisation known to encourage innovations?

These are a few illustrative questions. The audit can also focus on collecting anecdotes, stories and information about critical incidents.

The importance of OCTAPACE values in HR Leadership has been amply illustrated in a recent study by Agrawal and Rao (2022). E When HR leaders exhibit and promote values and they are shared by the organisation it becomes a part of the culture.

Recent Studies in Values and Culture

The study by Agrawal and Rao (2022) found the following as characterising the HR leaders:

- Trust and trustworthiness
- Integrity and honesty
- Disciplined, fair and firm with people
- Inclusive
- Respectful of people, service oriented, sharing, self-renewing and reflective
- Have service/superordinate goals and a higher purpose
- Humanitarian: Humane, caring and supportive of people
- Talent and people management and positive thinking

- Humility
- Hard work and commitment
- Sense of ownership
- Openness
- Authenticity and transparency
- Courageous, risk taking and independent
- Continuously Learning
- Proactivity
- Initiative and optimism
- Confronting and assertive when needed
- Purposeful
- Empathetic, customer and employee-centric
- Collaboration
- Experimentation innovativeness

Most of these values fit into the OCTAPACE or POCTAPLACED values outlined earlier by Pareek and later by Rao.

OCTAPACE and HRD Climate: There Are a Number of Studies on HRD Climate Mainly Consisting of OCTAPACE Culture

In a recent survey of HRD Climate in Bokaro Steel Plant Durlav Sarkar and Syed Miraz Hussain (2015) concluded that employees at higher levels, i.e., executive level are more satisfied with the existing HRD climate. But a level of dissatisfaction was seen within employees at non-executive level. They are very much satisfied with the interpersonal openness within employees and there was also high level of trust, which represent that employees within BSP are having a good interpersonal relationship and team spirit. One important factor revealed was a level of dissatisfaction within employees in the area of top management commitment to HRD. The employees also had negative attitude toward the reward and recognition policies, competencies development & personal policies. They felt that there should be a proper system to recognise the competencies and performance of employees so that they can understand their position better in the organisation. There should be proper ways to evaluate their weaknesses and strengths, and training programmes should be developed accordingly. Based on the survey, it was found that overall human resource climate in BSP is good but it needs improvement. They found that workers expected more from the top management than the management actually thought. They suggested that the management should reconsider its policies and regulations so that the workers remain happy and work more aggressively for the betterment of the company. Dadhabai and Mounika (2018) in a correlation analysis of the study variables revealed that HRD Climate and all its dimensions were positively and significantly correlated with employee engagement. Regression analysis revealed that considerable variance in employee engagement is contributed by HRD. The overall impact of HRD Climate was significant on engagement level of employees and suggestions were given for attaining better employee engagement.

Conclusion

The culture of any organisation has a tremendous impact on its success and, therefore, culture building is a critical function. It is the top management and other influential people in the organisation who create an OCTAPACE culture through their roles and styles of functioning. The styles are assessed separately. However, the organisational culture in terms of various other parameters is assessed here.

HRD audit includes interviews, questionnaires and observation, on the basis of which consultants suggest mechanisms to improve the HRD style and make it more facilitating and congruent to HR philosophy and outcomes.

An appropriate HRD culture carries with it HRD values and integrates into it empowering or developmental styles of managers. The HRD Score Card therefore emphasises HRD culture and values.

6

HRD STRUCTURES

Structure is essentially an instrument or a tool. It is not an end in itself; it is only a means to facilitate HRD. It has a characteristic of assuming permanence on its own, and sometimes without serving any purpose. It has also a tendency to multiply itself if unchecked (see Box 6.1). It therefore needs to be reviewed, audited and sharpened periodically. Dynamic organisations periodically review their structures to rejuvenate the HR function.

BOX 6.1 SOME INSIGHTS FROM PREVIOUS AUDITS

Some organisations have established HRD departments with a lot of expectations. They begin by recruiting a high-profile HRD manager or a senior manager. Soon the manager is able to get a department established with a few assistant managers and supporting staff. They soon get busy with one or other requirement of the corporation. This used to be recruitment in the past, but in recent years this is getting to be retrenchment, downsizing or voluntary retirement scheme (VRS). The author has found that most HRD departments focus on the subsystems of HRD irrespective of the needs of the company. For instance, a company may have needed to recruit manpower in heavy doses at one point of time but the HR department continues with the recruitment process by force of habit, or an HR department may continue with some subsystems created in the past for a particular single activity (e.g., preparing the tests, training the interviewers, maintaining the database, etc.). The structure becomes a factor to be reckoned with rather than a facilitating factor. Sometimes this happens because the HRD staff recruited at one point of time had strengths in one of the

---

DOI: 10.4324/9781003530534-8

components of HR and they have not grown beyond it subsequently. In such cases it is important to look at the HRD needs of the organisation in the context of the current and future business goals of the organisation and evaluate the activities undertaken by the company. The HRD activity checklist can be used to evaluate the activity requirements of the company and examine the structures needed by it (see Rao, 2008b).

Developing HR strategies, designing and implementing various HR systems, and monitoring the alignment of HR processes with business goals require the services of a full-time professional staff. HRD departments were established to give an impetus to the HR function, which has now become quite specialised. Appropriate structures are required to manage this function, which can be institutionalised through departmentalisation. However, in small organisations the function can take different forms. Some common practices in structuring the HR function are discussed as follows.

Current Structures and Structural Alternatives

HRD structures can take many forms. Some of these include the following:

- A dedicated and fully manned HRD department
- A corporate HRD department with HRD cells in the units or locations
- A high-profile HRD chief with limited staff
- An HRD task force largely drawn from line managers with an HRD trained chairman
- The CEO himself handling HRD
- The training manager handling HRD
- The personnel chief handling HRD
- HRD being handled at the corporate level by the HRD staff and at the unit level integrated into the personnel department

Other forms and designations like Chief Talent Manager, Chief Human Resources Officer (CHRO) are also common.

Dedicated and Fully Manned Department

Depending on the size of the organisation and needs, the HRD departments may get developed. It is not uncommon to have fairly large HR departments in large-sized organisations. For example, the size of HR departments in some public sector undertakings (SAIL, NTPC, Indian Oil, etc.) runs into hundreds. In large organisations the HR tasks may be subdivided with separate sets of HR staff dealing with different HR tasks.

Corporate HRD with Unit HRD or Location HRD Cells

In this structure there is normally a corporate HRD function at the head-quarters and there are separate independent HR departments at the plant/geographic regions/zones. The plant or location cells normally have dual reporting relationships – one to the location head and the second to the corporate HR chief. Policy responsibilities normally lie with the corporate HR, and implementation responsibilities are entrusted to the location HR cell.

This structure introduces its own dynamics. For example, the corporate HR may be insensitive to the local needs, whereas the locational HR may be too engrossed with routine matters and immediate needs. The locational HR may tend to downplay and neglect long-term strategies and HR policies. There is often conflict between the unit HR and central HR on some of the issues. A high degree of maturity is required on both sides to manage such differentiated HR function. Often the unit HR has dual reporting relationships with the unit operations and central HR creating further issues.

Sleek Department

Another structural variation practised by some organisations is to have one or more high-profile HR chiefs with fewer staff. This structure is more common in software, financial services and other companies with a high proportion of professional staff. In such cases the competencies of the HR chief become more critical than the structure itself. Outsourcing HR implementation is more common in such structures. The audit should focus on the adequacy of this model as well as the cost-effectiveness of outsourcing practices.

HRD Task Force

In smaller organisations that do not require a full-fledged HRD department, a group of competent line managers can form a task force with one of them as the chairperson. The group can meet periodically to plan, implement and monitor HR interventions. In some instances they could be assisted by a full-time HRD manager. In this structure the ownership is with the task force. This kind of structure is possible in smaller organisations.

CEO as HRD Manager

In yet another variation, the CEO himself or herself may be handling the various HR functions and taking all strategic HR decisions. In such a case he or she can take the help of the corporate planning cell or the TQM cell or other related role holders. This kind of structure is possible in relatively smaller organisations. The personnel function is separated out in such cases and is entrusted with only routine, establishment, work.

Other Structures

There can be other models, which include the training manager or personnel manager handling the HR function. Each of these has its advantages and disadvantages.

The HRD department plays a significant role in making the HRD systems and processes work. While conducting an HRD audit one of the factors to be seen is whether the HRD structure is in place. Box 6.1 presents some of the experiences from previous audits and demonstrates the need for evaluating the HRD structure.

The HRD structure includes the following:

- The task structure, including the activities, their grouping and their linkages
- The manpower, including the levels and their competencies, experience, etc.
- The roles, role relationships, role clarity, role effectiveness and inter-role linkages
- The competency structure
- The infrastructure and infrastructure facilities for effective functioning of the HRD departments
- The organisational structure, including hierarchies and hierarchical relationships
- The organisational process, including the systems, processes, norms, values and culture, which governs the department

The following are typical questions that need to be answered in auditing the structure of an HRD department:

What Kind of Structure Does the Company Need?

This is the first important question to be asked in the HRD audit. In the mid-seventies HRD departments were started to promote competence building and work motivation. The personnel departments were not required to focus their attention on the developmental aspects, and it was felt necessary to have a specialised group to promote learning among individuals, dyads and teams. The CEOs were requested to pay attention to the human aspects of the organisation. The HRD department became, in a way, an instrument for taking care of the human dimension, which was fulfilled to a large extent by the late eighties. By the early nineties, however, the focus of HRD changed from HR for its own sake to HR for business. Today, in a globally competitive environment the assumption that the human resources in an organisation deserve attention so that they can be harnessed and developed to help the organisation achieve its goals is well understood and needs no further emphasis. The important issues to be looked into are as follows:

- Given the current and future needs of the company, what kind of HR systems and processes are required?
- Given the HRD processes and systems, what kind of structures are required?
- Does the organisation have the appropriate structure required to carry out the HRD tasks to meet the current and future HRD needs of the company?

The following principles need to be kept in mind while evaluating the structure and their adequacy:

- HRD departments have the capability like any other department to multiply on its own. Such 'self-multiplication' is not always in the interests of the company. Every activity has to have a value addition
- HRD department should be high competency based and business driven rather than be merely HRD system driven
- It is possible to implement the HRD systems and strengthen the HR processes in a corporation without a formal HRD department

Do the HRD Activities Contribute Directly or Indirectly to the Business Goals of the Corporation? And do the Organisations Assess the Level of Importance of the Activity to Business Goals?

The activities should contribute to one of the following:

- The competencies required to execute or conduct the current (this year and the next year) business effectively and efficiently and meet business goals (profits, cost reduction, increased market share, quality of products, market image, new markets, customer satisfaction and delight, appropriate use of current resources, including technology, people, organisational capabilities, etc.)
- The competencies needed to contribute to the future (the next three years and above) and the business goals of the company – this may flow from the business strategies and the long-term plans (diversification, new product development, new technologies, new markets, new processes, new culture, etc.)

- Building employee motivation, satisfaction, commitment and account-abilities so that the business activities are undertaken with zeal and enthusiasm and achievement motivation – the activities should contribute to employee satisfaction, and building morale and task commitment and accomplishment. It should create a sense of pride and involvement in the employee. Employee motivation should subsume all levels – at the individual level, dyad level and at the team or departmental level and the entire organisation. Employees should be adequately motivated to carry out the various business transactions effectively and efficiently. The activities may deal with any function – procurement, production, marketing, technology, finances, product quality, management processes, information, customer service, etc.
- Building a culture (values, norms, patterns of behaviour expected to be shown by all the employees), including work culture, that is valued by the organisation and enables it to have a sustainable impact and continue to achieve its goals and grow. The culture should be defined by the organisation itself. The culture may deal with the values attached to internal and external customers, product quality, quality of services, speed and quality of decision-making, discipline, integrity, punctuality, trustworthiness, cost consciousness, etc. The HRD model of Pareek and Rao (1981, 1992a) promotes an OCTAPACE culture (Openness, Collaboration, Trust, Authenticity, Proaction, Autonomy, Confrontation and Experimentation)

Box 6.2 suggests a list of steps to be used in HRD activity audit. The activity audit provides the necessary insights for evaluating the structures and their functioning.

BOX 6.2 ASSESSING THE HRD ACTIVITIES AND THEIR RELEVANCE

The following steps can be used for the audit to ascertain if the HRD department is performing the important activities and if they are performing them well.

Step 1: List all the activities undertaken by the HRD department (e.g., conducting performance appraisal workshops or providing feedback to employees on training sponsorship decisions). Use the HRD activities profile given in Chapter 11 on HRD Audit Instruments.

Step 2: Add to the list if there are any significant activities that the HRD department should undertake but is not doing at present. The auditor can gather this from preliminary discussions with the line managers.

Step 3: Prepare a questionnaire to assess the perceptions of the importance of each activity and the effectiveness with which it is currently being performed. Use the scaling methods given as follows.

Scale to assess the importance of the activity to the corporation

5 = This activity is extremely essential (for competency building [A or B], commitment building [C] or culture building [D]. Without it the critical competencies/culture/commitment needed to run the business efficiently or effectively will be missing and the business is likely to suffer).
4 = This activity is essential.
3 = This activity is somewhat essential.
2 = This activity is not essential but if it is there it can be of help.
1 = This activity is not needed and the corporation can do without it.

Scale to assess effectiveness with which it is being performed

5 = This is being performed with extremely high effectiveness. There is no scope to do it better.
4 = This is being performed very effectively but not near perfection.
3 = This is being performed somewhat effectively – it is at 50 per cent level of effectiveness.
2 = This is not being performed well – it could be performed far better.
1 = This is not being performed at all – it is poor performance.

The following is an illustrative table for the checklist.

S. No.	Activity	Level of importance of this activity				Effectiveness with which it is performed today
		A	B	C	D	
1.	Conducting performance appraisal workshops					
2.						
3.						
4.						
5.						

Step 4: Administer this questionnaire to a random sample of line managers and executives. If possible, ask each department or unit to discuss the questionnaire and give their collective or team perceptions of the importance as well as effectiveness. Tabulate the data to identify the following:

Category 1: The activities that are very critical and not being performed well
Category 2: The activities that are not at all important to achieve any of the goals (A, B, C, D above) but are being performed well

Category 3: The activities that are not very important and are not being performed well

Category 4: The activities that are very important and are not being performed well.

Categories 1 and 3 should continue as they are. Category 2 gives the time-wasters of the HRD department. Category 4 gives the neglected and high-priority areas.

Step 5: Using this analysis, identify the manpower needs or rationalise the task structure of the HRD department. For example, too many activities in Category 2 call for some downsizing of the HR department. Similarly, too many activities in Category 4 call for fresh recruitment of competent people in HRD or for an intense competency-building effort.

Does the Organisation Have HRD Competencies of the Required Nature, Quality and Magnitude to Carry Out the HRD Activities and to Monitor the HRD Processes?

To answer this question one needs a good competency assessment. The ideal thing would be to run an assessment centre for the HR staff. However, as most audits are not elaborate and such centres may become time consuming (though cost-effective), the auditor has to use a number of methods to gather data on this dimension. The HRD audit questionnaire data assessing the HRD function will provide some inputs into these. The auditor must make an effort to find out the perception of the competencies of the HRD staff. The auditor must also interview the HR staff to assess their competence base. More details are presented in Chapter 8 on the competence assessment of HRD staff.

How Is the HR Department Placed? Is It Placed Under an Appropriate Top-level Manager or the CEO to Facilitate Its Work and Align Itself with the Business Goals?

The placement of the HR department has a lot of significance. It should preferably be headed by a board-level functionary who directly reports to the CEO. This is because most HR decisions are strategic in nature and/or have strategic implications, which need continuous communication with the top management groups. The positioning of the HR department itself reflects the importance given to HR in the organisation.

Is the HR Department Headed by a Person of the Level or Competence Required for HRD in the Organisation?

The level, experience, competence, credibility, vision and leadership qualities of the HRD chief have a lot to do with the effectiveness of the function and the impact it can make. These need to be assessed by looking at the experience, positioning and power equations of the HRD chief. It is extremely important and sensitive step in HRD audit to take a close look at the competence levels of the HRD chief.

How Are the Roles Defined? Are the Roles Clear?

The task assignments and role clarity of the HRD department also need to be studied. The distribution of tasks, the linkages, intradepartmental processes, etc., give insights into the functioning of the department.

The following are the other questions to be answered through interviews with the line managers and the HRD staff:

- What are the current tasks performed by the department?
- Are they value adding?
- Are they moving in the direction that contributes to the business goals of the company?
- How is the HRD department staffed?
- Are the competency levels of the staff appropriate?
- Are the reporting relationships well defined and facilitating effective task performance?
- Is the distribution of tasks within the department appropriate?

Auditing the Structure

The structure-related issues of HRD become linked to business goals. The structure and staffing of the HRD department are determined by the following considerations:

- The business goals of the company – both immediate and long term
- The competencies required at all levels to achieve the goals
- The competency gaps and requirements to achieve them
- The HRD systems and processes required to meet the immediate competency requirements and business goals of the company
- The HRD competencies needed to meet them
- The cost-effectiveness of outsourcing the same and the advantages over a long term of having an in-house capability to manage the competency requirements
- The feasibility or the advantages of having an in-house team and task force to manage or facilitate the processes as against having a full-fledged HR department

Through the HRD audit, the auditor attempts to answer the following questions:

- Given the competency requirements of the corporation, what seems to be the appropriate structure for this organisation?
- How well defined is the existing structure (roles, role relationships, task structure, reporting relationships, facilities, budget, power and authority, coordination mechanisms, integration mechanisms with other functions and business goals of the corporation, etc.) to meet the business goals of the organisation?
- What are the most appropriate structures that can take the organisation into the future and ensure that the goals are met?
- What are the strengths and weaknesses of the existing HRD structure?
- What is suffering and what is getting done under the existing structure? At what cost?
- What are the most appropriate elements of the existing HRD structure?
- What are the steps to be taken to align the HRD structure with the business goals of the company?

The answers to these questions can come from interviews of auditors with the line managers, top management, the HRD staff, related departments (personnel, industrial engineering, quality, corporate planning, etc.) and the like apart from the auditor's own insights.

Conclusion

Ulrich and team (Ulrich et al., 2013b) identified 12 key attributes of effective departments:

1. Robust training
2. Clear roles
3. Credible board interaction
4. Aligned structure
5. Integrated HR solutions
6. Accountable line managers
7. Managing outsourced activities/vendors (continuous appraisal of vendors or outsourced activities)
8. Cultural role models
9. Measured impact
10. External stakeholder focus
11. Aligned HR strategy
12. Aligned HR initiatives

According to a study by Ulrich et al. (2013b), an effective HR department has four times the impact of the skills and competencies of effective HR professionals. ulrich and team conclude from their global research that gaining competence as an individual HR performer is necessary but not sufficient. 'Being individually competent and being a part of a highly effective HR Department, taken together, will create a winning team both for HR and global business' (p. 252).

The HRD structure is vital to the organisation and deals with the task structure, role relationship, manpower, competence, infrastructure facilities and organisational processes. It is a means or a tool but not an end in itself. Structures have self-multiplying tendencies. They need to be reviewed and reoriented. The kind of HR structure an organisation needs depends on the HR strategies. Answers to questions on the needs of business, competency requirements, role clarity and top management attitude, etc., provide the inputs needed to evaluate the structure. The HRD audit attempts to highlight the current status, strengths, weaknesses, cost-effectiveness and other vital elements of the HR structure and aligns it in accordance to the business goals of the organisation. Innovative and cost-effective structures and structural mechanisms are needed to make the HRD function effective.

The HRD Score Card takes into consideration the appropriateness of the HRD function and the way it is structured. This is treated as a part of the HRD competency score.

7

HRD SYSTEMS

Systems are organised ways of making things happen. They help in planning and to bring in predictability, discipline and security. A system must be imbued with spirit and be governed by norms, values and rules. While all these can be part of a system, they cannot replace the system itself. For example, an 'HRD spirit' is essential for effective implementation of HRD. Without spirit, no one can be committed to development – either one's own or that of others. However, there is no way of ensuring that the HRD spirit is present in each individual in terms of effective implementation of HRD. Nor is there a way to ensure that the minimum degree of the spirit is demonstrated by every person. HRD, or for that matter a number of things in organisational life, cannot be trusted to the spirit of individuals. Similarly, norms are very specific and are related to behaviour of people in an organisation. It is difficult to propose norms for development. Norms mainly deal with compliance. There can be compliance sans spirit, in a mechanical way. Values are more lasting patterns of behaviour. Some useful values were mentioned in the previous chapter. They deal with something more internal, based on one's (individual or organisational) philosophy. They can be observed, measured and questioned. They cut across the system boundaries. Every system can have certain values behind it. For example, a management information system can be based on certain values. HRD values are important for the systems to work.

HRD Systems and Subsystems

A system has its own objectives, components or elements and a process. It has inputs, an output and a throughput. The purpose of any HRD system is

DOI: 10.4324/9781003530534-9

broadly to build the competencies and/or commitment of individuals, dyads, teams and the entire organisation as a whole through a variety of instruments. Its objective is to also build a lasting culture so that the employees learn and give their best on a continuous basis. Culture can be defined in terms of values and norms. The instruments available for an organisation are put into subsystems and become HRD systems or subsystems. The following are some of the HRD systems most commonly used.

1. Competency mapping
2. Recruitment and placement
3. Induction and integration
4. Performance management
5. Learning and development or training
6. Coaching and mentoring
7. Potential appraisal and development centres
8. 360-degree or multisource feedback
9. Rewards and recognition
10. Job rotation
11. Career and succession planning and development
12. OD

These are the most frequently used instruments or subsystems, which are propagated to ensure maximum achievement of the HRD goals. Some of them get grouped either for administrative convenience or to ensure synergy in terms of value. For example, induction training and training get normally grouped to form the training system. The training system attempts to ensure that the instrument of training is used efficiently, cost-effectively, appropriately and not misused. It becomes a system by formulating its own objectives, elements, inputs, output and process. It is the inputs and the output of the systems/ subsystems that link it to the other subsystems. A representation of the training system showing the various components has been provided in Box 7.1.

The following subsystems have been extensively used in the last 35 years of HRD in India.

BOX 7.1 TRAINING SYSTEM AND ITS ELEMENTS

Objectives

- To ensure that technical, managerial, human and conceptual competencies are developed in the employees on a continuous basis to enable them to perform their current jobs effectively and also prepare them to perform the new jobs as they come

- To offer the necessary competency-building inputs to all employees in a systematic, scientific and cost-effective manner
- To offer the required value- and attitude-based training to ensure that a lasting and self-sustaining culture is built in the organisation

Inputs

- Training needs identified on the basis of performance gaps in the previous year and performance opportunities for the next year – these are assessed through performance appraisals and come as inputs to the training subsystem
- Training needs assessed on the basis of potential appraisal exercises and assessment centres
- Training needs assessed on the basis of technological changes in the organisation, strategic moves and other changes in the environment
- Training needs assessed on the basis of the norms, values and other cultural aspects the organisation wants to develop in its members.

Output

- New competencies acquired by the employee
- New competencies acquired by the dyads, teams and the organisation as a whole

These new competencies are expected to become the inputs for improved performance, cost reduction, speed, efficiency and quality improvement in the products or processes.

Elements

- Methods of identifying training needs: performance appraisals, training need identification surveys, organisational diagnosis surveys, etc.
- The training department or training centre in the case of large organisations
- The training managers or the HRD staff handling the training subsystem and their own competencies
- The faculty and their competencies
- The training methods and strategies used
- The trainers and their competencies
- Training evaluation methods

These are just a few elements; there can be several more. Moreover, each of the above can be further broken into sub-elements.

Processes

The processes essentially deal with the organisation of the aforesaid elements and the rules, procedures and steps that govern their use.

- Method of determining training needs
- The timing
- The method of using the training needs to prepare training plans, etc.
- Methods of sponsoring the employee for training
- Pre-training preparation required
- Process of conducting the training
- Process of evaluating it
- Follow-up methods

This rationale can be followed for all HRD subsystems.

Competency Mapping

Competency mapping is the process of identification of the competencies required to perform successfully a given job or role or a set of tasks at a given point of time. It consists of breaking a given role or job into its constituent tasks or activities and identifying the competencies (technical, managerial, behavioural, conceptual knowledge, attitudes, skills, etc.) needed to perform the same successfully.

Competency assessment is the assessment of the extent to which a given individual or a set of individuals possess these competencies required by a given role or set of roles or levels of roles. Assessment centres use multiple methods and multiple assessors to assess the competencies of a given individual or a group of individuals. In order to enhance objectivity they use trained assessors and multiple methods, including psychometric tests, simulation exercise, presentations, in-basket exercises, interviews, role-plays, group discussions, etc. The methods to be used depend on the nature of competencies.

Who Identifies Competencies?

Competencies can be identified by one or more of the following categories of people: experts, HR specialists, job analysts, psychologists, industrial engineers, etc., in consultation with line managers, current and past role holders, supervising seniors, reporting and reviewing officers, internal customers, subordinates of the role holders and other role-set members of the role (those who have expectations from the role holder and who interact with him or her).

What Methodology Is Used?

The following methods are used in combination for competency mapping: interviews, group work, task forces, task analysis workshops, questionnaire, use of job descriptions, performance appraisal formats and key result areas (KRAs) and attributes.

TVRLS has developed a Role Set-based Competency Mapping (RSBCM) methodology and has been popularising it through their certificate programmes. In this methodology all role-set members are interviewed for mapping the competencies required for a role. A role set consists of all those who have expectations from a focal role holder and all those towards whom the focal role holder has obligations. The role-set members share their perceptions and expectations on the role holder's job, its purpose, activities and competencies required. The RSBCM methodology makes the role profile and competency profile exhaustive and also uses participative methodology and, hence, enhances acceptability of the output. TVRLS has used this method successfully both in India and its neighbouring countries like Sri Lanka. Training the internal resources through competency-mapping workshops to use RSBCM methodology has been found to be cost-effective. Illustrative lists of the corporations that have used this methodology include Wockhardt, HDFC, Dodla Dairy, Sampath Bank (Sri Lanka), etc.

Competency mapping is a starting point for building a competency-based organisation. Most organisations make the mistake of using competency mapping for developing competency models and stop there. A number of corporations do not have the right idea of the use of competency mapping and are unable to get the best out of their consultants. A good audit will go a long way in ensuring the ROI on competency mapping (see Rao, 2011, *Hurconomics*).

Training

This is the most frequently used and focused subsystem of HRD. This has been so significant that in the past HRD was equated in some of the companies with training. Even today it is not uncommon for an organisation to re-designate their training centre as HRD Centre or Training Department as HRD Department. In Pareek and Rao's model (1981, 1992a) it was treated as one of the HRD subsystems. Rao and Pareek (1994, 1998) re-titled it as Training and Learning System. Its scope extends beyond offering training programmes to facilitate learning and from classroom to continuous learning through distance learning (see Box 7.1 for a list of elements of the training system).

Performance Management

In the past, performance appraisal was an independent system to ensure role clarity, performance planning, job-related competency identification and development, development of critical attributes required by the job as well as those valued by the organisation and identification of training needs. In the last few years this system is slowly being replaced by a better one called *performance management*, which include the following:

- Performance planning or work planning
- Performance development
- Performance analysis
- Performance review discussion (coaching/counselling)
- Performance appraisal or monitoring
- Performance rewards and recognition

Of these, the first four are developmental and the rest are both developmental and monitoring activities that ensure accountability. In Pareek and Rao's model (1981, 1992b) performance management is split into the following: role analysis and performance appraisal as part of work planning, performance coaching as part of the development system and rewards and recognition as part of the culture system.

For more discussion on the PMS and recent developments, read Rao (2008a, 2010). The following conclusions have been drawn in these articles:

- You can make your PMS a change management tool and high-performance work culture development tool by redesigning it as a learning and development system than as a personnel administration tool
- As a first step identify the extent to which it is facilitating work planning and competency building at the employee level, among his or her seniors and in the team
- Redesign the PMS to include performance planning, performance analysis, and participative learning as integral parts
- Performance planning should include a listing of all key activities along with time in hours taken for the entire period of performance (year or half-year or a quarter year)
- The plans should also outline priorities of activities with weightages
- The plan should be discussed with the supervisor or seniors to whom you report so as to ensure mutuality and understanding. PMS works as a role clarification and mutuality-building tool
- It should be designed to include the scope for every employee to apply his or her key competencies in select projects

- The performance review sessions should be used as upward-learning sessions than as mere performance improvement discussion sessions. The focus of such reviews should shift from performance enhancement of the performer to the learning upliftment of his or her senior. A good performance review should enhance learning of seniors from their juniors
- The performance review session should also focus on identifying the factors contributing to the individual performance through an analysis of the performance and preparation of action plans
- The performance analysis details collected from groups and team of employees should be consolidated and used for initiating organisational improvements through OD facilitators
- PMS thus if redesigned and implemented well gives rise to enhanced human capacity utilisation, competency building and human capital value of an organisation.

Coaching and Mentoring Systems

In the earlier years feedback and counselling were regarded as an independent system. The assumption was that every senior should be conducting feedback and counselling sessions for his or her juniors periodically to aid their development as well as for mutual development. The periodicity was left for the organisation and the level of seniority. It was recommended that at senior levels, the sessions should be held at least every quarter and even monthly, and at junior levels it could be half-yearly. It was meant to be a system for communicating expectations, understanding difficulties, empowering, influencing, communicating, problem-solving, and mutuality building. It was also recommended as part of the performance appraisal system as it was felt that annual performance appraisals were an ideal time for holding these sessions on a mandatory basis. Unfortunately, by grouping the feedback and counselling system with performance appraisals, some organisations have limited them to performance feedback and counselling, which has led to some misunderstandings. Today, most organisations treat the feedback and counselling system as part of their PMS. Keeping this in mind, Rao and Pareek (1994, 1998) treat it as a subsystem of the overall development system.

Mentoring and coaching are becoming more acceptable and even desired systems. Executive coaching is becoming increasingly popular.

Career Development and Career Planning

Hope and advancement in one's career is one of the main motivating factors at any level of management. Some expectations of possible future opportunities of the individual is necessary to keep the manager's motivation high. Career planning does not mean predicting or envisaging what higher jobs will be available for each person. It essentially means helping the employee to plan his/her career in terms of his/her capabilities within the context of organisational needs. Career planning need not imply any specific commitment on the part of the management to promote an employee. It only implies that the individual after becoming aware of some of his capabilities and career opportunities and development opportunities chooses to develop himself in a direction that improves his chances of being able to handle new responsibilities. ... Career development means the development of general technical and managerial career in the organisation, career planning implies planning of specific career paths of employees in the foreseeable future in the organisation with the help of the superior.

(Pareek and Rao, 1975, 1998)

A number of organisations have followed this practice. Some of them have worked out career paths and linked promotion policies to career-planning development. In the changed context where the employee turnover is high and the average tenure of an executive in an organisation has reached its lowest levels (e.g., in the software industry and for HRD professionals it is stated to be two to three years), career planning takes a different meaning. Succession planning becomes more relevant. Career information also becomes more critical as a motivating factor. In the new model career planning and development is treated as a part of the career system and is linked to potential appraisals, manpower planning and recruitment.

Potential Appraisal and Development

Potential appraisal and development deals with the assessment of competencies of the employee in relation to likely jobs for him or her at higher levels in the future. The assessment can use primitive models such as asking the appraiser to assess the promotability of an individual to the next higher level or more modern methods like the use of assessment centres. In any case developing competencies of employees for handling future jobs is an integral part of the career development system and, hence, in the new model is represented as a part of the career system.

Assessment centres have become popular tools of high-performing organisations that try to ensure that competent people occupy higher-level positions.

An assessment centre is a comprehensive, standardised procedure in which multiple assessment techniques such as situational exercises and job simulation (business games, discussions, reports and presentations) are used to evaluate individual employees for a variety of manpower decisions.

> An Assessment centre consists of a standardised evaluation of behaviour based on multiple inputs. Several trained observers and techniques are used. Judgements about behaviour are made by these specially trained observers. At the end of the assessment the assessors get together to share their data which is scientifically recorded on a set of evaluation forms. They come to a consensus on the assessments of each candidate. Most frequently the approach has been applied to individuals being considered for selection, promotion, placement or special training and development in management.
>
> *(Ganesh, 2004)*

It is only after liberalisation in the nineties that interest in assessment centres got renewed. Many organisations have started setting up their assessment centres. This was a natural response to the need to ensure competent people manning strategic positions.

A large number of Asian companies have established assessment centres and many others are still exploring the same. The companies that are trying out include: RPG Group, Escorts, TISCO, Aditya Birla Group, Eicher, Cadburys, Castrol (India), Glaxo, Grindwell Norton, ONGC, Mahindra & Mahindra, SAIL, Siemens, Wipro, Wockhardt, J & J, etc.

Different organisations initiated assessment centres for different purposes such as recruitment, selection, placement, promotion, career development, performance appraisal, succession planning and development purposes like identification of training needs, identification of high-potential managers, creating a pool of managerial talent and multifunctional managers who would be available across the business group, employee recognition and fast growth. INFOSYS, WIPRO, Philips, Dr. Reddy's Laboratories and Global Trust Bank are some of the other organisations that have been using the assessment centres. Some of these organisations are in the process of developing measures to quantify managerial talent and measure the same periodically. Ganesh (2004) lists a number of organisations like HLL, Ranbaxy, Citibank, Tata Group, Tera Nova, HSBC, ICICI, Colgate and Motorola as having well-defined assessment centres in India.

Earlier assessment centres were used essentially for selection purposes since the traditional methods of interviews and considering educational qualifications were thought to be inadequate. The assessment centre method since then has been subjected to scrutiny and research much more than any other personnel practice. Due to the high-quality research done in this area and high reported validity, the methodology finds widespread use in a number of organisations. Besides selection, it is used for a variety of purposes, such as (*i*) early identification of management talent, (*ii*) promotion and (*iii*) diagnosis of developmental needs.

Every corporation needs competent managers in all their strategic roles and positions for the following reasons:

- To become more competitive as they are increasingly being required to compete with multinationals and locals with better organisational designs, technology, more competent people and rationalised organisational structures
- To prepare more and more of middle- and senior-level managers for senior- and top-level positions that could give strategic advantage to these organisations
- Due to a large number of vacant positions in top and senior levels arising from retirements and resignations
- The pressure on organisations to do business more effectively and efficiently through fewer but competent people and rationalised structures
- Increased pressure on corporations to perform and benchmark with international standards in terms of per employee productivity and contribution.

Under these conditions, there is no substitute for having competent managers to handle strategic roles and contribute continuously to organisations. Corporations cannot escape the reality and the need to have competent managers occupy strategic roles for the survival of organisations. Seniority has to get replaced by competence and merit.

It should not be mistaken that having an assessment centre means having completely objective decisions. Assessment centres certainly help in making employee promotions and placement decisions more scientific. Their contributions are more in creating a competence culture rather than mere best-fit decisions. Continuous competence building is a better aim rather than making promotion decisions with short-term objectives.

Auditing a potential appraisal and career development programme and assessment centres requires a thorough understanding of the theory and practice of assessment enters and how they are to be conducted and implemented.

Induction and Integration

Inductions have traditionally focused on new recruits at the entry level. This is partly because newcomers fresh out of college often need to know a lot about the company and make the transition from an institutional learning mode to an organisational action mode. Also, there are a large number of such graduates inducted into the company, and it is both feasible and economical to induct new batches in groups. The induction of employees recruited at senior levels has not attracted much attention in the past. It is still not considered an important issue in most companies. However, let us pause to consider the experiences from the West that show the significance of induction of new employees at senior levels. Studies have linked the retention capacity of a firm to the induction and assimilation process. The new economy and the need to be competitive require people to be inducted into a company even before they join it (Rao, 2002). If a new employee joining at the top level enters the organisation with a full understanding of its culture and his or her role, attrition rates can be checked.

Integration is a system of ensuring that new recruits are integrated into the system fast and start contributing soon. This is carried out by having role set-based discussions in the early stages of the life of a new entrant.

The induction and integration processes are to be audited by interviewing the new recruits and assess the effectiveness of the processes or systems and the time taken by the new comer to start contributing.

360-Degree Feedback and Development

In recent years, 360-degree appraisals have become very popular because it has long been felt that one person's assessment of another cannot be free of bias. In addition, with the focus on customers (both internal and external) and an emphasis on the softer dimensions of performance (leadership, innovation, team work, initiative, emotional intelligence, entrepreneurship, etc.) it has become necessary to get multiple assessments for more objectivity. A 360-degree appraisal is a multi-rater appraisal and feedback system. Almost every Fortune 500 company uses it in some form or the other. According to this system, the candidate is assessed periodically (once a year and sometimes even half-yearly) by a number of assessors, including his or her boss, immediate subordinates, colleagues and internal and external customers. The assessment is based on a questionnaire specially designed to measure behaviours considered critical for performance. The appraisal is done anonymously by others, and the assessment is collected by an external agent (e.g., a consultant) or a specially designated internal agent (e.g., the HRD department). The assessment is then consolidated, and feedback profiles are prepared and given to the participant after a workshop or directly by his or her boss or the HRD department at a performance review discussion session. Due to the innumerable variations possible in 360-degree feedback and appraisals and its potential as a competency identification and development tool, it is important to understand the process and its dynamics (for details on 360-degree feedback see Rao and Rao, 2000).

The following are some of the objectives of 360-degree feedback:

- Providing insights into the strong and weak areas of the candidate in terms of the effective performance of roles, activities, styles, traits, qualities, competencies (knowledge, attitudes and skills) and impact on others
- Identification of developmental needs and preparing development plans more objectively in relation to current or future roles and performance improvements for an individual or a group of individuals
- Generating data to serve as a more objective basis for rewards and other personnel decisions
- Reinforcing other change management efforts and interventions directed at organisational effectiveness (e.g., TQM efforts, customer-focused interventions, flat structures, quality-enhancing and cost-reducing interventions, decision process changes)
- Creating a basis for performance-linked pay or performance rewards
- Aligning individual and group goals with organisational vision, values and goals
- Culture building
- Leadership development
- Potential appraisal and development
- Career planning and development
- Succession planning and development
- Team building
- Planning measures to improve internal customer satisfaction
- Increasing role clarity and accountability

For auditing 360-degree feedback the auditors should be familiar with the theory behind the same. The audit should focus on the way 360-degree feedback is conceptualised and implemented. Most companies use external consultants to do this. Whether the way it is used is helping the organisation achieve the objectives envisaged needs to be ascertained. The auditors may examine some of the 360-degree feedback formats and interview line managers to decide the benefits and process improvements if any in administering the 360-degree feedback.

A More Rationalised Systems Approach

This is the era of professionalisation and professionalism. Professionalism means a scientific way of looking things. It promotes scientific temper and a systems approach. Nothing that is not defined gets done and nothing that is not monitored reaches its peak performance. Hence, it is important to use systems to define the objectives, inputs, output and processes. It is only well-defined systems that stand a chance of getting implemented. It is with this view that the new HRD systems model has been outlined in the earlier chapters. This model is an improvement over the earlier models and takes into consideration the contextual factors for HRD. It also takes into consideration the various developments that have taken place across the world that have some implications for the HR systems. For example, the last decade has witnessed a quality revolution through quality circles, TQM and the like. The importance of values and culture is being increasingly recognised. Organisation diagnosis surveys and employee satisfaction and customer satisfaction surveys are also becoming the basis for organisational change and change management programmes. OD interventions and team-building exercises are also becoming common. With increased stress, management programmes are becoming popular. The HRD systems model offered here forms the framework for HRD systems audit. The model is comprehensive and takes into account all the recent developments.

The new model separates career systems from work-planning systems, development systems and self-renewal and culture systems. Career systems deal with recruitment, promotions and placement of individuals. It is the starting point for any HR system. It provides the HR context for HRD. If done well, there is rationalisation of manpower and continuous utilisation and planned development of manpower. It ensures high motivational levels owing to the scientific way in which employees are recruited, promoted, placed and helped to develop capabilities for the unseen future jobs. Its main relevance to HRD audit is in terms of its scientific, systematic, approach of matching people and their competencies with organisational requirements. The work-planning system deals with ensuring role clarity on a continuous basis and helping employees deliver effective performance in their jobs by providing them an organisational or business context. If the business opportunities are not known or the environmental changes not shared with employees, a proper context cannot be provided for them either to plan their performance or to decide on their priorities. Thus, this system deals with both the business context and the role-related performance.

The development systems include most of the earlier stated elements: training, learning, feedback and counselling, job rotation, and mentoring, which has become popular in the last few years. Worker development has been included especially because any development effort is incomplete without the development of those who are the most critical performers in an organisation. For a variety of reasons, organisations neglected this aspect in the past but can no longer afford to do so.

Self-renewal systems essentially deal with the renewal processes at individual role level through efficacy exercises and at the group level through OD and action research interventions. These include all forms of OD interventions that are periodic and through which more immediate results can be expected. Exercises related to role efficacy, stress management and team building and annual or periodic organisational diagnosis surveys are attempts to bring about changes in the organisation.

Long-term cultural changes are effected through other mechanisms such as HRD climate surveys, quality circles, rewards and recognition, improvements in communication, etc. These can be grouped under culture systems, which is in tune with the definition of HRD as focusing on culture building besides competencies and commitment. The last set of subsystems deal with the culture-building subsystems. There can be some disagreement on whether some of the components classified under culture systems would be better placed under self-renewal systems. It is best left to the opinion and practical considerations of those conducting the audit. There is also no rigidity in the sequence or order and this too can be changed. What is more important is the component itself and not the system to which it belongs. Each component has its value.

Auditing HRD Systems

The HRD audit questionnaires described in Chapter 11 are probably the most appropriate instruments to audit the subsystems of HRD. However, as stated in the earlier sections it is useful to combine the various methodologies. Questionnaire data are not likely to give a full sense of the spirit with which each of the component subsystems are being implemented in an organisation. It is the interviews, observation, informal discussions and the examination of the formats and other documents that can tell a lot about the systems and their functioning. See Table 7.1 for details.

The systems audit is essentially meant to find out which systems are being effectively used to bring about improvements in the subsystems. Since this entire book is devoted to this subject, we will not discuss it further here. Table 7.2 presents what to observe while auditing HR systems.

Some guidelines for using the interviews, observation and documentation are given under each of the subsystems in Tables 7.1, 7.2 and 7.3. Table 7.3.

For a detailed discussion on these lines for competency mapping, 360-degree feedback and assessment centres, etc., see Rao's (2008b) *HRD Score Card 2500*.

TABLE 7.1 Interview Areas, Dimensions and Questions for Assessing HRD Systems

HRD System	Possible Interview Areas, Dimensions, Issues and Questions
A. *Career system*	
A1 Manpower planning and recruitment	• What is the process of manpower planningplanning, and recruitment? • How do the line managers participate in it? • What has it resulted in? • Are there differences in the workload of different departments? How is manpower being rationalised? • Is the manpower planning being done scientifically? • Are there adequate mechanisms to ensure the availability of the right competencies? • Is the competency listing appropriate and given adequate attention? • What are the strengths, weaknesses and suggestions for improvement?
A2 Potential appraisals and promotions	• Is there a system of potential appraisal? • How is it being implemented? • Is it scientific? • Is there a promotion policy? • Is it widely shared with all employees? • Are the promotions based on competency assessment? • What are the subjectivity levels of assessment? • What is the thinking on assessment centres? • What are the strengths, weaknesses and suggestions for improvement? • If there are assessment and development centres, how well are they designed, communicated and administered?
A3 Career planning and development	• How is the system of career planning and development operating? • What is the process of succession planning? • Are there well laid-out career paths? • If the organisation has made structural changes in the recent past, have the implications for careers been explained? Have they been thought out? • Are people aware of the implications of flat structures? Do they see the advantages and link it with careers? • What are the strengths, weaknesses and suggestions for improvement in career planning and development?

(Continued)

TABLE 7.1 Interview Areas, Dimensions and Questions for Assessing HRD Systems (*Continued*)

HRD System	Possible Interview Areas, Dimensions, Issues and Questions
B Work planning	
B1 Role analysis (goal setting)	• What is being done to clarify roles on a continuous basis? • Is role clarity an objective of the PMS? • Are there mechanisms for periodic dialogue between the seniors and juniors to give direction? • Are there mechanisms for sharing performance expectations between senior managers and their juniors? • Is the goal-setting and performance-planning process in place? • What are the strengths, weaknesses and suggestions for improvement in work planning systems (KPAs, KRAs, etc.)?
B2 Contextual analysis	• Are there mechanisms to inform employees about the performance of the company? • Are there mechanisms for formulating and communicating annual or periodic performance plans and thrust areas to all employees? • Do these communications help employees in planning their work and give them a sense of direction? • Do heads of departments and other senior managers take pains to communicate organisational plans and ensure that they are translated into work plans at the individual level? • What are the strengths, weaknesses and suggestions for improvement?
B3 Performance appraisal	• What is the current system of performance appraisal? • What are the components? • What are the objectives? • What is it currently being used for? • How is it linked to other systems? • Are the line managers taking it seriously? • What are the roles being played by the system? • Are the line managers adequately trained by it? Are there efforts made to constantly keep educating the line managers? Are the objectives clear to all? • Are there too many perceived biases if it is linked to rewards? • What are the strengths, weaknesses and suggestions for improvement?

(*Continued*)

TABLE 7.1 Interview Areas, Dimensions and Questions for Assessing HRD Systems (*Continued*)

HRD System	Possible Interview Areas, Dimensions, Issues and Questions
B4 Work from home or work from anywhere?	• Is WFH needed in this organisation? • Does it suit all jobs or some jobs? • Is the ROI better for jobs where work can be done from anywhere? • How were the policies evolved? Need based or trend based? Or ad hoc? • Were the employee preferences taken into consideration? • Is the policy communicated to all employees? • Is the policy being applied uniformly to all relevant employees? • Have employees working from home been provided enough technological and other infrastructure support? • How are the monitoring mechanisms evolved? Has it enhanced employee morale and motivation? • Has it impacted cost savings? • Has it enhanced the quality of products and services? • Have employees been equipped with the necessary coaching to manage disturbances? • Are the policies structured appropriately to enhance human resources utilisation? • Have the policies been reviewed and modified from time to time? • How is it working as a system or strategy?
C. *Development system*	
C1 Training and learning	• What are the suggestions for improvement in the training? • What is the training budget? • Do line managers take the training seriously? • What is the process of sponsoring employees for training? • What are the other learning mechanisms being used for competency building? • What are the new learning mechanisms that can be used? • What are the attitudes of the line managers and the top management for training? • What are the strengths and weaknesses of the training as it is being managed?

(Continued)

TABLE 7.1 Interview Areas, Dimensions and Questions for Assessing HRD Systems (*Continued*)

HRD System	Possible Interview Areas, Dimensions, Issues and Questions
C2 Performance coaching/ counselling	• What is the system of giving performance feedback and counselling? • Are the feedback and counselling sessions conducted seriously? • Do line managers take it seriously and give it the importance that is due? • Are adequate time, infrastructure (e.g., meeting rooms) and other facilities provided for the feedback and review sessions? • Is research done and the data utilised for bringing about improvement? • What are the strengths, weaknesses and suggestions for improvement of the system?
360-degree performance feedback	• Is there a 360-degree feedback system in operation in the company? For how long? • What has been the experience of managers with the system? • Is anonymity being maintained? Has it resulted in development or created interpersonal issues? • Are the agents administering trained to ensure development? • Is it adequately understood and being administered without violating the principles of feedback? • What are the strengths, weaknesses and suggestions for improvement of the system?
C3 Others like job rotation, mentoring	• What are the other noticeable mechanisms being used for competence building and commitment building in the company? • How is job rotation being used? • How is mentoring being used? Are people trained adequately? • Is the success experienced communicated to others to enhance the effectiveness of the system? • What are the strengths, weaknesses and suggestions for improvement in job rotation and the mentoring system?

(*Continued*)

TABLE 7.1 Interview Areas, Dimensions and Questions for Assessing HRD Systems (*Continued*)

HRD System	Possible Interview Areas, Dimensions, Issues and Questions
C4 Staff (worker) development	• What is the level of seriousness attached to worker and staff development? • Is there a separate person in-charge? What are the competency levels of the persons dealing with worker and staff development? • What is the range and appropriateness of the training and other development activities undertaken for the workers and staff? • Do they go beyond the statutory requirements? • How seriously are the statutory requirements of training taken up by the company? • Is there a special training budget for the workers and the staff? • What are the strengths, weaknesses and suggestions for improvement in the systems of training and worker development?
D. *Self-renewal system*	
D1 Role efficacy	• Are there mechanisms for periodically examining the effectiveness with which employees are performing their roles? • Are there any role efficacy programmes conducted in the company? What is the level of role efficacy? Is there adequate decentralisation and delegation? • Are there periodic reviews of roles and efforts made to improve the scope for role effectiveness? • What are the strengths, weaknesses and suggestions for improvement of role efficacy mechanisms?
D2 OD	• What OD exercises have been undertaken in the past? What have been the results? • Is the diagnosis shared widely? • What are the interventions used in the past and how did they work? • What are some of the top management attitudes to OD interventions? • What is the scope for OD exercises? • What should be the focus in future? • What are the priority areas for OD work? • What are the strengths, weaknesses and suggestions for improvement in relation to OD activities?

(*Continued*)

TABLE 7.1 Interview Areas, Dimensions and Questions for Assessing HRD Systems (*Continued*)

HRD System	Possible Interview Areas, Dimensions, Issues and Questions
D3 Action orientation research	• Is there a research orientation? • Have there been any researches in the past? What is the scope for action research in the company? • What is the level of HR research orientation in the company? What are the competency levels of employees in the company to conduct such research? • What are the strengths, weaknesses and suggestions for improvement in action research and research-based interventions?
E. *Culture systems*	
E1 HRD climate	• What are the main characteristics of the HRD climate? • How do the line managers characterise the learning environment in the company? What are the salient features? • What is the level of OCTAPACE in the company? • How free, frank and open are people with each other? • What is the level of trust? Are people generally reliable and counted upon to say what they feel and do what they say? • Is there a lot of chasing and monitoring to be done of each other? Is there a collaborative spirit and 'we' feeling? • What are the strengths, weaknesses and suggestions for improvement of the HRD climate?
E2 Values	• Are there some stated values? What are these values? • How are these communicated, monitored and practised? • How related are these values to the organisational goals or to larger-level community- or country-related goals? • What are the strengths, weaknesses and suggestions for improvement in the process of articulation and practice of values?

(*Continued*)

TABLE 7.1 Interview Areas, Dimensions and Questions for Assessing HRD Systems (*Continued*)

HRD System	*Possible Interview Areas, Dimensions, Issues and Questions*
E3 Quality orientation	• What efforts have been made in the past to improve the quality of products and services? • How extensive are the quality-related efforts? • Have all employees become quality conscious? • Is ISO 9000 or such other systems followed only for certification purposes or also for genuine improvement of quality? • What is the level of tolerance of poor quality of internal customer services? • What are the various quality-related systems in use? • How are they being taken? What are the attitudes of line managers to these? • Have these systems been focusing on continuous competence building of the employees? • Are these enhancing the commitment of employees to quality and other dimensions? • What are the strengths, weaknesses and suggestions for improvement for each of these systems?
E4 Reward and recognition	• What are the various reward systems in use? • What impact have they made in the past? • Are people happy with these? • Are the negative effects or side effects of these systems and mechanisms small enough and do the positive effects outweigh these? • What do people feel about these? • What aspects often go unrecognised and unrewarded? • Are the reward systems adequate and appropriate? • What are the strengths, weaknesses and suggestions for improvement?
E5a Information	• What are the informational needs of employees at the various levels given the nature of business or business plans of the company? • Is the information given up to the desired level? • What more information needs should be taken care of? • What are the strengths, weaknesses and suggestions for improvement in the information needs of employees and the way they are being met?

(*Continued*)

TABLE 7.1 Interview Areas, Dimensions and Questions for Assessing HRD Systems (*Continued*)

HRD System	Possible Interview Areas, Dimensions, Issues and Questions
E5b Communication	• What are the communication needs of people? • Do they get regular communication about the company, groups, etc., and their performance? • Are the communication needs being met effectively? • Are there efforts made to use information as a developmental, context-providing and commitment-building tool? • What are the strengths, weaknesses and suggestions for improvement?
E6 Empowerment	• What is the level of empowerment? • Are the line managers and particularly the seniors tuned in terms of their attitudes to empowering their subordinates? • What are some of the practices or efforts made in the past to empower employees (e.g., delegation of powers, use of committees and task forces, etc.)? • What are the strengths, weaknesses and suggestions for improvement?
F Competency mapping	• Are all jobs defined appropriately with details of competencies? Are critical competencies (knowledge, attitudes, skills and other qualities required) stated appropriately? • Are competency maps available for each role? Are they being used in all appropriate HR systems, such as recruitment, induction, PMS and training? • Are there competency models developed and used appropriately for leadership development and succession-planning pipeline?

TABLE 7.2 HRD System – What to Observe for Auditing

HRD System	Secondary Data	Steps and Observation Pointers for Audit
A.	Career system	
A1	Manpower planning and recruitment	Analyse recruitment data (number of applicants in relation to those recruited and whether it is worth the effort and if there are other mechanisms available), exit data, retirement data, age profile, etc., and assess the extent to which these are used for manpower planning.
A2	Potential appraisals and promotions	Analyse the rate of promotions department wise, grade wise, location wise, etc., to ascertain if there are any visible biases and to assess the pattern of promotions.
A3	Career planning and development	Study the past internal promotion patterns and career patterns of employees in the organisation. How have the roles, salary structures, etc., of those with the company changed over time and what do they reveal about the company? The proportion of internal versus external promotions in the organisation can be studied to assess the trends.
B.	Work planning	
B1	Role analysis (goal setting)	Study the performance appraisal forms and examine the extent to which the KPAs and KRAs, tasks, targets, etc., differentiate the roles and responsibilities and the extent to which duplication exists in the roles and responsibilities. Examine if there are any role directories, competency directories and skill inventories and examine the extent to which they differentiate the roles and provide role clarity. Also examine the data available from any role analysis exercises in the past.
B2	Contextual analysis	Examine the extent to which data is provided to employees about the changing context of the business. Is it adequate to set priorities of individual role holders? What is the nature of information shared or made available to different departments and functions in the beginning of the performance year to ensure that the departmental and individual work plans are made with full and detailed contextual understanding? Is it adequate? Are the technological changes, management practice changes, market changes, etc., properly communicated to individuals to enhance role clarity and set the priorities right? Examine documents circulars, performance appraisal forms and departmental plans, if any, for this purpose.

(*Continued*)

TABLE 7.2 HRD System – What to Observe for Auditing (*Continued*)

HRD System	Secondary Data	Steps and Observation Pointers for Audit
B3	Performance appraisal	Study the pattern of ratings for leniency, rater-wise trends and department-wise trends to ascertain the leniency and conservativeness in assessment. Study interdepartmental variations in ratings and rewards to ascertain the possible biases, etc. Investigate this only if necessary.
C.	*Development system*	
C1	Training and learning	Assess the expenditure on training level wise, department wise and location wise. Assess if the training programmes sponsored are in line with the training needs stated in the appraisal formats. Analyse the training budget to assess if the budgets are prepared appropriately and the full expenditure is taken into consideration in the assessment.
C2	Performance coaching/ counselling	Find out the time spent by each appraiser in performance counselling for each of his direct reports. Analyse the facilitating factors and difficulties mentioned by each of the appraisees or in each of the counselling sessions. Tabulate them department wise and find out what has been done in relation to them.
C3	Others like job rotation and mentoring	Analyse the job rotation data of the past to see if job rotation is being carried out according to the stated norms or policies. Analyse the trends in job rotation; for example, is it being carried out only in some departments and sections, and is it following the rationale stated or some other rationale or is it ad hoc and convenience based? Examine the mentoring data in terms of the number of meetings held, results of the evaluations conducted, if any, and the regularity and seriousness with which the mentoring system is being implemented.
C4	Staff (worker) development	Calculate the per employee training hours per year and the per employee expenditure per year. Study the distribution of these statistics for various departments and categories of workers. Focus attention on the staff. Examine the adequacy or inadequacy of the training. Examine the training inputs and sessions from the available documents and data.

(*Continued*)

TABLE 7.2 HRD System – What to Observe for Auditing (*Continued*)

HRD System	Secondary Data	Steps and Observation Pointers for Audit
D.	*Self-renewal system*	
D1	Role efficacy	Examine if any role efficacy seminars or workshops have been conducted. Have any surveys been conducted in the past to assess role efficacy? If yes, then what do the results indicate? Have there been any action plans drawn to improve role efficacy? Have they been followed up systematically? If not, what is being done to examine role efficacy and delegation? Any secondary data dealing with this can be examined.
D2	OD	Study any documents available from the OD exercises.
D3	Action-oriented research	Study the research reports and any circulars, communications, etc., using these.
E.	Culture systems	
E1	HRD climate	Examine the earlier climate survey data and compare with the current survey, if available.
E2	Values	Examine the values, statements and any comments, notifications and critiques in relation to values. Examine the extent to which these are being followed.
E3	Quality orientation	Examine data on TQM and ISO 9000 certification, minutes of QC meetings, Kaizen, etc., to ascertain the quality of implementation and possible improvements.
E4	Rewards and recognition	Study from the available documents the patterns, variations, coverage, etc., in relation to rewards. Examine the exact circulars, announcements and their wordings, etc., to examine the appropriateness of language and their motivational potential.
E5a	Information	Examine if there are any secondary data maintained for these.
E5b	Communication	Observe meetings, memos, notice boards, circulars and celebrations for communication content.
E6	Empowerment	Observe the level of confidence with which the staff speaks/decisions are taken.
G	Assessment and development centres	Observe the assessment and/or development centres in operation and ascertain the way the principles are followed: two assessors at least for each assessee and same assessor not assessing more than twice the same candidate and how well the exercises are conducted.

TABLE 7.3 HR Systems-related Documents and Facilities to Be Observed

HRD subsystem	Documents and physical facilities to be observed	Audit points for observation and analysis
A.	Career system	
A1	Manpower planning and recruitment	• Manpower-planning documents for their thoroughness and appropriateness • Tests used • Interviews and the way they are conducted • Assessment in the interviews • Process of recruiting from the time of receiving request for recruitment till the time recruitment is completed and appointment letters issued
A2	Potential appraisals and promotions	• Assessment centres in operation • Physical facilities and the tests used for assessment centres • Feedback process in assessment centres • Promotion interviews • Potential appraisal formats and interviews, if any
A3	Career planning and development	• Career path documents and development. Designation-associated facilities (size of room, office accommodation, perks given and the distance they are likely to be creating between the various levels) • Career counselling sessions, if any
B.	Work planning	
B1	Role analysis (goal setting)	• Role directories • KPAs or KRAs or job analysis or role clarity reports • Workshop documents, if any; role clarity and role negotiation workshops conducted in the past • Performance appraisal reports
B2	Contextual analysis	• Circulars and communications issued to employees explaining company performance and plans • Internal information-sharing circulars • Newspaper cuttings about the performance and plans of the company and internal communications issued in relation to these

(*Continued*)

TABLE 7.3 HR Systems-related Documents and Facilities to Be Observed (*Continued*)

HRD subsystem	Documents and physical facilities to be observed	Audit points for observation and analysis
B3	Performance appraisal	• Performance appraisal forms and appraisal manuals • Circulars issued in relation to these • Consultancy reports • Filled-in forms • Research and analysis reports
C.	*Development system*	
C1	Training and learning	• Induction manual • Training policy document • Training centre, hall and other facilities for training • Literature circulated for employees • Circulars regarding follow-up of training • Attend any seminars or presentation sessions after training
C2	Performance coaching/ counselling	• Feedback and review rooms • Feedback sessions in progress, if any, if the dyads agree to let you sit in their discussions • Post-counselling action plans or noting on the forms
C3	Others such as job rotation, mentoring	• Manuals, policies and circulars • Mentoring meetings or sessions in progress
C4	Staff (worker) development	• Physical facilities • Training material • Time tables and so on • Attend some of the training programmes in session • Observe shop floor committees, quality circle and Kaizen meetings and so on in progress
D.	*Self-renewal system*	
D1	Role efficacy	• Documents and reports
D2	OD	• Documents and reports
D3	Action-oriented research	• Documents and reports
E.	*Culture systems*	
E1	HRD climate	• Documents and reports
E2	Values	• Physical facilities • Observe the extent to which the values are being practised, the way people behave with you and with each other in their informal or formal transactions

(*Continued*)

TABLE 7.3 HR Systems-related Documents and Facilities to Be Observed (*Continued*)

HRD subsystem	Documents and physical facilities to be observed	Audit points for observation and analysis
E3	Quality orientation	• Observe the general quality of service and care taken by the people • Observe the quality orientation in the canteen, organisation of workplaces, library, shop floor, playground, rooms and so on
E4	Rewards and recognition	• Newsletters, announcements on the noticeboards

Conclusion

The importance of systems cannot be underplayed in the present era of professionalisation and quality consciousness. HRD subsystems such as planning, career, work planning, development, self-renewal and culture systems are extremely crucial to the organisation since they focus on competence building and have a lasting impact on the organisational culture. The HRD audit helps to assess the orientation, processes and mechanisms, degree of participation, cost-effectiveness and efficiency of the overall system and helps to point out areas of modification for meeting the organisational needs. This forms another significant dimension of the HRD Score Card.

8

HRD COMPETENCIES

Competent and committed employees produce quality products and services and get delighted and loyal customers. HRD is in fact defined as competence, commitment and culture building. Organisational culture and values provide the milieu in which competent employees make things happen. HRD interventions aim at building the three on a continuous basis. The HRD department and staff are instrumental in conceiving, designing and implementing systems and processes that result in continuous competence, commitment and culture building. This requires competent HR staff. However, if senior and top management are not supportive and have the required philosophy and styles, it might lead to demoralisation of HR staff as well as all other employees. While the impact of HRD depends largely on the competent HR staff, it also requires learning-oriented employees. In some corporations when employees do not have the required learning attitude and orientation, HR staff struggle a lot to make an impact. Hence, in the HRD audit, all these components are assessed.

Any HRD audit is incomplete without an assessment of those involved in HRD. The HR personnel are the principal actors in the HRD field. They are expected to spend all their time studying the HR needs of the company, designing the HR strategies, aligning and realigning HRD systems to suit the business strategies, implementing HR practices, etc. Their knowledge level, attitudes and skills play a critical role. The HRD audit, therefore, looks at the competency base of its staff and assesses their adequacy to suit the current and future HRD needs of the corporation. In addition to the HR staff, line managers, top management and other strategic persons like union representatives should also possess the right awareness, attitudes and skills.

DOI: 10.4324/9781003530534-10

The HRD audit also attempts to assess the level of these characteristics and their adequacy for good HR.

The HRD audit assesses the competencies of HR staff, the learning attitude of line managers and other supervisory staff, empowering and development styles of top management, learning attitudes of workmen and their representatives and the credibility and competence of the HRD department. Thus, the HRD competence audit proposed in this book is unique and comprehensive.

This chapter focuses on these various aspects and discusses the competency requirements of the HR staff and their evaluation. To begin with, the chapter outlines the challenges faced by the HR profession. A case is made for the need on the part of HR professionals to possess a high level of competencies. Next, the list of competencies is highlighted and then the methods to assess them. This is followed by an approach to assess the HRD styles of top management. Line managers' competence in terms of attitudes towards learning is assessed by the extent to which they use various sources of learning. The sources of learning include both the opportunities provided by HR instruments and systems and self-initiated learning through Internet and other mechanisms. The workmen's HRD orientation is assessed by measuring the extent to which they learn from various opportunities provided for them, including quality circles, shop floor councils, training programmes and so on.

Challenges for HR Champions

HRD competencies and their requirements need to be analysed in the context of business challenges and the role of HRD professionals in meeting them. In this context the following competitive business challenges as identified by Dave Ulrich (1997b) are worth noting:

Challenge 1. *Globalisation*

'Globalisation entails new markets, new products, new mindsets, new competencies, and new ways of thinking about business. In the future, HR will need to create models and processes for attaining global agility, effectiveness, and competitiveness' (Ulrich, 1997b: 2).

Challenge 2. *Value chain for global competitiveness and HR services*

This is what Ulrich has to say on building customer-responsive organisations: 'Responsiveness includes innovation, faster decisionmaking, leading an industry in price or value, and effectively linking with suppliers and vendors to build a value chain for customers. To support the value chain argument, research indicates that employee attitude correlates highly with customer attitude' (Ulrich, 1997b: 5).

Challenge 3. *Profitability through cost and growth*

Leveraging growth through customers involves efforts by the firm to induce customers to buy more of its products and services. Leveraging growth through core competencies involves the creation of new products and turning research knowledge into customer products. Mergers, acquisitions and joint ventures are the third growth path.

The issues for HR managers arising out of these are as follows:

- How can executives create a commitment to rapid growth and the culture that supports it while simultaneously controlling its costs?
- How can executives be sure that they hire people who can grow the business while reducing overall labour costs?
- How can executives create an organisational structure that provides both the autonomy needed for growth and the discipline needed to control costs?
- What are the HR implications of entering new business, of leveraging core technologies that lead into unfamiliar business, and of building the intimate customer relationships that bring an ever-increasing percentage of customer's purchases into the same provider? (Ulrich, 1997b: 9)

Challenge 4. *Capability focus*

'Organisation capabilities are the DNA of competitiveness' (Ulrich, 1997b: 10). Capabilities may be hard, such as technological, or soft, such as quality or organisational, speed of response, etc. The HR professional needs to address these in terms of the following:

- What capabilities currently exist within the firm?
- What capabilities will be required for the future success of the firm?
- How can we align the capabilities with business strategies?
- How can we design HR practices to design the needed capabilities?
- How can we measure the accomplishment of the needed capabilities?

Challenge 5. *Change, change and change some more*

Managers, employees, and organisations must learn to change faster and more comfortably. HR professionals need to help their organisations to change. They need to define an organisational model for change, to disseminate that model throughout the organisation, and sponsor its ongoing application. As cycle time gets shorter and the pace of change increases, HR professionals will have to deal with many related questions, including the following:

- How do we unlearn what we have learned?
- How do we honour the past and adapt to the future?

- How do we encourage the risk taking necessary for change without putting the firm in jeopardy?
- How do we determine which HR practices to change for transformation and which to leave the same for continuity?
- How do we change the hearts and minds of every one to change?
- How do we change and learn more rapidly? (Ulrich, 1997b: 11–12)

Challenge 6. *Technology*

'Managers and HR professionals responsible for redefining work at their firms need to figure out how to make technology a viable and productive part of the work setting' (Ulrich, 1997b: 13).

Challenge 7. *Attracting, retaining and measuring competence and intellectual capital*

In this fast-changing world, attracting and retaining talent becomes the battleground of competitiveness. Securing intellectual capital and developing it becomes a critical task. The most sought-after managers will possess intellectual capital to do global business. A firm's success depends on not only the economic criteria but also on the capability to attract and retain intellectual capital. This changes the measurement criteria of a firm's success, and seeking, finding and using such measures becomes another challenge for HR professionals. Post-pandemic challenges to HR: The pandemic has demonstrated the need for HR professionals to extend their scope of work from employees to all stakeholders and create and facilitate mental and physical health at all times to come. The work of HR extending from individual employee to their families, their place of living and neighborhood to ensure that they return to work happy and healthy poses a major challenge.

Challenge 8. *Turnaround is not transformation*

Many organisations in the past have undertaken turnaround exercises using downsizing, business process reengineering, consolidations, restructuring, etc. They have become more profitable. Such turnaround is not transformation. Transformation involves some fundamental changes. It may involve identity changes. Creating fundamental and enduring changes may become another challenge for HR professionals.

Professionalism in HR

Meeting these challenges requires the HR professionals to act professionally. What does professionalism imply? Ulrich (1997b: 7) states that

Professionals in other functional areas share the following characteristics:

- Focus on defined outcomes (e.g., physicians commit themselves to the Hippocratic oath and to healing)

- A shared body of knowledge (e.g., attorneys learn the canon of law)
- Essential competencies (e.g., engineers have the skill to build bridges, design machinery or create computers)
- Ethical standards maintained by collegial jurisdiction (e.g., licensed psychologists must adhere to an established set of ethical standards)
- Clear roles (e.g., comptrollers help monitor the economic performance of firms)
- Outcome definition, knowledge, competencies, standards, and role criteria enable these occupations to be recognised and accepted as professions.

The HR staff therefore needs to be professionally prepared to perform their roles effectively. In the last decade companies have recruited and placed employees without adequate professional preparation as HRD managers. As a result of this, the HRD function has suffered and lost credibility in quite a few organisations. Adequate professional preparation is essential (see Box 8.1).

BOX 8.1 PROFESSIONALISM IN HRD AND PROFESSIONAL PREPARATION OF HRD MANAGERS

HRD managers need to be prepared professionally. The Academy of Human Resources Development (AHRD) has prescribed the following minimum standards to qualify as a sound HRD professional: the candidate should have studied and passed a minimum of the following 10 courses:

1. Introductory Course on Organisations: Structure and Dynamics
2. Human Behaviour in Organisations
3. Integrated HRD Systems: Introductory course in HRD
4. Performance Planning, Analysis, Review, Appraisal and Development
5. Career Planning, Dynamics and Development
6. Potential Appraisal and Development
7. Training and Development
8. OD and OD Interventions
9. HRD Strategies and Interventions for Workmen
10. Personal Growth Laboratory

In MBA programmes the first two courses are normally offered as compulsory courses, and hence, the additional eight courses are needed to be completed to get qualified as a trained HRD professional.

In order to be a qualified HR professional the candidate needs to complete the following additional courses:

For Industrial Relations Competencies

- Labour Laws
- Employee Welfare
- Collective Bargaining
- Trade Unions
- Work Redesign and other HR Interventions for Organisational Effectiveness

For Personnel Management

- Recruitment
- Manpower Planning
- Human Resources Information System
- Wage and Salary Administration and Reward Management

Separate standards are prescribed from time to time through diploma programme run by the NIPM along these lines.

The two-year programmes offered by institutions like the XLRI, Jamshedpur; Tata Institute of Social Sciences, Mumbai; Symbiosis Institute, Pune, etc., and soon provide comprehensive programmes on HR, including HRD, IR and HRM. The specialisation in HRM may or may not include a full HRD component depending on the institution offering the course.

Challenging the Myths about HRD Is the First Role of HR Managers

A number of myths and misconceptions exist about HRD. Some of these are highlighted in Box 8.2. The first and foremost important role of HR is to ensure that such myths are not perpetuated and that the reality of HRD (see Box 8.3) is understood by all the employees in a corporation.

Dave Ulrich (1997b) has identified several myths that keep HR from becoming a profession. ulrich's challenges to the HR profession are also worth noting here. These are presented in some detail in Box 8.4 for the relevance they have for auditing the HR managers and their context.

BOX 8.2 EIGHT MYTHS ABOUT HRD

1. *HRD means training.* This myth has been perpetuated by those organisations that have renamed their training departments as HRD departments or their training managers as HRD managers. It is also perpetuated by

those who do very little beyond training. While training is important and has a significant role to play, HRD is far more than training

2. *HRD means promotions.* This myth is perpetuated by line managers who put the onus of their promotion (or not getting the promotion) directly or indirectly on the HRD department or HRD systems like appraisals. No one gets promoted or not promoted because of HRD. Biases do not automatically get reduced, nor do rewards get increased because of HRD. HRD may change the nature of recognition and reward systems and align them with the performance culture. This is not always a process without pain

3. *HRD means fat salaries.* This myth is perpetuated by some CEOs and top-level managers who go on communicating to their employees that salary revisions are not being undertaken since the company does not have a good and competent HRD manager and also by those who chose to give this as the first important task to a newly established HRD department

4. *HRD means planning the careers of people.* This myth is partly perpetuated by the team itself and partly by line managers who are incapable of planning their own careers. A fair number of employees seem to expect the companies to plan their careers and yet are not willing to share any of their own career aspirations with their seniors

5. *HRD means rewards.* This myth is perpetuated by those companies that overpublicise the linkage of their performance appraisal systems with rewards. Most line managers think that the moment the performance appraisal system in their company changes they will now become eligible to get rewards

6. *HRD means having a good time.* It is not unusual to come across some managers commenting that though their HRD department has come into existence about eight years ago, they have not been sponsored for a single training programme outside the company. Some of them even refuse to recognise the numerous in-house programmes they attended as training programmes. It must be outside their city and in a good place. It has got to be a memorable outing. In fact, in one organisation the HRD department was nick-named the Holiday and Recreation Department

7. *HRD depends on the top management.* This myth is perpetuated by a number of incompetent HRD managers who keep on attributing their own inefficiencies and ineffectiveness to the lack of commitment of the top management. This is also perpetuated by some of the CEOs and other top-level managers who treat HRD as a fashion and establish HRD departments without knowing what they can do.

8. *HRD is the job of the HRD department alone.* This is the most widely shared and misunderstood myth. It is also normal human tendency to assume if you have a department everything is to be done by that department only. Most managers get disappointed that the HRD department is not able to change their employees (direct reports) and their attitudes. In HRD it is the

responsibility of each employee to develop himself or herself and facilitate the development of at least one level below. The HRD department equips line managers with instruments for development

BOX 8.3 THE HRD REALITY

- HRD means learning
- HRD means self-development
- HRD means creating conditions for others to develop and remain motivated
- HRD means creating new development tools and their use
- HRD means more accountability
- HRD means more initiative, teamwork and collaboration
- HRD means trusting and trustworthiness and creation of a trusting environment
- HRD means autonomy and experimentation
- HRD means effort
- HRD is contextual

In sum, it means competence, commitment and culture building at individual, dyad, team and organisational levels in the contexts applicable to each organisation.

Ulrich (1997b: 237) observes: 'The tools for creating competitive organisations come from redefining and upgrading human resources'. HR policies and practices should create organisations that are better able to execute strategy, operate efficiently, engage employees and manage change, all of which are elements of a competitive organisation.

The HR professional of the future will be dramatically different from the HR employees of the past. under the rubric of becoming business partners, HR professionals will think more about results than programmes. They will focus on and guarantee deliverables from deployment of HR practices that create value for their organisation, developing organisational architectures and using them to translate strategy into action. They will perform organisational diagnosis by applying their organisational architectures to set organisational priorities. HR professionals reengineer HR work through the use of technology, process reengineering teams and quality improvements. They will be the employees' voice in management discussions, ensuring that employees feel that their issues have been heard. They will be catalysts, facilitators and designers of both cultural change and capacity for change, establishing a vision for the HR function that excites clients and engages HR professionals (Ulrich, 1997b: 235).

BOX 8.4 MYTHS AND REALITIES AFFECTING THE HR PROFESSION (ULRICH, 1997B)

Old Myths	New Realities
People join the HR function because they like people.	HR departments are not designed to provide corporate therapy or as social or health and happiness retreats. HR professionals must create practices that make employees more competitive, not more comfortable.
Anyone can do the HR function.	HR activities are based on theory and research. HR professionals must master both theory and practice.
The HR function deals with the soft side of business and is therefore not accountable.	HR professionals must learn how to translate their work into financial performance.
The HR function focuses on costs that must be controlled.	HR practices must create value by increasing the intellectual capital within the firm. HR professionals must add value, not reduce costs.
The job of the HR professional is to be the policy police and the health-and-happiness patrol.	The HR profession does not own compliance – managers do. HR practices do not exist to make employees happy but to help them become committed.
The HR function means a lot of fads.	HR practices have evolved over time. HR professionals must see their current work as a part of an evolutionary chain and explain their work with less jargon and more authority.
The HR function is performed by nice people.	At times, HR practices should force vigorous debates. HR professionals must be confrontational, challenging as well as supportive.
The HR function is only for HR professionals.	HR work is as important to line managers as are finance, strategy and other business domains. HR professionals should join other functional managers in championing HR issues.

The following seem to be the priorities for HR professionals.

Priority 1: *HR theory*

HR professionals must master the theory behind HR work. Theories of learning, motivation and organisational change should lay the foundation.

Priority 2: *HR tools*

Improvements must continue in HR core technologies such as executive development, recruiting and staffing, training and education, rewards and recognition, performance management, employee relations, labour relations and diversity. Six HR tools will become issues for the future: global HR (focusing on the ramifications for HR of global business strategy), leadership depth (defining and creating leaders for the future), knowledge transfer (creating systems that will transfer knowledge throughout the organisation to reduce cycle time, increase innovations and quality decisions), cultural change and customer-focused HR.

Priority 3: *HR capabilities*

The new HR capabilities, in addition to the traditional ones, should include the following:

- *Speed*: Quickness in doing HR work without sacrificing quality
- *Implementation*: Turning ideas into actions
- *Innovation*: Thinking creatively about problems
- *Integration*: With customer goals, strategic plans, employee needs, etc.

Priority 4: *HR value proposition*

The HR investments in the future must focus on value creation and developing a value equation for HR services and products. HR practices affect

- Employees in terms of their morale, commitment, competence and retention
- Customers in terms of their retention, satisfaction and commitment
- Investors in terms of profitability, cost, growth, cash flow and margin.

Priority 5: *HR governance*

How is work coordinated? The HR professional must see if the work is organised and coordinated in the organisation. For this purpose he or she needs to be well-versed in organisational structures and the dynamics generated by them. He or she needs to master work organisation, theories of differentiation and integration, etc. He or she should be able to examine the current work organisation systems, evaluate them, be sensitive to functionalities and dysfunctionalities of various structures and benchmark with the best practices. He or she needs to understand flat structures, matrix structures and their suitability to different contexts and businesses.

Priority 6: *HR careers*

The HR professional can be located in one of the following four locations: the (plant), the business unit (product line or country), corporate HR or outside the HR function. He or she may be a specialist or generalist. He or she may be a contributor (working alone), integrator (coordinating the work of others) and a strategist (directing policies and procedures).

Priority 7: *HR competencies*

- Knowledge of business (financial, strategic and technological variables and their influence on business)
- Knowledge of HR practices (staffing, development, appraisal, rewards, organisational planning, communication, etc.)
- Management of change (creating meaning, problem solving, innovation, transformation, relationship influence and role influence)
- Business mastery (knowing the business, financial, strategic, technological and organisational capabilities of the organisation)
- HR mastery
- Change and change process mastery
- Personal credibility (accuracy in all HR work, consistency, predictability, meeting commitments on schedule and within the allotted budget); good chemistry with colleagues, subordinates and supervisors; appropriate behaviour during disagreements or confrontations; integrity; out-of-the-box thinking; maintaining confidentiality; ability to listen and focus on problems of employees)

In addition to the aforesaid priorities and competency requirements of HR professionals globally, an analysis of some of the outstanding performers in the HRD profession in India can also indicate some important lessons. An analysis of the list of National HRD Award Winners has indicated the following characteristics. As the process of selecting outstanding performers in HRD set up by the National HRD Network is rigorous, it can be taken as a fairly credible list.

Lessons from Award-Winning Indian HRD Managers

There were 11 National HRD Award Winners between 1989 and 1997. The list includes P.K. Sarangi (1989, Indian Oil), M.R.R. Nair (1989, SAIL), D.F. Periera (1989, L&T), Susan Varghese (1990, Crompton Greaves), S. Chandrasekhar (1990, L&T ECC), Anil Sachdev (1991, Eicher), Arvind Agarwal (1991, Modi Xerox), K.N. Sharma (1992, Godrej Soaps), R.R.

Nair (1993, Hindustan Levers), Aroon Joshi (1993, Cadbury's) and Major Narayana Murthy (1993). Some of the prominent HRD professionals awarded in the subsequent years include Dr Anil Khandelwal (Bank of Baroda), Anji Reddy (CEO, Dr. Reddy's), Azim Premji (CEO, Wipro), Santrupt Misra (Birla Group), Pritam Singh (Academic, MDI), Ratan Tata (Group Chair, Tata Group), Adesh Goyal (Hughes Software), Dileep Ranjekar (Wipro), R.A. Mashelkar (Chief, CSIR), Rajendra Pawar (CEO, NIIT), Venu Srinivasan (CEO, Sundaram Clayton), B. Muthuraman (CEO, Tata Steel), Anand Nayak (ITC), Hema Ravichandar (Infosys), P. Dwarakanath (GSK), K.V. Kamath (CEO, ICICI Bank), Aquil Busrai (IBM), G.P. Rao (JK Tyres), Kumaramangalam Birla (Group Chair, Aditya Birla Group), Pankaj Bansal (People Strong), Visty Banaji (Godrej Industries), B. Santhanam (CEO, Saint-Gobain), C.S. Venkatarathnam (Academic, IMI), N.S. Rajan (E&Y), P.V.R. Murthy (Exclusive Search), Tanaya Mishra (ACC), Vivek Paranjape (Reliance), S. Varadarajan (Quatrro Global Solutions), Marcel Parker (IYKYA Solutions), Leena Nair (Hindustan unilever), Rajeev Dubey (Mahindra & Mahindra), Sonali Roychoudhury (P&G), Vineet Nayar (CEO, HCL Technologies) and Fr. E. Abraham (XLRI, Jamshedpur). The award winners in subsequent years include: K. Ramkumar, Ritu Anand, Ashok Ramchandran, Deepak Kumar Hota, Anand Nayak, Pritam Singh, Indira Parikh, Prem Singh, B. Ashok Reddy, Meenakshi Davar, N. Chandrasekharan, Shika Sharma, Vineet Kaul, H N Srinivas, and Aquil Busrai.

The HRD managers who won awards continued to do well. Of the 11 awarded up to 1993, nine of them have moved on to boardlevel positions in subsequent years. One of them became Chairman of SAIL, Mr. M.R.R. Nair, and has taken SAIL from strength to strength nationally and internationally. Subsequently, he was heading a multinational conglomerate in the steel industry in Mexico and worked for the world-famous ArcelorMittal Group. Mr. Anil Sachdev set up the Eicher consultancy division, then Grow Talent and now SOIL, an education company, and is helping a large number of other organisations in HRD, TQM, LSIP and OD. Arvind Agarwal has become the CEO of a manufacturing unit and subsequently as an advisor to RPG group and is doing very well. Another HRD manager, P.K. Sarangi, became an adviser to the top management of a pharmaceutical company (Ranbaxy) and has assisted that company to go global. Another has moved on to the board of his multinational company and is continuing to steer organisational changes and, post-retirement, is working as a CEO coach. An examination of the professional life and accomplishments of these individuals offer excellent role models for upcoming HR managers. Some of their common traits and characteristics are given here based on the author's observations and personal knowledge about these individuals.

Among those awarded in the subsequent years there are three categories: CEOs, CHROs and Change Leaders in Academic. All the CEOs awarded are those who are known for their HR orientation and excellent people management practices. One of them has even written a book called *Employees First*, published by Harvard Business Publications. Another HR manager, Dr Anil K. Khandelwal, later became a CEO and has documented his experiences in a book called *Dare to Lead* and has received international recognition for his work. Almost all of these HR professionals are placed in board-level positions and are known for their leadership and change management skills. Some of them have even become the main promoters of professional bodies like the National HRD Network. From a detailed knowledge of tracking their professional careers the following conclusions are drawn about effective HR.

They are role makers rather than role takers.

They have not looked for guidance from the top management about what they should do as HR managers. Rather, they provided guidance to the top management and steered their respective companies to adopt good HRD practices. The citations of these individuals prepared at the time of awards indicate these characteristics. They have developed themselves into persons of stature in the HR function by making things happen. They are action-oriented people. They shared their success stories inside and outside their organisations and enthused people to learn and change.

They have integrated HR policies and practices with the company business.

They held a high degree of concern for their company's business and growth. They were constantly concerned about their company's growth and business plans and kept in touch with all aspects of the business. They made efforts to study and understand the challenges faced by the company and aligned themselves and their work to the company needs. This is what gave them credibility from the top management.

They are versatile and can shift with ease from one HR task to another.

Their professional life indicates the versatility and ease with which they can shift from one area to another depending on the organisational need and situation. On one particular day they may be working on performance appraisals, and on another day they may be training the managers on the managerial grid or TQM or internal customer orientation. Another day they may be reviewing the wage structure or negotiating with the unions or conducting a worker development programme. Yet another day they may be getting experts to examine their company or making presentations to the line managers about the findings of their HRD climate survey or giving feedback to the CEO about his or her managerial style and their impact on the company.

They are learning individuals and use various sources of learning.

Their definition of HRD seems to have been influenced by the organisational needs and the context rather than textbook formulae of what should be done. It is not that they are opposed to learning from books; they are continuous learners and good readers. They are also good listeners. Almost all of them attend seminars and conferences, address them and stimulate the thinking of the participants and in the process also get stimulated to do new things. They are also known to enjoy talking to people and learn from their experiences. They can interact with equal ease with a shop floor worker and the CEO and learn from both the interactions and put such learning to the advantage of the company.

Those who were recognised for their outstanding contributions as CEOs are highly HRD oriented. Some of those who are CHROs may not even have HR designations.

Some of them were HR managers and the terms meant very little for them in defining their roles. They also did not limit their work to managerial staff; they focused equally on the workers.

They have been ready to handle line responsibilities due to their constant interaction with and learning from the line managers.

Some of them have handled or have been handling subsequently line responsibilities rather well.

They have a high applied behavioural science orientation.

Interestingly, most of the awardees are professional members of the Indian Society of Applied Behavioural Sciences (ISABS) or Indian Society for Institutional and Social Development (ISISD). All of them have been interested in human behaviour and are value-driven individuals.

Over and above all this they are committed, hardworking individuals who travel a good deal, are receptive to new ideas, are secure individuals and have a change orientation.

The previous description should be a good guide to provide role models for effective HR managers. These are only some individuals whom the HRD Network has recognised and awarded. There are several more HR managers who are equally or perhaps even more effective. Most of them are constantly initiating change and innovations in HR tools and systems.

Santrupt Mishra, Arvind Agarwal, Rajeev Dubey, Aquil Busrai, P. Dwarakanath, P.V.R. Murthy and many other are known be change masters. They have introduced some change or the other. The HR professionals in academics are change leaders. All of them are initiative takers and credible activists.

Future Strategies

The following attitudes need to be developed for HR managers to become effective.

Six Principles for HRM Effectiveness

1. *Respect the individual through respect for his or her time*
   Our respect for each other is indicated by the respect we show to each other's time. The HRD manager has to learn to respect each individual and the contributions each can make to the organisation. The analysis in Box 8.5 indicates the importance of time.

BOX 8.5 RESPECTING EACH OTHER BY RESPECTING EACH PERSON'S TIME

We have been wasting our human resources since we show scant respect for other people's time. Once I started calculating the economics of time and came up with some startling figures. I calculated the economic value of time of a manager working in a company with a turnover of ₹2,000 million and employing 500 individuals. In this company a middle-level manager has an annual salary of ₹300,000. Putting all the benefits together the company spends ₹400,000 on him or her. The total annual expenditure of the company on salaries and perks is about ₹80 million. The company works for 250 working days, and therefore, the time of this manager could be valued as ₹1,600 a day. He or she is expected to work for eight hours a day. This means that every hour of his or her work costs the company ₹200. This means that every minute of his or her time costs ₹2.50. This means that every time he or she makes a phone call to the personnel department to sort out his or her leave matters or for expediting recruitment or every time the personnel manager makes a call to him or her, it has cost the company more than ₹25, assuming that both speak to each other for five minutes. It would have cost the company at least ₹600 if the person has to visit another office site and spend an hour to sort out a leave matter and another hour for travelling back to his or her office and another hour thinking about it. In addition, you need to count the time of the personnel manager and the time of a few of his or her fellow managers with whom he or she will be sharing his or her encounters with the personnel department. All this may be to get a ₹100 medical bill passed or a ₹400 petrol bill sorted out. We can see how much we waste each other's time through our own inefficiency, use of poor technology, lack of systems and lack of mutual trust. Some HR managers enjoy this and do not give the facilities due to the line managers unless they pay a visit to their office.

As I thought about this it occurred to me that I was perhaps making a basic mistake in my calculations. I was looking at the value of time in terms of the cost to the company calculated from salary bills and using the input of the company as an indication of the cost. In reality the company expects a certain output from each individual. So the value of time should be measured in terms of the value of the output expected. That means the value of time is equal to the value of the output expected. By this reasoning if an individual draws a salary and perks of ₹400,000 and it constitutes 0.5 per cent of the salary bill, the value of his or her time is 0.5 per cent of the total annual turnover. If the company is a ₹2,000 million company the value of the time of the individual is in fact ₹10 million per annum. By this argument every day costs ₹40,000 and every hour costs ₹5,000. Thus, every minute of this manager costs ₹83.33 as against our earlier calculation of ₹2.5. Now you can imagine the quality of services we need to render to each other so as not to waste each other's time (for a detailed discussion of how HRD managers should value time and talent see the book on Hurconomics by T. V. Rao; Rao, 2011).

2. Become trustworthy and promote trust by being trustworthy

Ours is a relationship-oriented culture (see Box 8.6 for some illustrative experiences on how our relationship orientation is expensive). We like to please each other and prefer not to offend the other in a face-to-face meeting. However, we do not hesitate to speak ill of the other person behind his or her back. We maintain two faces. We find it difficult to be forthright and straightforward.

I have begun to believe that this has become our culture. As a result, most of us seem to have two faces – what we mean or what we think privately and what we say publicly are different; similarly what we promise to do and what we attempt to do are also different. As we grow we seem to discover more and more of these differences and tend to become less trusting of others. When we do not trust others we also become less trustworthy. If others can be so unreliable why can I not be unreliable for a change? Why should I inconvenience myself? Why should I be the one to sacrifice my conveniences? This attitude sets in and as you grow older you tend to learn from the low trustworthiness of others and become less trustworthy yourself.

To get over this, in other countries human beings are substituted by technology and systems. In these countries, you cannot enter the railway station unless you have the right kind of ticket. The machine decides whether you have the right ticket or not.

If we respect each other the next important thing we need to do therefore is to create a culture of trust. We can only do this by becoming more and more trustworthy. We should not make promises that we cannot keep and when we make a promise we should keep it at any cost. The HR manager should make efforts to create a trustworthy and trusting culture. This should become an important HR agenda of organisations. If we have to change society it has to begin in our organisations first and should begin in HR departments even earlier.

BOX 8.6 TRUST AND TRUSTWORTHINESS

Many expected that after liberalisation with increased opportunities and customer orientation, our people will become more trustworthy. My experience over the last few years has indicated that we have a long way to go. The car you buy on the basis of advertisements is not trouble free. The sales engineer who promised to deliver the refrigerator at your house on a specified day and time does not turn up and you postponed your other work and wait for him or her. The computer company delays the delivery of the computer for which you have paid a full advance by as much as two months and they give you the printer first and the computer two months later, upsetting all your plans and making you spend an extra ₹5,000 on the DTP work. Your driver and secretary frequently go on sick leave even if they are not sick and you discover that they are working somewhere else for some extra money. The administration does not arrange the carpenter on the promised day to work at your office while you made all plans as per their promise. The vendor does not deliver the items on time. The personnel department does not arrange the labour on time for some important work. There can be hundreds of such examples of low trustworthiness of people. Those who are not trustworthy do not realise the extent to which the other person is made to suffer or incur losses. For them it is just a term, but, for the other person, it may have cost a fortune. This is the weakest aspect in our public services.

---

3. *Continuously introspect on the roles you perform and undertake self-renewal exercises at both individual and group levels*

If we have to achieve a cultural change and build our profession, organisations and the nation we need to introspect. Our self-perceptions and others' perceptions about us may not be the same. Introspection is a good tool to move our perceptions closer to those of others. When we introspect we should ask ourselves the question, 'Why have I behaved the way I have behaved?' Such self-examination is the first step to growth. It leads to discovery and lays the foundation for the future. Self-examination can also be a painful process. No change is possible in the directions I have suggested earlier without introspection. It is the introspection that will put us in touch with our weaknesses and helps us to improve. It is the introspection that helps us to understand others better as most others are also like us.

While we as individuals should introspect, as teams we need to conduct periodic renewal exercises and take the help of outsiders to facilitate this process. Organisational and team-renewal exercises are building blocks for sustained development of organisations and groups.

4. *Learn from your neighbours by using them as sounding boards for change and reflection*

Such introspection can get tremendously facilitated if we can take the help of an external agent. The external agent could be a consultant, a fellow HRD professional, a line manager or even someone not at all connected with your field. When the National HRD Network was started one of the intentions was to facilitate networking among HRD professionals so that they could learn from each other and also work as facilitators for HRD in each other's units. We have not yet been able to establish fully the culture of HRD managers serving as consultants to each other. We seem to think only successful HR managers make good consultants. I believe that those who have attempted but could not do well may also make good consultants. At least they can put us in touch with the realities and complexity of the problems involved in change. It is high time our organisations learned to grant professional leave to every HR manager to enable him or her to work as a consultant for some other organisation. If there is a fear of helping a competitor the HR manager can be spared to work for compatible or sister organisations. It is worthwhile even if they can be spared to work with an NGO or an educational institution. It will rejuvenate the HR manager and at the same time may do some good to the client organisation where the HR manager spends some time.

5. *Pay adequate attention to the culture and values in the company and the country*

There is no one other than the HR manager who can pay attention to the values and cultural aspects of the organisation. If one thing can be learned from successful companies and successful organisations, it is the attention they pay to the values and culture of the organisation. HR managers should get themselves trained to understand the cultural dimensions of organisational life. They should get themselves prepared professionally by going through appropriate professional development programmes. The doctoral fellow programmes offered by the AHRD and XLRI as well as the Indira Gandhi National Open university (IGNOu) programme or the diploma in

HRD offered by AHRD are some avenues available for such higher studies. Periodic surveys of organisational culture and using the feedback to initiate change are some of the things that can be done.

6. *Use personnel policies for empowering people and promoting managerial effectiveness rather than for blocking creativity and innovation*

Finally, an important question that HR managers should ask themselves is regarding their role in the organisations. In the past their role focused on maintenance functions. As experience shows this is a very narrow way of looking at the HR function. I consider the main role of HR people as 'to create conditions for empowering people in the organisations so that they can make things happen'. Such an empowering role requires a constant examination of the factors that are motivating and facilitating managerial effectiveness. They should therefore keep examining the structures, systems, styles, skills, technology, attitudes, personalities, etc., that block effective managerial performance and planning and undertake activities that remove such blocks. This is the single most important task of the HR manager. An HR manager will be able to transform himself or herself into a transformational leader if he or she undertakes some of the things mentioned earlier. If the HR manager follows these principles, he or she will not only enjoy his or her work and job but will also take the organisation forward.

In the context of the previous discussion it is clear that HR professionals need to develop the right kind of attitudes, besides their strategic thinking and professional expertise. Given the criticality of the role of HR professionals, the HRD audit naturally focuses substantially on the background and preparation of HR professionals. There are many methods for assessing this. The most important ones are whether they have the required professional preparation to meet the HRD challenges faced by the organisation. In the context of the country as a whole their preparation goes beyond the organisation and should also look into the societal culture. It should assess whether the HRD manager has the understanding of the country's culture and whether been prepared adequately to diagnose, face and change the same. A list of competencies emerging out of this discussion is presented here.

Dave ulrich and team identified three sets of competencies in 1987: knowledge of business, delivery of HR practices and managing change. In 1992 personal credibility was added. This included working well with seniors, communicating with excellence and delivering results with integrity. Change management became more heavily weighed and HR professionals from high-performing organisations spent more time on strategic issues while those in low-performing organisations spent more time on operational issues (Ulrich et al., 2013b: 19).

By 1997 the focus shifted to culture management, and HR professionals of high-performing firms were found to focus on culture management wherein HR professionals identified organisational cultures that helped implement business strategies. By 2002 HR's role as a strategic contributor asserted itself. This competency consisted of integrating fast change, strategic decision making and market-driven connectivity. Through this competency HR professionals helped their organisations successfully navigate changing customer, competitive and shareholder requirements (Ulrich et al., 2013b: 21). By 2007 building organisational capabilities had become a defining feature of HR competencies. By 2012 Dave ulrich and team evolved a six-domain HR competency model:

1. Credible activist (professionally credible, interpersonally competent, develop positive chemistry with all stakeholders and contributes to business results through grounded data and opinions)
2. Strategic positioner (understands business context – global, social, political, economic, environmental, technological, demographic, customer, competitor and supplier trends and translates such trends into business implications)
3. Capability builder (creates, audits and orchestrates an effective and strong organisation)
4. Change champion (develops organisation's capacity for change and manage the same)
5. HR innovator and integrator (innovates and integrates HR practices systems and processes into business imperatives and results)
6. Technology proponent (constantly keeps in touch with technological developments and leverages them for HR to deliver results)

All these qualities seem to be so true with most of the awardees of National HRD Network.

Out of its own research and experience, TVRLS Pvt. Ltd has identified the following 10 set of competencies as required by HR professionals to be successful and make a difference.

1. *Business knowledge*: Knowledge of business (products, services, customers, technology, competitors, developments, R&D) and all functions (sales and marketing, production and operations, finance, systems, MIS, logistics, services, etc.), knowledge of business capital (intellectual capital) and its constituents and methods of building business capital
2. *Functional excellence*: (*i*) HR knowledge and (*ii*) HR delivery, including culture sensitivity, empathy, coaching and facilitation
3. *Leadership and change management*: (*i*) Communication, (*ii*) initiative (*iii*) creativity and (*iv*) change management

4. *Strategic thinking*: Analytical ability, cost and quality sensitivity, ability to spot opportunities, anticipate and find alternate ways of solving problems
5. *Personal credibility*: Delivering results, honouring commitments, communicating and trustworthy
6. *Technology savvy*: Including HR technology and research methods
7. *Personnel management and administrative skill*: Dealing with labour laws, statutory requirements, attendance and leaves, employee benefits, logistics and infrastructure management (transport, living, etc.)
8. *Vision of the function and entrepreneurship*: Ability to think long term, see opportunities and articulate future directions and aspirations
9. *Learning attitude and self-management*: (*i*) Self-awareness and desire to learn, (*ii*) time management, (*iii*) networking and (*iv*) research and analytical skills
10. *Execution skills*: (*i*) Planning and monitoring skills, (*ii*) cultural sensitivity, (*iii*) persuasive skills, (*iv*) behaviour modification techniques and group dynamics, (*v*) ability to craft interventions for implementation and (*vi*) cost and quality sensitivity

Agrawal and Rao (2022) in their study of 30 HR leaders identified the following sets of competencies:

A. **Business Leadership:** contributions to business which deals with Business acumen, business information, business decision making, entrepreneurship, knowledge of all functions like finance and accounts, marketing, production, logistics and information technology.
B. **Functional Leadership:** Dealing with HR function and includes expertise in the HR function, its strategy, systems, processes, technology, talent management and execution etc. A good part of people management skills get classified here as it is a part of the HR profession.
C. **Professional Leadership:** Largely dealing with contributions to the profession in the country and across the globe, adding to professional knowledge, dissemination, membership and leadership in professional forums and bodies and professional innovations that go beyond the organisation and benefit to the profession and Professional bodies, writing, influencing Govt. etc.
D. **Personal Leadership:** Which largely starts with self and self-management, self-renewal, initiative, drive, creativity and such other personal qualities that put the person in the leader's seat. These are also required for functional leadership but these are more of Individual competencies going beyond the function.

E.   **Social Leadership:** Which largely deals with contributions to the society and humanity at large and is also contributions to society and larger causes.

The 2021 Model of HR competencies of Dave Ulrich: The HRCS 8 study – hosted by The RBL Group, Ross School of Business at the University of Michigan, and 19 regional partners across the globe – surveyed over 27,000 participants rating the competencies and performance of more than 3,500 HR professionals and more than 1,500 organisations. Below is the new HR competency model.

Accelerates Business and results:. This includes: generate competitive market insights, have personal capital, have the skills to influence the business, and get the most important things done and build agility throughout the. Additionally, they must help drive agility throughout the organisation.

Advances Human Capability: This includes: the extent to which HR professionals can successfully advance human capability in the organisation, deliver solutions, that improve both individual talent (human) and organisation performance (capability) with specific focus on championing diversity, equity, and inclusion in the workplace to improve overall organisational performance.

Simplifies Complexity: This includes the extent to which HR professionals can think critically and objectively about the challenges their organisation think independently, and discover opportunity even during times of uncertainty or crisis.

Mobilises Information: This includes the extent to which HR professionals are able to access, analyse, and act on information by using technology to solve problems and influence decisions, and understanding of social issues that will impact the organisation.

Fosters Collaboration: Includes successfully fostering collaboration of working together, being open and self-aware, inspire trust and respect, and how effectively they build relationships that bring people together.

The SHRM Competency Model: Provides the foundation for talent management throughout the HR lifecycle and helps organisations ensure that HR professionals are proficient in the critical behaviors and knowledge necessary to solve today's most pressing people issues. The model is based on input from 1200 professionals from 29 cities and 111 focused groups from different cities. It is validated by 32000 subject matter specialists. The model consists of the following nine competencies: Human Resource Expertise (HR Knowledge); Ethical Practice; Leadership and Navigation; Business acumen; Consultation; Critical evaluation; Communication; Global and Cultural effectiveness; and Relationship Management. SHRM research indicates that LBIT model explains largely success of HR Professionals. T stands for technical knowledge, and three clusters including L for leadership, B for Business and I for Interpersonal relations. HR Leaders in our study undoubtedly LBIT competencies to a large extent. There could be minor individual variations in each of the components but in general there is a good fir.

CIPD's Professional Map: Designed to respond to the changing role of people professionals, the map aims to help people professionals face the future with confidence, by setting out the knowledge, values and behaviors they'll need to thrive in a changing world. CIPD claims for those working in HR or L&D, it will help them to make good decisions, perform at their best, further career and drive change in their workplace.

There are four key elements at the heart of the Profession Map.

1. **Purpose:** Having a shared purpose
2. **Core knowledge:** (six core areas of knowledge create value, drive change and positively impact workplace: (*i*) culture and behaviour, (*ii*) . business acumen (*iii*) analytics and creating value, (*iv*) digital working and (*v*) change)
3. **Core behaviours:** (eight ways of thinking and acting that enable one to become an effective professional: working inclusively, commercial drive, valuing people, passion for learning, change, focus on insights, ethical practice, professional courage and influence and situational decision-making.
4. **Specialist knowledge:** (9 areas of specialist knowledge within the people profession include: organisational development and design, people analytics, resourcing, rewards, talent management, employee experience, employee relations, diversity and inclusion and learning and development) (CIPD, 2021) (https://www.coursesonline.co.uk/everything-you-need-to-know-about-cipds-new-2021-qualifications/)

National HRD Network: HRScape includes 4 behavioral competencies and 8 functional competencies.

1. Credible Champion denotes the ability to demonstrate high integrity in personal and professional transactions: Integrity and fairness; building trust; emotional maturity and ethics
2. Diversity and Inclusion: This refers to the comprehensive set of organisational policies, processes and practices that respect, value and support differences and diverse perspectives at the workplace for leveraging and maximising the potential of all employees' context of diversity, cross-cultural sensitivity and inclusive practices
3. Service Orientation: This refers to the ability to imbibe and demonstrate readiness to respond to the needs and concerns of internal and external

customers; customer orientation, problem solving and process orientation and improvement and service delivery

4. Managing Change: This refers to the ability to diagnose, design and deliver change processes for individual and organisational transformation; designing change interventions, managing resistance and communicating change

Functional Competencies Include: Employee relations; strategic HRM; organisational design; workforce planning and staffing; talent management; total rewards; learning and development and performance management.

Auditing HRD Competencies

HRD competencies can be audited using several methods. The more important ones are given as follows.

- Knowledge testing
- Attitudes and values
- Self-assessment by HR professionals
- Peer-level assessment or 360-degree assessment
- Assessment of the HRD function or department by line managers
- Assessment centres

Knowledge Testing

The HRD profession in India has come of age. There is a body of knowledge available in India for the HRD profession. There are full-time master's programmes, doctoral programmes and various other short-term courses. A good HRD manager is expected to have a basic minimum knowledge in HRD. The knowledge forms an essential component of HRD competencies. Without this knowledge base the HRD manager is not likely to perceive the roles needed and may not be able to perform them well. Just as knowledge of anatomy and physiology are important for becoming a doctor or a surgeon, the basic knowledge of HRD, including that of adult learning, HRD tools, conditions of learning, etc., is essential for becoming a skilled HRD professional. Tests can be developed for assessing the knowledge base of any candidate. TVRLS, an HRD company, has developed a series of tests for assessing the knowledge base of HRD professionals. Some sample items from this test are presented in Chapter 9. The TVRLS–HRDKA Test deals with the basic knowledge required for HRD professionals.

Attitudes and Values

Some basic attitudes and values are needed for effective performance of HRD roles. These include a faith and self-confidence in one's own ability to influence and make things happen – also known as the internal locus of control (LOC). Without faith in HRD, personal effectiveness attitudes, empathy and the right work values, the HRD manager will not be able to function well. There are a number of tests available to measure some of these variables. Some of these are presented in Chapter 11. These include TVRLS–HRD–LOC, the work values scale, personal effectiveness questionnaires and empathy questionnaire. Some questionnaires can be used from other sources as well.

Self-Assessment and 360-Degree Appraisal

HRD managers can assess themselves on the aforementioned checklist. Such self-assessment can indicate the competence areas and competence gaps. This can be supplemented further by a 360-degree assessment. This may include the peers, bosses, direct reports and other internal and external customers. Two questionnaires in Chapter 11, entitled 'Professional Preparation in HRD' and 'HRD Profile Questionnaire', are also self-assessment questionnaires that provide information about the nature and extent of the professional preparation of the HRD manager.

Assessment of the Department or Internal Customer Satisfaction Surveys

The HRD audit questionnaires given in Chapter 11 have a section dealing with the assessment of the effective functioning of the HRD department or function. This assessment is made by the line managers and other respondents from the organisation and is likely to give a good evaluation of the effectiveness of the department. Internal customer satisfaction surveys also can be developed and used.

Skill Assessment through Assessment Centres

The HRD skills of the staff can be best evaluated by an assessment centre. However, such assessment centres cannot be organised as a part of the HRD audit as they require special attention and focus, which makes them expensive and time consuming. However, if the organisation has a large number of HR employees and is interested in building their competencies, it is useful to conduct an assessment centre for them to test their skill base. Such an assessment centre may use a variety of methods, including simulation exercises such as an in-basket.

Extracts of an illustrative audit report of the HRD function in an organisation is presented in Box 8.7. The extracts are taken from the audit reports of some of the companies that were audited by TVRLS. The report is not based on any one company but reconstructed from a few to provide an illustrative example of the kind of dimensions covered. This does not give all details but is illustrative of the kind of competency audit done for the HRD department. Similar audit was done to assess the competencies of the line managers, top management, workmen, secretarial staff and supervisors and office-bearers of the unions.

BOX 8.7 EXTRACTS OF AN ILLUSTRATIVE AUDIT REPORT ON HRD FUNCTION

Strengths of HRD Department

- The department is adequately staffed in terms of numbers
- The chief of HRD is highly committed and motivated in regard to HRD implementation
- A few of the staff are well-versed in one of the subsystems of HR
- There is good degree of understanding of the technical and business aspects of the company
- The plans made by the HRD managers for some of the departments (e.g., materials and production) are in the right direction and are need based
- The materials department plans deal with internal customer satisfaction surveys and 360-degree appraisals
- The HRD plans of production deal with training, manpower planning, job descriptions, appraisals, diagnostic survey of projects, improvements in recruitment and induction, visiting officers to assess training needs and training of trainers

Weak Areas

- Most HRD staff is assigned to three of the five divisions
- The HRD managers are mostly preoccupied with routine administrative tasks and have little time to pursue important and relevant tasks
- The internal customers of the divisional HR managers seem to be the corporate HRD department rather than the line managers. Most of the time is spent in interacting with each other than with the line managers
- Dual reporting is creating confusion and divided loyalties

- The inefficiencies of the head office HRD or corporate HRD are passed on to the lower levels; for example, a lot of the HRD managers' time is spent for sorting out appointment letters, etc.
- There is no planning
- Too many initiatives are taken up with inadequate follow-up
- There is no systematic maintenance of records

Competency Requirements: HRD

- The HRD staff needs to build the following competencies: knowledge of HRD systems and their significance to company vision, induction, training, performance management, role clarity and role efficacy, career planning and development, OD and self-renewal systems
- Implementation skills
- Internal customer orientation
- Attitudes and values, including empathy
- Speed
- OCTAPACE
- Probation – at present they are reactive, they merely respond to requests.

The profile and competencies of the HRD staff have been examined for their age, professional qualifications, experience, training and competency levels. The analysis is given as follows:

Age Profile of HRD Team

The average age is 44 years, and seven of them are above 50 years of age. Three are above 55 years and this needs to be taken into account in manpower planning of HRD.

Qualifications

None of them have HRD qualifications from a reputed institution that prepares focused HRD professionals. Eight have an ISTD diploma in HRD, which is more of a training course and is not a full-fledged HRD course. Six of them have an engineering background, which gives them a technical advantage in the business of the company. Of the six, only three have had some professional preparation in HRD through an ISTD diploma. Two of them possess qualifications in personnel management, but with a highly inadequate preparation in HRD. Four of them have no appropriate qualifications. On the whole the professional preparation of all the HRD staff put together in the department is weak.

Training

Out of the 16 officers analysed, eight have experience in handling training in the past. They have a cumulative training experience of 57 years. Six officers have an all-round experience in integrated HRD. Their cumulative experience is 16 years (average = 2.7 years). Ten officers have experience in recruitment with a cumulative experience of 20 years. Five officers have experience in personnel administration with a cumulative experience of 45 years. Four of them have experience in quality circles and ISO 9000 and their cumulative experience is 22 years. The experience profile indicates that the HRD staff as a team is very inexperienced. Their experience is predominantly in training, and the few that have a broader exposure also do not have high-experience profiles.

Training Received by the HRD Officers

Taking all the training programmes the HRD officers have attended in the past into consideration, following conclusions can be made:

- All of them together have attended a total of about 175 programmes of a total duration of 600 training man-days during the last five years
- Only two of them did not attend any programme
- Most of the programmes they attended were of short (one or two days) duration
- Of the 600 days of training they received only 70 days (about 12 per cent) of training directly related to HRD (the other training programmes were largely general and contextual and not related to HRD). Four of them are members of ISTD, five are members of NIPM and three are members of the HRD Network

Self-Assessment

The self-assessment of the team indicates the following:

- Strengths include: worker development, quality circles and small groups, recruitment, training systems and, to some extent, performance appraisals
- In all these areas the self-assessed proficiency is only above average and not excellent
- There are several areas where the competencies are weak: potential assessment, OD and culture building, career planning and development, job evaluation, vision and mission exercises, HR information systems, strategic planning, job evaluation and redesign, etc.
- There are only four individuals in the entire team who have a relatively high confidence level about their own HRD competencies

HRD Function Assessed by Line Managers:
HRD Audit Questionnaire

Positives or areas above average score = 60 per cent
- Importance given by the top management to this department (score = 66 per cent)

There are a few areas where the function could improve substantially (scores below 55 per cent) These are given as follows:

- Importance given by the senior-, middle- and supervisory-level officers as well as the personnel department (52–55 per cent range)
- Assistance given to line managers in enhancing their work effectiveness (42 per cent)
- Value addition of HRD activities (47 per cent)
- Contribution of HRD activities to climate building (45 per cent)
- Making an impact in the company through its work (43 per cent)

Importance of Top Management Styles

An OCTAPACE culture can be built only by an enlightened top management. Top management refers to all those who are decision makers and event makers in the organisation. This includes the owners, board of directors, unit heads, heads of departments and even section heads. It also includes office bearers of unions and associations.

All heads in formal and informal organisations who have the capability to influence the course of action of the organisation, its units, subsystems or functions can be considered as top-level managers. It is these influential people who set the tone for creating an OCTAPACE culture. They do it through the roles they perform or do not perform and the styles with which they perform these roles. Their style of functioning has a larger impact on culture creation.

Indian managers have been found to exhibit the following styles (Rao, 1986):

Benevolent or paternalistic style. This style is indicated by a belief and behaviour that treat all subordinates affectionately – like a parent or father figure treats his children. In this style, the manager is highly relationship oriented, treats his or her subordinates with affection, takes care of their needs, rewards and punishes employees on the basis of relationships, is protective and a giver of resources. His or her general belief is that the paternalistic style is the one that gets people to work. He or she believes in generating loyalty and getting work done through admiration for himself or herself and the fear of losing his or her favours. He or she guides his or her employees constantly, decides more often what is good for them and what is not, corrects their mistakes and salvages the situation, is always available when they are in trouble, gives his or her judgements about who is right and who is wrong when two or more parties are in conflict, generates resources for the employees, distributes favours on the basis of his or her likes and dislikes and is primarily governed by relationships, though tasks are important.

Such a style, I have found through research, creates feelings of dependency and high-relationship orientation. The work culture is good, but it lasts as long as the boss lasts. The absence of the boss is felt strongly as people are accustomed to work to please him or her. Personal loyalties govern the actions more than organisational loyalties. However, in crisis situations, these managers do extremely well and people stand by them. Such a style promotes OCTAPACE only to some extent. Trust and trustworthiness are elicited by the leader alone and others may have difficulty in getting trust and trustworthiness from the same group.

Critical style. This style is the second most frequently exhibited style. Those with this style are of the Theory X type. They believe in close supervision and constant monitoring. They perceive employees as those who avoid work and, hence, impose close supervision. They are oriented towards meeting short-term goals. They want immediate results and are impatient. They criticise, reprimand and provide directions more frequently, to control and influence employee behaviour. They cannot tolerate mistakes and complain bitterly if conflicts arise. They are even willing to take action on the erring parties. They have a very low tolerance for mistakes. They tend to use punishment and fear more than reward and encouragement. They are quite directive in their approach. They constantly monitor their employees. Such styles have been found to create morale problems and motivational issues. The OCTAPACE culture gets least developed in units, departments and functions with such leaders.

Developmental style. This style is the third style of management. It is a highly mature style and can be considered as the real HRD style of management. Research shows that the top managements of most Indian companies profess this style, few practise it fully and even fewer are perceived as practising it. In this style, the manager believes in empowering the subordinates or the employees who work with him or her to such an extent that they become fully autonomous and independent in working out their growth and competence. Such managers believe that people are generally responsible and the best way to get their commitment is to build their competence. These managers, therefore, believe that their main job is to build the competence of their staff. They invest a lot of their time in competence, culture and commitment building.

These managers are system oriented and very professional. They are more guided by the long-term interests of the organisation or the unit than short-term results. They prefer that employees learn from their mistakes and resolve conflicts on their own. They also devote their time on empowerment. Such a style has been found to create an OCTAPACE culture to a great extent.

Auditing the Styles of the Top Management

The effectiveness of various HRD systems and the extent to which they are likely to get the desired results depend on the style of the top management. In a research study of the effectiveness of HRD implementation, Nagabrahmam (1980) found that department heads had a high degree of moderating effect on the effective implementation of HRD systems. Their styles seemed to make a tremendous impact. Thus, any HRD audit has to take into consideration the styles of the top management and whether or not they are congruent with the HRD philosophy. While the developmental style is most congruent with HRD philosophy, other styles may have to be used occasionally depending on the situation, person and nature of issue. While a developmental and empowering philosophy should constitute the core of the styles, effective use of other styles may be needed to run the system or its subsystems.

In case of lack of congruence, the audit should indicate the currently dominant styles used by most managers and their impact on the people. The Leadership Styles Questionnaire described in Chapter 11 can be used to selectively measure these styles. If practical considerations such as cost and feasibility affect such a detailed study of the styles, the auditors can interview employees about the styles of the top-level managers. If a 360-degree feedback system is in operation and it focuses on leadership, the auditor may have an opportunity to study the congruence of the leadership styles with the HRD philosophy.

The following method may be used for assessing leadership styles.

Step 1. First determine and draw out a list of strategically important individuals in the organisation who seem to influence its decisionmaking, systems and various processes. Specially select those who seem to determine or influence the values and culture of the organisation. Such a list can be drawn in consultation with the top management or by the HRD department itself.

Step 2. Administer the questionnaire to these key individuals. Take their consent to collect 360-degree feedback on them to find out their styles.

Step 3. Collect the questionnaire for 360-degree feedback. Tabulate the data and draw conclusions about the congruence of their style with the HRD implementation in their units or functions.

In case it is not feasible to study the styles by a questionnaire, interview the managers, individually and in groups, to ascertain the style of management and how it is influencing competence, culture and commitment building in the organisation. Give special focus to the OCTAPACE culture and see which styles are facilitating it and which ones are blocking it. Names of individuals should not be reported in the audit report, unless a conscious decision is made to study individual styles. Even if individuals are studied, the reporting should be on trends in the company rather than on individuals. The individual data should be given only to the concerned individuals.

Step 4. Make observations about the style of the top management and its implications for creating both a learning and HRD culture. Specially comment on (*i*) the general beliefs and attitudes of top-level managers with regard to people and the HRD function, and (*ii*) their style of assigning tasks, monitoring performance, managing mistakes and conflicts as well as rewards and punishments, communicating the vision, sharing information and so on.

Step 5. Suggest mechanisms to improve the HRD styles so that they facilitate the HR function and are congruent to the HR philosophy and outcomes.

The HRD Score Card takes into consideration the extent to which the managerial and supervisory staff exhibit an empowering (developmental) style and the extent to which such styles are integrated into the culture and values of the organisation.

Line Managers' Learning and HRD Orientation

Line mangers and other supervisory staff need to have the attitudes to learning. If they have the job of HRD staff it becomes much easier. However, some times the line managers also may have a great learning orientation and HRD department may not be up to expectations. Hence, it is necessary to audit line managers' attitudes independently. In the HRD Score Card adequate weightage is assigned to this component (100 out of 500 points while the HRD staff competencies are assigned 200 points). The extent to which the following are used as sources of learning may be assessed:

* Performance planning and review discussions
* Departmental meetings, in-house communications
* Books
* Internet
* Project reports, including consultancy reports, diagnostic studies
* Outside visitors and others
* Each other through presentations, discussions, meetings, etc.

- Newspapers and magazines of business
- Functional journals and other literature
- Training programmes: in-house programmes and seminars
- Training programmes: outside programmes
- Seniors and mentors from inside the company or outside
- Mistakes

Similarly, workmen's and union representatives' learning orientation can be assessed by the extent to which they learn and develop from various sources like the following:

- Training: in-house and outside
- Multi-skilling activities
- Job rotation, cross-functional teams and work groups
- Health-, safety- and environment-related activities, including training
- Quality circles, shop floor councils and such other small group activities (not meant for skills upgradation)
- Suggestions schemes
- Communications from HRD, top management, etc.
- Self-initiated activities of the union and other bodies
- Other activities unique to your organisation

These may be assessed both through interviews and also through observation and questionnaires.

Competencies of HR Department

As mentioned earlier while discussing the HRD structure the HR department as a whole can make an impact if they work together. This can be audited for its credibility through interviews and observation. The following dimensions can be assessed through interviews, questionnaires and observation:

- HR department is adequately and appropriately structured
- HR staff works collaboratively as a team
- HR staff is relied on for what they say. They are trusted to speak the truth
- HR staff is seen as professionally competent
- HR staff is seen as humane and helpful
- HR policies are viewed by employees with respect and positively
- HR staff is seen as genuine and not indulging in politics
- HR policies are seen as unbiased and not favouring any one group or team
- HR communications are trusted for what they say
- HR systems and practices are viewed with interest and taken seriously

Conclusion

The HR professionals today face many challenges in areas of conceptual knowledge, capabilities, value proposition, HR governance and career paths. Higher the level of competence in HRD, greater is the efficiency of the systems. The HRD audit, therefore, assesses the competence of HR managers through knowledge testing, attitudes and values testing, 360-degree assessment, HRD function assessment and assessment centres. This helps to discover the areas of strength as well as the areas of development, thereby strengthening the HR effectiveness in the organisation. This is a significant dimension of the HRD Score Card. The score card covers the competency levels of the HRD department, line managers, the top management, union representatives and the HRD staff. It also covers the professional preparation of the HRD managers and the competency levels of the HRD department as a whole.

SECTION 3

HRD Audit Methodology and Issues

Any HRD audit that is conducted should be comprehensive; that is, it should be able to assess all the possible aspects, while focusing on the critical ones. Comprehensiveness also requires the involvement of all those who matter in HRD – including the suppliers, disseminators, and users of HRD. Because of its comprehensive nature HRD audit has to depend on multiple methods. These include interviews, observations, questionnaires and analysis of records, reports and other secondary data. These are discussed in detail in this section.

Each method is suitable for studying certain aspects. The questionnaire methods are useful for managers. Although most questionnaires described in this book are meant for managers, it is possible to design questionnaires for workmen and other staff. However, there are certain limitations for the use of questionnaires for all categories of staff, owing to language variations and education levels. Where questionnaires cannot be used, interviews can be a good substitute. Interviews with a skilled interviewer can also throw up a lot of data as they provide opportunities for respondents to express themselves better. A number of issues relating to motivation of employees and building their commitment cannot be obtained by questionnaires. They need to be observed. For example, some aspects of work culture as well as the quality of work life can be assessed using observational methods. In addition, every organisation maintains a lot of data in the form of internal reports, manuals, information, etc. An analysis of these can also give insights into HR practices, issues and needs. All these methodsmethods, when used synergisticallysynergistically, can yield a good-quality audit. These are presented in detail in this section. A special feature of this section is that it includes a number of questionnaires that can be used in an HRD audit.

DOI: 10.4324/9781003530534-11

9

HRD AUDIT METHODOLOGY

Interviews

Interviewing various stakeholders can give considerable data about the current areas and directions for improvement. The main advantage of the interview method is its capacity to capture the primary concern of the stakeholders. Interviews make the assessment dynamic and also provide an opportunity for the auditor to contextualise the audit. The context is provided by the stakeholders.

This chapter provides the objectives of these interviews with each of these groups, lists the interview questions and concludes with some guidelines. Guidelines are presented both for individual and group interviews. Even if no other method is used, the interview method is quick and adequate for a comprehensive HRD audit.

Individual Interviews

The interviews can be conducted individually or in groups. Interviews with different individuals can cover different aspects. The following are the categories of stakeholders who can be interviewed for HRD audit: CEOs and the top management, the HRD chief and HRD staff, line managers and workmen, operators, field staff, etc., and their representatives.

Interview with the CEO and Top Management

Individual interviews should begin with interviews with the top management. It serves a number of purposes:

DOI: 10.4324/9781003530534-12

- Helps the auditor to get to know the expectations of the top management
- Provides an opportunity for the expert to explain the scope and limitations of the HRD audit
- Prepares the ground for getting cooperation from the staff for the audit and legitimises the exercise
- Provides an opportunity to sow the seeds for effective utilisation of audit results.

Over and above these, the interviews with CEO and top management become the starting point for the audit in terms of clarifying the strategic long-term plans as well as the short-term plans of the organisation. These plans may or may not have been articulated fully and may not be known to all the staff. It is these plans that provide the backdrop for assessing the competency gaps and needs of the organisation.

The CEO or managing director or president must be interviewed separately. If he or she so wishes, a group session with all members of the top management can be organised. The group session can be a briefing session of about one or one-and-a-half hours for introducing HRD audit to all the senior or top-level managers so that they are clear about its purpose. The briefing session can answer the following questions:

- What is HRD?
- What is HRD audit?
- What is the methodology of HRD audit?
- What is required of the line managers in individual or group interviews?
- What have been the findings of group?

The briefing by the auditor to the CEO may cover the following:

- Explain HRD audit and its methodology
- Explain the schedule
- Ask the CEO of his or her expectations
- Clarify if any of the expectations cannot be met

The following may need to be stressed in the briefing exercise:

- HRD audit is not a problem-solving exercise. It may not be able to provide any solutions to specific problems the organisation is faced with, be it an industrial relations problem or a problem of poor discipline or poor performance, etc. However, it can give insights into the sources of the problem. Also, while it may not give feedback about specific individuals, it can provide feedback about the HRD department, its structure,

competency levels, leadership, processes, influence of the HRD on the other systems, etc. HRD audit is conducted against the HRD framework
- HRD audit is comprehensive. However, it is possible to sharply focus on one or more systems
- Action on the HRD audit is entirely in the hands of the CEO; the auditor has no control over it

Questions for Individual Interview with the CEO

The questions can be formulated as follows:

We will be starting our audit with a view to assess the competency requirements for the future of your organisation. You may have in your mind or in some document form the short-term and long-term plans of the organisation. These may be in terms of diversification, scale of operations, new product lines, new markets, new businesses, new areas, exports or any other forms of change or expansion or consolidation. To assess the adequacy or inadequacy and the preparedness of HR for these, we would like to assess the competency requirements of the organisation in the next three years and if possible even in the long term. Please share with us your thoughts and plans.

- What do you see as the competency requirements for the future?
- What competency gaps do you see as existing in the staff at present?
- What new competencies need to be developed in the staff? At what levels? How are you proposing to do it?

Interview with the HRD Chief

The objective of the interview would include the following:

- To understand the current systems, structure, skills existing in the HRD staff, top management styles and their congruence with the HRD philosophy, problems, etc.
- To plan out sampling and other details of the study
- To prepare a checklist of documents for the audit checklist
- To find out about the linkages with the personnel department
- To understand the internal customer framework of the HRD department
- To find out the time division and how time is spent by the department
- To ascertain views on how various systems are working
- To get a SWOT analysis of the HRD systems
- To find out the HRD chief's perceptions of the top management and the support required

- To understand his or her perceptions of the competencies of the HRD department and staff, the chief's perceptions of the line managers, their competencies and their involvement in HRD matters as well as his or her perceptions of the unions and their involvement in HRD-related issues

Appropriate questions may be framed on all these dimensions. The following is an illustrative list.

- What are the objectives of this department?
- Why was it set up? When? How? What are some of the significant milestones in the history of this department and its contributions?
- What are its current activities?
- What are the most important current activities? What is the organisational structure? Who reports to whom?
- How are the strategies of HR and HR plans formulated? What is the role played by the department in strategic planning?
- Please take each of the following systems and outline the strengths and weaknesses of each of these systems and their functioning: (*i*) performance appraisal, (*ii*) counselling, (*iii*) training, (*iv*) career planning and development, (*v*) succession planning for strategic roles, (*vi*) job rotation, (*vii*) OD and team-building interventions, (*viii*) research and systems development, (*ix*) mentoring, (*x*) worker development and (*xi*) culture-building exercises and (*xii*) quality improvement interventions
- What are the main competencies of HRD staff? What do they excel in? What do they need to develop more?
- How do you characterise the styles of the top- and senior-level managers? How conducive are they for developing a learning culture?
- What are the main blocks for developing a learning culture?
- How are the line managers tuned to play development roles for their juniors? How supportive are they to HRD? What needs to be done to make them more supportive?
- What is the nature and magnitude of support given by the top management to HRD?
- Is there a separate budget for HRD? How is it formulated? What has been the response of the top management to budget allocations to HRD?
- Is there a well-articulated HRD philosophy and values? What is it? How is it disseminated?
- What in your opinion are the core competencies of each of the departments and the organisation as a whole?
- What are the linkages between the personnel and HRD units or sections? Is there a need for further strengthening, integrating or differentiating the functions or activities of the two?

Interviews with Line Managers

The objective of these interviews would be to understand their perceptions of the HRD needs, the current status, expectations, competencies, commitment to HRD, etc. The questions to be asked are as follows:

- What kind of HRD needs do you have for yourself or for your department?
- What kind of help do you get from the HRD department for competency and commitment building?
- What help do you get for culture building?
- What are the HRD systems that you feel happy about?
- What are the HRD systems that you feel have contributed or are contributing to the business goals of the organisation?
- What are the weak areas of HRD?
- What are the expectations you have from HRD?
- What are the training needs?
- Are your training needs being taken care of?
- What are your career growth needs? Are they being taken care of by HRD?
- What do you see as the future growth opportunities and business directions of the company?
- What are the core competencies or skills and knowledge the company has that you are proud of?
- What skills and knowledge do you require to run your business more effectively (or to perform better on your current job)?
- What are the strengths of your HRD function?
- What are the areas where your HRD function can do better?
- What is good about your HRD subsystems: Performance appraisal? Training? Job rotation? Career planning and development?
- What should the HRD department start doing (or do more)? What should the HRD stop doing (or do less)?

Interviews with Workers and Their Representatives

Here the objective would be to find out the current status of their development needs in relation to the business goals of the company, their motivational levels and the culture prevailing in the organisation; as also to list the good practices in the organisation that are keeping their commitment levels high.

The questions that may be asked are as follows:

- How do you feel working in this organisation?
- What are the strengths of this company?

- What are the areas that need improvement?
- What do you know about the business plans and opportunities for this company?
- What do you know about the competition this company is facing today or is likely to face in the future?
- What are some of the things this company should do to face the changing environment?
- What is being done to ensure that you all have the skills needed to meet the current needs or future challenges of this company?
- What motivates you here?
- What more do you think needs to be done to help you contribute better to the organisation?
- What kind of training do you get here? Are you satisfied? What more do you think needs to be done in the interest of the company?
- What are the facilities available for you all? What are they in the plant and in the colony?
- What do you think can be done to improve quality, save costs and make people feel happy to work for the organisation?
- What are your expectations from the HRD department? What are you happy about? What are your suggestions for them to serve you better?

Group Interviews

While individual interviews give a lot of personalised inputs and reveal a number of things, group interviews ensure the coverage of a wide variety of areas. They also enhance a wider participation of employees in HRD audits. It is always a useful strategy to interview senior managers, leaders and opinion makers individually and the others in teams. Group interviews on HRD audit have the following advantages:

- Wider coverage of issues and, therefore, the possibility of not missing out any significant one
- Larger involvement of employees
- Verification of data and significant points
- Assessment of the intensity of feelings associated with any issues and problems or satisfiers and dissatisfiers
- Education of employees about their own roles and responsibilities as line managers

Sampling for Group Interviews

The group interviews could be conducted with a group size not exceeding eight respondents. The ideal size for an in-depth group interview is about four to five respondents. However, where there are a large number of employees in a department, unit or a level, it can be extended to include a maximum of eight. The larger the number, the wider the participation, but at the same time it reduces the scope for in-depth understanding.

The groups can be drawn from the same department if the audit has to focus on interdepartmental variations in the HRD implementation or perceptions. Otherwise, it can be cross-functional. Drawing respondents from across functions ensures a freer atmosphere as respondents most often feel free to talk with people whom they may not have to work with or interact with all the time.

The groups should preferably be drawn from the same levels of hierarchy since juniors may feel inhibited from expressing their views and opinions about HRD freely in the presence of their seniors.

Guidelines for Selecting Samples for Group Interviews

The following guidelines may be used in drawing samples for group interviews.

Top Management

Only individual interviews, each lasting about an hour, may be conducted. However, if it is a very large organisation, the total interviews may be limited to 50 per cent or so. One group briefing session by the top management team to the auditors in the beginning of audit may be held.

Managers

Individual interviews may be held with senior-level managers and heads of department, divisions, SBUs, sections, etc., as well as with strategic and experimental units, sections, departments, etc. In special cases individual interviews with managers with demonstrated strong positive attitudes and skills or strong negative attitudes and issues may be held, if suggested by the top management or the HRD department.

Group interviews may be held with middle-level managers sampled department wise or group wise. A minimum of 10 per cent of the managers in each department, level, group or section must be covered. It can go as high as 100 per cent if the size of the managerial manpower in the company is below 100. In any audit it is useful to interview about 100 managers individually or in groups. This number can go up to 300 for large organisations.

Supervisors and Staff

A sample of about 10 per cent or about five to six groups representing different functions and workplaces may be selected for the audit.

Workmen

They can be interviewed in relatively large groups. About 5 to 10 groups are sufficient to indicate the trends.

Golden Rule: Conduct interviews until you begin to get no new information or insights from any three successive group interviews for respondents at the same level.

Guidelines for Interviews in Groups

The auditors should first introduce themselves and their background. (It is always useful for someone from the HR department to come to the group meeting and introduce the auditors to the group and leave the rest of the introductions to the auditors.) They should then introduce the concept of HRD audit and why it is being conducted in the company. The auditors should also mention about how the audit is likely to be useful to the company and the intended outcomes.

The auditors may then ask the following question going from system to system:

What in your view are the strengths and weaknesses as they exist today in relation to the following components of HRD?

- Top management commitment to HRD (MD, presidents, VPs, GMs, directors, etc.)
- Recruitment of competent people into the company
- Retention of competent people
- Identification of fast-track employees
- Mentoring system (if it exists; if not, is it useful to have one and why)
- Training (in-house and outside)
- Induction
- Career planning
- Succession planning
- Job rotation
- Performance appraisal
- Performance review discussions
- Separations
- Quality circles
- Participative management
- Systems, if any
- Shop floor committees
- Delegation
- Personnel policies
- HRD departments, including the staff

- Communications
- HRD culture
- Linkages between personnel and HRD
- HR information system
- Others

The interviewer should take notes and consolidate them after all the interviews are completed. Sometimes, the group can be requested to answer these questions through a questionnaire for about 30 minutes and the rest of 30 minutes can be used for discussions to gauge the intensity of feelings and to gain an in-depth understanding.

10

HRD AUDIT METHODOLOGY

Observation

What Is Observation?

Observation is a way to look at the things as they exist. It involves the use of various senses and drawing meanings to the things we see or hear. There are a number of things that can be observed by an evaluator. These may be classified under the following categories:

- Physical facilities and living conditions
- Meetings, discussions and other transactions
- Celebrations and other events related to organisational life and culture
- Training and other HRD-related facilities, including the classrooms, library, training centre, etc.
- Forms and formats, reports, manuals, etc.

Physical Facilities

The Rationale

A good work environment with good work technology and facilities, a healthy, clean and well-organised workplace, the necessary tools for effective functioning, and good living conditions have a great motivational value. They save the energies of employees from avoidable problems, irritants and tension and are prime-movers to get them to give their best.

DOI: 10.4324/9781003530534-13

The Objective

The objective is to assess the current status of the physical facilities and their organisation in the work as well as the living environment and examine their motivational or facilitating (or demotivating or inhibiting) value to employee satisfaction, productivity and effectiveness.

The aspects to be observed and assessed for their current status in terms of work facilitation and motivational value are listed as follows:

- Physical layout of the factory and the work environment
- Physical layout of the office and seating arrangements
- Work conditions and work facilities
- Housekeeping
- Record-keeping and filing
- Toilets and their upkeep
- School and other educational facilities
- Hospital and medical facilities
- Canteen and other facilities
- Housing and housing facilities
- Transportation and other conveniences
- Sports, games and other facilities

Meetings, Discussions and Transactions

The Rationale

Most organisations today have been extensively using small groups, task forces, committees, cross-functional teams, quality circles, open houses, communication meetings and such other mechanisms in an effort to bring change or to improve themselves. Most of these methodologies are based on the assumption that participation has a motivational value and groups always contribute greater value than individuals put together. Thus, a group is meant to improve productivity both in terms of the quality of decision making and motivation to implement decisions. However, there is not adequate preparation to help the groups function well. The observations of a sample of these groups and the way they are functioning can help to ascertain the value addition, human competency or motivational losses or gains that may arise from the conduct and processes of meetings and discussion groups.

Meeting management and teamwork skills are required. Also, a right atmosphere needs to be created for the effective functioning of the groups. Observation of meetings in progress can help to ascertain their effectiveness.

Some of the possible meetings that can be held include

- Quality circles and other small group activities
- Shop floor councils and meetings
- Departmental meetings
- Cross-functional teams and task forces
- Open houses and open forums
- Communication meetings
- Daily production meetings
- Presentations by outsiders, insiders, vendors, etc.
- Performance review committees

Specialised Sessions

- Performance appraisal and counselling sessions
- Conflict resolution sessions
- Union negotiations and meetings
- Union and association meetings
- Training need identification sessions
- Classroom sessions
- Communication meetings by the CEO or the top management
- Other specialised sessions of certain departments: unique practices

What to Observe in Meetings

Observing meetings is essentially meant to evaluate the extent to which they are serving the purposes they are meant to serve. Most meetings are performance improvement meetings. Some of them attempt to provide information that can have motivational value. Others try to provide information that is essential to perform the job. Some others, such as identity establishment meetings, are intended to ensure that the employees feel that they are a part of the company. Some meetings place considerable emphasis on participation and human resource utilisation. Hence, the evaluation should be preceded by an understanding of the purposes of the meeting and then the observation should focus on the extent to which they are serving the purpose. The following guidelines can help in the evaluation process:

- Do people come adequately prepared for the meetings?
- Is the agenda circulated well in advance?
- Are the objectives clear to all?
- Do people share the goals?
- How well are the meetings being coordinated?
- Are people participating well?
- Is the leader of the meeting sensitive to individual differences in participation and other group dynamics? Does he or she ensure equal participation by all?

- Do the members try to get the best out of the meetings?
- Is internal networking taking place?
- Do the people listen to each other?
- Is there learning by groups?
- How are conflicts being handled?
- Are people receptive? Are people only habituated to speak or do they also listen to each other?
- Are there too narrow functional or departmental loyalties hindering organisational problem solving and effectiveness?
- Are they resulting in clear action plans? Do people seem to learn from each other?
- Are the meetings a waste of time or are they adding value?
- What critical competencies will make the meetings more productive?

Celebrations and Events

The Rationale

On an average every employee spends more than 60 per cent of his or her waking life in the organisation every day. The organisation is his or her first home. Besides putting in eight hours of work, an employee spends considerable time travelling to and returning from office, in discussions with friends and relatives, in recreation time, etc.; hence, it is the organisation that dominates his or her thinking. The organisation is the first family in many ways. If the organisation has to get the best out of an employee, it is important to ensure that his or her personal and social needs are attended to. Also it is beneficial to create a family and social environment in those places, for example, company colonies, where employees live. Cultural events, community celebration of festivals, celebration of accomplishments by the employees and their families, annual days, etc., bring the employees together and create a family feeling. Such events are observed to assess the motivational and culture-building value.

The following are some types of events that can be observed:

- Annual days and other celebrations
- Cultural events
- Special days like the environment day, founder's day and other such celebrations
- Sports days, school functions
- Opening ceremonies of any new facilities, departments, etc.
- Celebration of festivals
- Birthday celebrations and other similar celebrations
- Celebration of accomplishments like the company getting a trophy for safety, sports, quizzes, exports, etc.

What to Observe?

- Participation – eagerness and enthusiasm and spirited participation?
- Organisational aspects – how well is it being organised? How much of it is being facilitated by the company? Are there efforts made to involve everyone?
- Status differences, if any, in terms of participation, seating, etc. – are they functional or dysfunctional?
- Ceremonial roles of top management – how well are they being performed? Do they indicate respect for labour and all employees?
- Does it help people to get closer and develop a 'we' feeling? (This can be inferred by observing the interactions of the employees at different levels and categories during the celebrations.)

Training and Other HRD-Related Facilities

The Rationale

The training room or complex is a symbolic reflection of the extent to which the organisation values systematic learning and competency building of their employees. Those who take some time off for learning new skills, attitudes, etc., have to be protected from external disturbances such as noise so that they can fully devote their time to learning. A good training facility needs to be well organised, neatly arranged and must have the right ambience that can motivate a person to learn. The way the training facilities are arranged can determine to a significant extent whether the learning will be productive or a sheer waste of time. The training facilities can create the right mind-set for change.

The following aspects in regard to arrangements, spacing, crowding, noise, acoustics, convenience and aesthetics can be observed to ascertain whether the training is imparted in the right atmosphere:

- Ambience of the training facility – surroundings, greenery, lawns, flooring, rooms, etc.
- Training rooms and training facilities
- Library, its organisation, books and facilities
- Meeting and discussion rooms and facilities
- Classrooms and classroom facilities
- Administrative facilities like photocopying and fax machines
- Audio-visual aids including overhead/LCD projectors and their conditions
- Flip-charts and other writing facilities like a white board
- Furniture, seating arrangement and their convenience

Forms, Formats, Reports and Manuals

The Rationale

The written material available in the company indicates a lot about the character of the company. A checklist of documents that can be used for observation is presented in Box 10.1. These are culture-building instruments that also transmit the culture of the organisation. Well-developed annual reports are an indicator of the external customer orientation while internal documents indicate the internal customer orientation. The language used in all these is itself an indicator of the organisation per se, that is, whether it has a formal or informal culture, systematic or ad hoc operation, professional or bureaucratic structure and so on. Written communications are the first signal to a new entrant or visitor about the organisation. In induction especially, these have considerable implications for socialisation, culture-building and commitment-building values.

Documents to Observe

- Annual reports – observe and assess the importance given to employees, mission statements and how much they reflect HR concerns, HR budget and its proportion to the total budget, innovativeness of the company, HR values, and so on
- Appointment letters – study the language, details, personal touch, motivational value of the contents, who signs it, delays in sending them, extent to which they treat individuals with dignity, etc.
- Transfer letters
- Training sponsorship, evaluation and follow-up formats – the language, values communicated to people; extent to which respect, dignity and commitment is promoted; accountability; and learning emphasis, etc.
- Product information and company information brochures – values, customer-centredness employee focus wherever feasible, etc.
- Newsletters – HR concerns, satisfaction-enhancing measures, quality-of-life-improvement measures, dignity given to individuals, depth and breadth of coverage, etc.
- Manuals (all types) – simplicity, language, culture as reflected in the language, systematisation, care, meticulousness, complexity, cost-effectiveness, etc.
- Notices on notice boards – degree of formality, personal versus impersonal and bureaucratic approach, etc.
- Posters, memos, announcements
- Appraisal forms, training nomination forms
- Claim forms, application forms for recruitment
- Joining formalities for new inductees

BOX 10.1 CHECKLIST OF DOCUMENTS REQUIRED FOR OBSERVATION AND ANALYSIS OF HRD DEPARTMENT FOR AUDIT

1. Personnel manual
2. Manpower-planning guidelines
3. Recruitment policies
4. Promotion policies
5. Performance appraisal manuals
6. TQM manuals
7. Quality circles, shop floor committees, their guidelines, etc.
8. Suggestion schemes and other guidelines
9. Training policy guidelines
10. Succession-planning and career-planning guidelines and methods
11. OD interventions, if any, taken by the organisation
12. Activities of the HRD department – annual reports, etc.
13. Training calendar and reports of training activities
14. Diagnostic and evaluation studies
15. Reward systems – policies and guidelines
16. Communication systems and reports
17. In-house newsletters and other mechanisms
18. Delegation manuals or guidelines
19. Job rotation and transfer policies and practices
20. Organisational structure of the HRD department
21. Small-group activities, shop floor committees and other details
22. Exit interview guidelines and data
23. Documents dealing with facilities offered to employees
24. Worker education and training programmes
25. Welfare schemes and facilities
26. Residential colony facilities – guidelines
27. Climate surveys, culture studies
28. Previous HRD audit reports
29. Other studies undertaken by summer trainees and students
30. Age profiles – grade wise and department wise for assessing retirements, etc.
31. Attrition rates, department or unit wise and exit interview data
32. Any other documents with implications for HRD strategies
33. Organisational structure charts, if required

What to Assess?

- Do they promote a sense of belonging or do they distance the employees from the organisation?
- Do they communicate a sense of respect and dignity for each individual, his or her time and contributions expected from him or her?
- Are they professional or bureaucratic in terms of language, tone and explanations?
- Are they clear or ambiguous?
- Do they indicate a lot of centralisation or decentralisation and autonomy?
- Are they prepared with thought and care? Are they aesthetic and well designed or casual?
- Are they readable and communicative or ambiguous and left to differing interpretations?
- How are they organised and displayed? Are they prominent or only fulfilling a formality?
- Are they genuinely intended to serve some purpose or merely routine?
- Are they informative or hiding details and prone to rumours?

11

HRD AUDIT INSTRUMENTS

Questionnaires

There are a number of questionnaires used for HRD audit. These questionnaires measure various aspects of HRD and provide inputs more appropriately for the HRD Score Card. There are questionnaires to measure HRD systems and their effectiveness comprehensively as well as individually, effective performance of various activities by the HRD department, HRD competencies of HRD staff, HRD styles or empowering styles of line managers and HR staff, and HRD culture. These questionnaires are described in detail here and most of these are also reproduced.

HRD Audit Questionnaire

This is the most comprehensive questionnaire available for HRD audit. This is to be administered to line managers and the HRD staff. The questionnaire discussed here is meant for supervisory and English-speaking categories. The questionnaire may be administered to all employees or on a sample depending on the exhaustiveness intended by the organisation. This questionnaire is available in *HRD Score Card 2500* (Rao, 2008b: 253) and a shorter version of this ublished in 1996 (aro, 1996).

This questionnaire has 279 items dealing with the following sections:

HRD Audit Questionnaire	*No. of Items*
Dimensions	
A. Career system	
A1. Manpower planning and recruitment	12

DOI: 10.4324/9781003530534-14

HRD Audit Questionnaire	*No. of Items*
Dimensions	
A2. Potential appraisal and promotions	10
A3. Career planning and development	7
B. *Work planning*	
B1. Role analysis	10
B2. Contextual analysis	10
B3. Performance appraisal systems	18
C. *Development system*	
C1. Learning systems/training questionnaire	28
C2. Performance guidance and development	15
C3. Other mechanisms	10
C4. Worker development	6
D. *Self-renewal systems*	10
D1. Role efficacy	
D2. Organisation development	11
D3. Action-oriented research	10
E. *HRD*	18
E1. HRD climate/top management commitment	
E2. Values in the organisation	10
E3. Quality orientation	12
E4. Rewards and recognition	8
E5. Information	14
E6. Communication	12
E7. Empowerment	10
F. *HRD function*	14
G. Competency mapping, 360-degree feedback and assessment and development Centres	21
H. *Strengths, weaknesses and suggestions*	3
Total	279

Benchmarking data are available from TVRLS for each item. The benchmarking data gives the highest and lowest scores along with the standard deviations for each item for the various organisations to whom the questionnaire has been administered so far.

Mapping the HRD Practices Profile

This questionnaire has 100 activities that can be undertaken by the HRD department in any organisation. The objective of the questionnaire is to assess the degree to which these activities are performed as well as the degree of effectiveness. Organisations with good HRD practices seem to perform a large number of these activities. It is hypothesised that performing all the 100 activities very well would be a characteristic of a world-class organisation. When all these activities are performed, it is obvious that the organisation is in sound health.

This questionnaire is to be administered to all the HRD staff as well as the representative staff of other functional managers. The dimensions covered by the questionnaire and the items are given as follows.

Dimensions	No. of Items
HRD philosophy and liaison with top management	10
Creating development motivation in line managers	15
Strengthening HRD climate through HRD systems	31
Directing HRD efforts to goals and strategies of the organisation	10
Monitoring HRD implementation	5
Inspiring unions and associations	7
Human process research	7
Influencing personnel policies	5
Strategic HRD	6
Networking and benchmarking	4

As mentioned in the earlier chapters, satisfied and motivated employees are likely to produce more (in terms of better services or higher number goods). Employee satisfaction can be directed to raise customer satisfaction. HRD systems are essential to create such employee satisfaction. Well-designed HRD systems reduce uncertainty, increase equity and predictability and reduce transaction costs. They also enhance professionalism and people's respect for the organisation.

The detailed tool is given in *HRD Score Card 2500* (Rao, 2008b).

HRD Climate Survey

An optimum level of a 'development climate' is essential for facilitating HRD. Such a climate can be observed in organisations consisting of the following tendencies and attributes:

- A tendency at all levels and specially the top management to treat people as the most important resource
- A perception that developing the competencies in the employee is the job of every manager/supervisor
- Faith in the capability of people to change and acquire new competencies at any stage of life
- A tendency to be open in communications
- A tendency to encourage risk taking
- A tendency to help employees recognise their strengths and weaknesses
- A general climate of trust
- A tendency on the part of employees to be generally helpful to each other and collaborate

- Team spirit
- A tendency to discourage favouritism and biases
- Supportive personnel policies
- Development-oriented appraisals, training, rewards, job rotation, career planning and potential appraisals

Organisations differ in the extent to which they have these characteristics. Abraham and I developed a 38-item HRD climate survey at the XLRI Centre for HRD. This is being used widely as an instrument to survey the HRD climate. These 38 items assess OCTAPAC (Openness, Confrontation, Trust, Autonomy, Proaction, Authenticity and Collaboration) culture and implementation of HRD mechanisms. The detailed questionnaire is available in *HRD Score Card 2500* (Rao, 2008b).

Training Effectiveness Questionnaire

This questionnaire is intended to assess the effectiveness of the training function in an organisation. Any formal training should contribute to the growth and development of employee competencies and motivation. For training to be effective, it has to be need based, well planned, evaluated, monitored and used. Both line managers and HRD staff have to become partners to ensure the effectiveness of training. The questionnaire measures the extent to which the training function is effective in the organisation.

Administration

This questionnaire can be administered to line managers as well as HRD staff. The results can be analysed to review the effectiveness of training function. The item-wise data can be used to identify areas that need improvement.

The ratings on the 25 items may be added for each respondent to compute the training effectiveness score. The score can range from 0 to 100. A score above 75 indicate that the training function is effective in the organisation.

Training Effectiveness Questionnaire

Indicate the extent to which each of the following items is true in your organisation using the 5-point scale given as follows.

0 = not at all true; 1 = a little true; 2 = somewhat true; 3 = true to a great extent; 4 = very true

1. Induction training is given adequate importance in this organisation
2. Induction training is well planned

3. Induction training is of sufficient duration
4. Induction training provides an excellent opportunity for newcomers to learn comprehensively about this organisation
5. The norms and values of this company are clearly explained to the new employees during induction
6. Senior executives/officers take interest and spend time with the new staff during induction training
7. The new recruits find induction training very useful in this organisation
8. Our induction training is periodically evaluated and improved
9. The employees are helped to acquire technical knowledge and skills through training
10. There is adequate emphasis on developing the managerial capabilities of management staff through training
11. Human relations competencies are adequately developed in this organisation through training in human skills
12. Training of workers is given due importance in this organisation
13. Employees are sponsored for training programmes on the basis of carefully identified developmental needs
14. Those who are sponsored for training programmes take the training seriously
15. Employees in this organisation participate in determining the training they need
16. Employees sponsored for training go with a clear understanding of the knowledge and skills they are expected to acquire from training
17. The HRD department conducts briefing and debriefing sessions for employees sponsored for training
18. In-company programmes are handled by competent faculty
19. The quality of in-company programmes in this organisation is excellent
20. Senior line managers are eager to help their juniors develop through training
21. Employees returning from training are given adequate free time to reflect and plan improvements in the organisation
22. Line managers provide the right kind of climate to implement new ideas and methods acquired by their juniors through training
23. Line managers in this organisation utilise and benefit from the training programmes
24. External training programmes are carefully chosen after collecting enough information about their quality and suitability
25. There is a well-designed and widely shared training policy in the company

Performance Planning, Analysis and Development Questionnaire

This questionnaire, also known as the Performance Appraisal Effectiveness Questionnaire, aims at assessing the extent to which the performance appraisal system in the organisation is HRD oriented. An HRD-oriented appraisal system promotes participative planning of performance, participative analysis of performance leading to the identification of factors facilitating and hindering performance, performance review discussions, relatively greater objective assessment through task and target orientation, identification of development needs, improved communication, openness, and mutuality and trust among appraisers and appraisees.

The extent to which some of these components are a part of the appraisal system is assessed in the first part of the questionnaire. The second part assesses how well the development-oriented appraisal system is being implemented in the organisation. This questionnaire is only meant for executing appraisals.

Administration

This questionnaire can be administered to managers/employees covered by the appraisal system. The responses may be tabulated and analysed itemwise. Items with low scores may be identified for discussion by HRD staff or top management or performance appraisal task force or performance review committee or any other appropriate body that has the responsibility to improve the appraisal system.

Performance Planning, Analysis and Development Questionnaire

Please answer the following items on a 5-point scale by assigning 0 to those items that you think are totally false for your organisation, 1 to those items that are only slightly true or true to a little extent (25 per cent true and 75 per cent false), 2 to those items that are somewhat true (50 per cent true and 50 per cent false), 3 to those items that are mostly true (75 per cent true) and 4 to those items that are completely true.

Part 1

1. The executive appraisal system in this organisation provides an opportunity for each appraisee to have a clear understanding of what is expected from him or her by his or her reporting officer during the performance year
2. The appraisal system helps each appraisee and appraiser to have a clear joint understanding of each appraisee's job

3. The appraisal system helps managers to plan their performance well
4. The appraisal system provides an opportunity for each appraisee to communicate the support he or she needs from his or her superiors to perform his or her job well
5. The appraisal system provides an opportunity for self-review and reflection
6. The appraisal system encourages the appraiser and appraisee to have a common understanding of the factors affecting the performance of the appraisee
7. The appraisal system provides an opportunity for a discussion between the appraiser and appraisee on the expectations, achievements, failures, constraints and improvements required
8. The appraisal system has scope for reflection and assessment of each appraisee on the personality factors and attributes required for the current job of the assessee
9. The appraisal system encourages open communication between each appraiser–appraisee pair through performance review discussions
10. The appraisal system provides an opportunity for each appraisee to express his or her developmental needs
11. The appraisal system has scope for correcting the biases of the reporting officer through a review process
12. The appraisal system aims at strengthening appraiser–appraisee relationships through mutuality and trust
13. The appraisal system helps interested appraisees to gain more insights into their strengths and weaknesses
14. The appraisal system has scope for helping each employee discover his or her potential
15. The appraisal system has scope for communicating the plans of the top management and the business goals to the staff

Part 2

16. The objectives of the appraisal system are clear to all employees
17. Periodic orientation programmes are conducted to explain the objectives and other details of the appraisal system
18. Line managers generally spend time with their subordinates and discuss their performance
19. Reporting officers help their appraisees to plan their performance in the beginning of the year
20. Discussions on KPAs/KRAs/tasks/targets between appraiser–appraisee pairs are very educative to both the appraisees and appraisers
21. The managers take the performance appraisal seriously

22. Executives do a thorough job on self-appraisal in terms of reviewing, reflecting and analysing the factors affecting their performance
23. Performance review discussions are taken seriously by the managers and they devote sufficient time to participate in them
24. Performance review discussions are of high quality and are conducted with care
25. The appraisers make special efforts to be objective in their appraisals
26. The HRD department follows up seriously on the training needs identified during the appraisals
27. The appraisal data are used by the HRD department for other development decisions like job rotation, job enrichment and the like
28. The appraisal data are used as inputs for recognition and encouragement of high performers and desirable behaviour
29. The reviewing officers take the appraisals seriously and educate their subordinates to overcome their personal biases and favouritism
30. The HRD department actively reviews each appraisal and discusses them with the line managers
31. The HRD department provides adequate feedback to the line managers on their rating behaviour and the decisions taken on their ratings
32. The performance review committees do a thorough job in reviewing and using the appraisal data
33. The appraisals facilitate growth and learning of both appraisees and appraisers in this organisation

Effective Counsellor Attitudes

Every line manager should have counselling or helping skills. These skills contribute substantially to managing the staff effectively and contributing to their development. The line managers are required to use these skills particularly during annual performance discussions. These skills bring the line managers closer to their subordinates, understand them better, motivate them and in the process also contribute to their development. The counselling skills are based on listening and diagnostic skills, empathy and faith in people and their competencies, positive attitude to the development of others, openness, self-disclosure, receptivity to feedback, etc. This questionnaire is meant to help line managers assess for themselves the extent to which they possess the attitudes required to be a good counsellor.

Administration

The 25-item questionnaire can be administered to line managers. Scores above 75 indicate effective counsellor attitudes. Low scorers may identify the items on which they score low and discuss among the group their beliefs and their sources.

The line managers can also attempt to rate themselves as their subordinates would rate them. The ease with which a rater is able to shift his or her frame of reference and look at himself or herself from the point of view of his or her subordinates is indicative of an 'empathic attitude', which is an essential quality for effective counselling. Some managers find it difficult to look at themselves from their subordinates' point of view.

The HRD manager should administer this questionnaire on himself or herself and clarify his or her own attitude before using it for other line managers. The HRD staff or a small group of people can get together, self-administer this questionnaire and study their own attitudes.

An interested manager can get himself or herself assessed on this questionnaire by his or her subordinates and use it for gaining insights into his or her own behaviour.

Effective Counsellor Attitudes

Read each question given as follows. Rate yourself on each question using a 5-point scale:

4 = definitely or always; 3 = mostly or most frequently; 2 = sometimes; 1 = seldom; and 0 = never

First, rate yourself as you see yourself. In the next column rate yourself as your subordinates or employees would rate you. Write 4, 3, 2, 1 or 0 against each question in both columns according to the scale just explained. You can also get yourself rated by your subordinates to assess the extent of similarity of your perceptions with theirs.

1. Do you feel your job requires the development of your subordinates?
2. Do you believe behaviour can be changed at any stage of life?
3. Are you a careful listener?
4. Do you let your employees try their ideas even though these may not be as good as yours?
5. Are you aware of your employees' feelings when you converse with them?
6. Do you communicate to your employees your understanding of their strengths and weaknesses?
7. Do you communicate your true feelings to others (as against telling them what they would like to hear)?
8. Do you offer specific and concrete suggestions to your employees?
9. Do you make it a point to give sufficient time to have periodic performance review discussions with each of your staff?
10. Do you feel that performance review discussions are learning opportunities for both the appraiser and the appraisee?
11. Have you found the performance review discussions useful?

12. Do you take time to reflect about your own behaviour and its impact on your subordinates?
13. Do you seek feedback from your subordinates about your own performance and the support you are able to give them?
14. Do you believe that it is your responsibility to initiate special counselling sessions with troubled employees?
15. Does your job offer you opportunities to help your employees?
16. Do you believe in leading by example?
17. Do you delegate and pass authority and responsibility down as far as possible?
18. Do you provide candid and data-based feedback without getting emotional?
19. Do your employees communicate their personal problems to you also?
20. Are you meeting your objectives?
21. Do you talk to your employees about their problems and offer suggestions when they talk to you?
22. Do you get concerned about providing them a proper emotional climate for growth?
23. How often do you think about them and their problems?
24. Are you aware of your own styles of interpersonal communication?
25. Do you believe that you are capable of becoming an effective counsellor through practice on your own?

The Supervisory and Leadership Beliefs Questionnaire

One of the most important tasks of a manager is to manage human resources. The effective management of human resources requires an understanding of the capabilities of subordinates, assigning them appropriate tasks, helping them to acquire new capabilities, maintaining their motivation levels and structuring the work so that people can derive some satisfaction from doing it. As managers climb up the corporate ladder, they are required to spend an increasing amount of time interacting with people. These interactions may be on the shop floor, in group meetings, in dyadic transactions, through telephone conversations or in formal or informal gatherings. Many managers spend more than 50 per cent of their time interacting with their subordinates.

The effectiveness of the manager depends on both the content of the interaction and the manager's style. The manager's technical competence, functional knowledge, skills and information are very important in determining his or her effectiveness in managing subordinates. A capable manager is able to influence a subordinate by providing technical guidance and clear directions when needed. However, if the manager is not sensitive to the emotional needs of subordinates and does not use the appropriate styles of supervision and leadership, there is a great danger of crippling the growth of the subordinates. For example, an authoritarian manager may arouse strong negative reactions by continually dictating terms to capable subordinates but may do extremely well with subordinates who are dependent and who are just beginning to learn their roles. Similarly, a democratic manager may be liked by capable subordinates but seen as incompetent by dependent subordinates. It is necessary, therefore, for managers to adopt different styles while interacting with different people.

Benevolent, Critical and Development Styles

In this concept, leadership or supervisory styles stem from three mutually exclusive orientations: benevolent, critical and self-dispensing.

Benevolent Supervisor

This type protects subordinates, tells them every time what they should and should not do and comes to their rescue whenever needed. Such supervisors cater to the subordinates' needs for security and are generally liked by their subordinates. They are effective as long as they are physically present. In their absence, workers may experience a lack of direction and motivation. Such supervisors tend to have dependent followers and do not reinforce initiative-taking behaviour.

Critical Supervisor

This type takes a critical approach to employees and gives little allowance to mistakes, low-quality work, indiscipline or individual peculiarities. Finding mistakes, criticising subordinates and making them feel incompetent are characteristic behaviours of critical managers. Subordinates may produce acceptable work out of fear, but they do not like this type of manager.

Developmental Supervisor

This type has confidence in the subordinates, helps them to set broad goals and allows them to work on their own. Such supervisors provide guidance to their subordinates only on request. Competent workers who have this kind of supervision feel confident about their work. They feel free to work both independently and interdependently with their colleagues. Employee competencies are also developed well.

Institutional Supervisor

Closely related to the developmental supervisor is what David McClelland of Harvard University refers to as an institutional supervisor because this type is involved in developing the department or unit (McClelland and Burnham, 1976). Such supervisors are also called institution builders because they ensure the growth and development of their units and subordinates by incorporating processes that help people to give their best and to grow with the organisation. The following are the characteristics of institutional supervisors:

- They are organisation oriented and feel responsible for building their organisation
- They are self-disciplined and enjoy their work
- They are willing to sacrifice some of their own self-interests for the welfare of the organisation
- They have a keen sense of justice
- They have a low need for affiliation, a high need to influence others for social or organisational goals and express their power needs in a disciplined or controlled way

Such supervisors have a developmental style and are flexible in their use of styles. They are likely to create highly motivating work environments in their organisations.

Implications of Supervisory Styles

No single supervisory style is universally effective. The effectiveness of the style depends on the employee, the nature of the task and various other factors. If a new employee does not know much about the work, a benevolent supervisor is helpful; a critical supervisor may be frightening. On the other hand, a capable employee may feel most comfortable with a developmental style of supervision and resent a benevolent supervisor who continually gives unwanted advice.

Employees with low self-discipline probably could be developed best by critical supervision, at least on an intermittent basis. Constant use of critical supervision, however, is unlikely to be effective. Flexibility and perceptiveness about when to use each style are useful attributes for leaders or supervisors. However, developmental philosophy should be the core philosophy to enhance learning among employees.

Administration and Scoring

These are 12 sets of items in the questionnaire. Each set of items contain one 'benevolent' style-related item ('A' in each item), one 'critical' style-related item ('B' in each item) and one 'development' style-related item ('C' is each item). A total of 6 points have to be distributed in every set of items depending on the extent to which the item characterises the belief of the respondent.

Add scores on all 'A's to get the Benevolent Score for the respondent. Add scores on all 'B's to get the Critical Score for the respondent. Add scores on all 'C's to get the Developmental Score for the respondent.

The total of all the three scores should add up to 72 as there are 12 sets of items. The highest score indicates the dominant style of the respondent. The next highest score indicates the 'back-up' style of the respondent. While a relatively higher score on developmental style is desirable, lack of flexibility in using other styles may not be desirable. Such 'flexibility' is not measured by this questionnaire, and this issue may be discussed in the group. A development style is congruent with the HRD philosophy.

This questionnaire can be administered with a few modifications to study the perceptions of subordinates. The items given as follows are for the assessment by others as they are used in 360-degree feedback. Interested managers can get themselves rated by subordinates anonymously, analyse the responses with the help of the HRD department and examine their own beliefs and styles.

Responses from 360-Degree Feedback

1. Beliefs about subordinates
    - Believes that the subordinates should be treated with warmth and constantly guided and helped, and, therefore, gives instructions regularly
    - Believes that the subordinates tend to avoid work unless they are closely supervised, and, therefore, keeps a close watch on them
    - Believes that the subordinates are capable of working on their own, and, therefore, leaves them to work on their own most of the time, providing support only if needed
2. Organisational and personal goals
    - Shows concern for the individual needs and personal goals of fellow employees; takes trouble to help them achieve their personal goals
    - Excessively concerned with immediate tasks and organisational goals; has no concern for individual needs and goals
    - Is readily willing to sacrifice personal goals for organisational goals and sets an example for others; helps employees see the linkage between personal and organisational goals
3. Vision
    - Thinks only in terms of his or her people and protecting them; at times organisational tasks are secondary and makes efforts to gain the personal loyalty of subordinates by satisfying them

- Thinks only in terms of the immediate tasks or short-them goals; does not mind dissatisfying a few employees if the immediate tasks are not accomplished
- Thinks in terms of the long-term goals and interests of the organisation, is a visionary and invests time in developing sub-ordinates for the future of the organisation

4. Support:
   - Expects subordinates to come to him or her whenever they are in difficulty and solve their problems
   - Treats the subordinates as a problem and grudgingly provides help whenever they ask
   - Expects the subordinates to develop competencies by working through their difficulties and by learning to solve their own problems but readily provides support when they need

5. Mistakes
   - Tolerates mistakes and salvages the situation; protects the subordinates as far as possible
   - Cannot tolerate mistakes; gets emotional at times even for minor mistakes
   - Encourages the subordinates to use mistakes as learning opportunities, discusses the mistakes with them, educates them and helps them become more competent

6. Conflicts
   - When conflicts arise, delivers a judgement on who is right or wrong; employees normally look up to him or her for such decisions
   - When conflicts arise, complains to others or takes action to pull up the erring side
   - When conflicts arise, calls the parties together and tries to help them solve the problems in a manner that enhances mutual understanding and builds their competencies for resolving conflicts

7. Decision making
   - Prefers to take most decisions himself or herself and informs only those who are loyal or close to him or her; prefers that subordinates consult him or her before they take any decision themselves
   - Takes all decisions by himself or herself as he or she does not have confidence in the ability of the subordinates to take decisions
   - Prefers the subordinates to take most decisions on their own; however, consults people in critical decisions and keeps them informed, giving them a sense of involvement and identification with the organisation

8. Assignment of tasks
   - Assigns tasks on the basis of personal preferences
   - Assigns tasks purely according to the organisational norms without any flexibility or concern for people

- Assigns tasks in such a way that they match the competencies of subordinates and at the same time provides them opportunities for developing their competencies

9. Significance
   - Likes others to treat him or her with respect, admiration and personal loyalty; can always be counted on to protect the interests of those loyal to him or her
   - Treats other employees or subordinates as less important or less significant people; prefers to go by designations and status
   - Treats other employees and subordinates with respect; believes that he or she can become significant or powerful only by making all those who work with him or her significant and powerful

10. Communication
    - Shares information about company policies, environmental changes, technology, strategies, etc., selectively with those close to him or her or whom he or she considers dependable
    - Keeps all information to himself or herself and uses it as a source of power to control people
    - Takes the subordinates into confidence and keeps them informed of company plans, policies, changes in environment, technology, strategies, etc., with a view to get them involved or prepare them for future challenges

11. Inspiration
    - Is interested in maintaining good relationships; highly relationship oriented
    - Is quite task oriented and cannot tolerate any delays or deviation; has no concern for people and their difficulties
    - He inspires people to give their best to the organisation; creates conditions to help people enjoy their work

12. Initiative
    - Gives freedom and opportunity for employees to take initiative; encourages a few who are close and loyal to take initiative
    - Prefers employees/subordinates to conform strictly to the rules, regulations, procedures and norms and enforces them, even with some coercion if required
    - Encourages all his or her employees to take initiative; believes that employees cannot develop unless they have some freedom to take initiative and experience personal worth

The TVRLS–HRD–LOC Inventory

A number of HRD managers in recent times have failed to make a mark as they lacked self-confidence and lost faith in their own ability to make things happen. The term 'locus of control' indicates the point of influence as perceived by the respondent. Researches have shown in the past that effective managers and leaders believe in their own capacity to influence the environment and make things happen. Managers who believe that they can make a significant impact on their own environment and have faith in their own capability to make things happen are called 'internals'. Those who believe that events that happen to them or to others in their organisation are influencing factors beyond their control are called 'externals'. It has been found that internals have a tendency to work hard, work more and work with confidence. It is internals who can make things happen. Externals, on the other hand, are less likely to put in as much hard work and dynamism.

HRD success depends to a large extent on the attitude of the HRD manager. If he or she is an 'external' and thinks that he or she cannot do much to create a learning culture or to make HRD succeed in the organisation and that it is the top management, unions, line managers and the powerful others who can make things happen, he or she is less likely to succeed.

The TVRLS–HRD–LOC inventory measures the extent to which the HRD manager or HRD staff member is internally oriented or externally oriented. A good degree of internality is indicative of the dynamism needed to make HRD succeed.

Administration

The following inventory can be self-administered. It can be administered to all HRD staff to determine the attitudes and the internality and externality levels of the HRD staff.

Scoring for TVRLS–LOC Inventory

The inventory has 32 pairs of items. Each pair has one internality item and one externality item. Two of the items are filler items and do not fall into either the internality or externality category. There are therefore 30 items for scoring. The number of times the respondent prefers an internal item to an externality-representing item is considered as the score. Higher levels of internality are desirable. A score above 20 is considered an acceptable score and scores above 25 are ideal.

The following are the internality items. Score one point for each of these alternatives preferred or tick marked:

1b; 2a; 4b; 5b; 6b; 7a; 8b; 9a; 10a; 11b; 12b; 13a; 14a; 15b; 16b; 17b; 18b; 19a; 20b; 21b; 22b; 24a; 25b; 26b; 27a; 29a; 30b; 31a; 32b

Item 3 and 23 are filler items and are not scored.

Which one of the pairs do you tend to agree more. Tick mark the one you agree more than the other in each pair.

1. (a) Most top-level managers (CEOs and Directors) have no genuine belief in HRD. They appoint HRD managers to convey an impression that they are modern and professional
   (b) CEOs are genuinely interested in HRD
2. (a) HRD budgets are cut because the HRD function has not established its credibility
   (b) No matter how credible the HRD manager is, organisations are bound to reduce the HRD budget when faced with a financial crunch
3. (a) A good CEO always has time to devote to HRD-related matters
   (b) CEOs should invest their time on matters other than HRD that contribute directly to profits of the organisation
4. (a) No matter how capable the HRD manager is, it is the CEO who decides how well he or she is going to be used
   (b) Effective HRD managers always find their way to make an impact
5. (a) Performance appraisals are difficult to succeed in India
   (b) A good manager always finds time to provide performance feedback to their subordinates
6. (a) Line managers have very little interest in HRD-related matters
   (b) Line managers should learn HRD to develop themselves
7. (a) Employees who cannot make use of the HRD function for their development have missed something
   (b) Employees should do the work assigned to them than to think of HRD. HRD contributes little to promotions
8. (a) Distance education can be of very little help to develop managerial capabilities
   (b) Good managers can be made; they are not born
9. (a) People get the rewards they deserve in the long run
   (b) No matter how effective you are, unless you are in the good books of your boss, you cannot get ahead
10. (a) Training programmes provide a good time to be away from job and get re-charged
    (b) A training programme that does not get the trainee to work hard has not made a good impact
11. (a) It is really not worthwhile to plan your work as you rarely have control over your time once in office
    (b) It is important to plan your work and time to make use of your talents
12. (a) Promotion decisions are mostly subjective
    (b) Most promotion decisions have some element of objectivity

13. (a) Good HRD managers can contribute to objectivity in appraisals
    (b) No matter how good an HRD manager you have, if your boss is not impressed with you, you cannot get ahead
14. (a) The organisational culture can be changed and modified with effort
    (b) Once established, the organisational culture is difficult to change
15. (a) Autocratic managers will remain always autocratic
    (b) Feedback can change the management styles of people
16. (a) HRD managers who do not succeed in one or two companies are not likely to succeed later
    (b) With introspection and effort one can succeed eventually
17. (a) A strong union leader can undo all the good work done by the HRD department
    (b) HRD can do a lot more to help organisations by focusing their attention on workers
18. (a) The HRD needs of workers are different from those of managers
    (b) Small investments on developing the workforce can give rich dividends
19. (a) There should be one HRD person for every 100 employees
    (b) In these days of cost-cutting it is enough to have one HRD manager for every 1,000 employees
20. (a) One loses faith in behavioural sciences when one looks at the way behavioural scientists behave
    (b) Peculiarities in behavioural scientists are due to the influence of their discipline on them
21. (a) Any effective line manager can be an equally effective HRD manager
    (b) To be a good HRD manager, one needs to have received professional training in HRD
22. (a) Commerce graduates should prefer finance and accounts courses than HRD
    (b) Arts graduates with a psychology background will do well as HRD managers
23. (a) Good HRD managers can be good CEOs
    (b) To be a good CEO you do not need any competencies in people management but you need the right breaks
24. (a) Good appraisal systems can create a new culture in organisations
    (b) Organisational culture is created by good CEOs rather than by HRD systems
25. (a) No matter what you do, managers cannot change their preferences for people from their own regions, communities, religion, etc.
    (b) With training it is possible to reduce biases in appraisals
26. (a) Most organisations have given up on appraisals
    (b) A number of organisations keep reviewing their appraisal systems

27. (a) Openness hurts. One should be open always
    (b) One should be open with open people and be careful with closed people
28. (a) Most people are not trustworthy
    (b) Trust is expensive
29. (a) Promoting trust is an important task of HRD
    (b) HRD managers should devote enough time to select the right people than on promoting trustworthiness, openness, etc.
30. (a) Textbooks can help very little to develop HRD skills
    (b) One can recognise a good HRD manager from a few interactions
31. (a) If workers take sufficient interest, they get union leaders who can really take care of their interests
    (b) No matter how much the workers try, it is difficult to get union leaders who can look after their interests.
32. (a) High achievements in HRD courses do not necessarily make good HRD managers.
    (b) Doing well in HRD courses lays a good foundation for HRD skills.

TVRLS–HRD–KA Test: Knowledge of HRD

This is a test to measure HRD knowledge and attitudes (K&A). Knowledge forms the basis of skills. Skills are easy to acquire and become meaningful if they are based on an understanding of their appropriateness. This test measures the extent to which the candidate has some basic professional knowledge in HRD. What is given in the following is a sample set of items. I have developed and used one version of the test in HRD audit programmes. The scoring key is not given here as it is a knowledge test and it needs continuous modification for an appropriate assessment. Interested persons can write to the author to get the scoring key and latest versions of this test.

TVRLS–HRD–KA Test: Knowledge of HRD

A. Attitudes
Please indicate your agreement or disagreement by using letters *A* for Agree and *D* for Disagree. Do not leave any item.

1. People can learn at any stage of their life
2. Age increases resistance to learning
3. Performance appraisals are not meant as learning tools
4. One can learn better in the training programmes than on the job
5. Monetary rewards play a critical role in learning

6. Employees will learn better if they have good career opportunities in the organisation
7. Openness (free expression of ideas and feelings, etc.) leads to more politics and interpersonal problems and hinders learning
8. Trusting people is more important than being trustworthy
9. Team spirit is high among Indians
10. Most Indians are influenced by caste, community and such other divisive parochial considerations

B. Learning sources: Ideation
List in the following as many different sources of learning as you can think of for employers (managers, workers, all categories).

1.	2.
3.	4.
5.	6.
7.	8.
9.	10.
11.	12
13.	14.
15.	16.

C. HRD Systems
Identify True and False items (mark *T* for True and *F* for False).

1. KPAs are observable; KRAs are not always easy to observe
2. KPAs deal with your own work; KRAs may include the work of others
3. KPAs are of Indian origin
4. KRAs are based on the management by objectives (MBO) approach
5. KPAs and KRAs are very similar
6. KPAs can be stated tasks and targets
7. KPAs are part of performance management systems
8. To be a good training manager, it is sufficient to be a good HRD manager
9. In a good performance review discussion the appraisee should speak more than the appraiser
10. Assessment centres are good ways of assessing the performance of an employee on a given job
11. Assessment centres have not worked well in the West
12. Career paths indicate to every individual the path that is carved out for him or her in the organisation
13. Career paths are broad indications of career progression from a given position to other positions

14. Job rotation means transferring the person compulsorily to another job periodically
15. Job rotation means planned change of jobs with the intention of developing different skills in the person
16. HRD is a new name for training. Training is a small and significant part of HRD
17. OD is a part of HRD roles
18. OD means giving new direction to organisations
19. HRD is an integral part of the personnel function
20. HRD has very little to do with the personnel function

D. HRD General Part (2)

1. Which of the following is an important component of HRD manager's preparation (tick one):
   (a) Learning theories
   (b) Personality development
   (c) Negotiation skills
   (d) Marketing skills
   (e) Computer technology
   (f) System designing skills
2. When an HRD manager joins the company one of his or her first important tasks should be (tick one):
   (a) To look at the performance appraisal system
   (b) Visit the training centre
   (c) Read the annual report and balance sheet of the company
   (d) Meet other HR staff
3. Which of the following are OD interventions (tick as many as relevant):
   (a) Wage settlement
   (b) Evaluating training
   (c) Conducting internal customer satisfaction workshops
   (d) Conducting role negotiation exercises
   (e) Presenting survey results on organisational culture
   (f) Revising the salary structure
   (g) Drafting the recruitment policy
4. Which of the following does not fall into the job of an HRD manager (cross the one that does not fit in):
   (a) Recruitment
   (b) Job rotation
   (c) Training
   (d) Designing performance management
   (e) Preparing appraisers for communication
   (f) Rewarding good performance

5. Which of the following systems requires a higher degree of employee participation (tick one):
   (a) Job rotation
   (b) Training
   (c) Performance management
6. Good performance counselling does not include (tick two):
   (a) Upward appraisal
   (b) Two-way discussion
   (c) Feedback by appraiser to appraisee
   (d) Identifying development needs
   (e) Performance ratings

E. Which one of the items in each pair should be the priority of the HRD manager (tick mark the item)?

1. (a) Understanding the product range of the company
   (b) Knowing the age profile of the staff
2. (a) Knowing the age profile of the staff
   (b) Knowing the business context of the company
3. (a) Designing the appraisal system
   (b) Participating in wage negotiations
4. (a) Understanding how people learn
   (b) Understanding labour laws
5. (a) Understanding people issues and concerns
   (b) Implementing HRD systems
6. Which of the following is a well-set KPA for a sales manager of a branch with 10 sales staff?
   (a) To sell 100 air conditioners a month
   (b) To establish mechanisms necessary to help the service engineer to attend to every complaint within 30 minutes of receiving the complaint
7. Which of the following increase speed in decision making?
   (a) Flat structures
   (b) Clear role definitions
8. Which of the following is essential for improving quality?
   (a) ISO 9000 certification
   (b) Creating a quality mind-set among all employees
9. Which of the following is a KPA and not a KRA?
   (a) To complete the project report taking into consideration all parameters
   (b) Completing project reports on time
10. Which of the following is more correct?
    (a) HRD is a recent management development
    (b) There is not much new in HRD – it has been in existence since the beginning

F. Given as follows on side a are some principles of management and human behaviour. On Side B are HRD subsystems. Identify the subsystem from Side B for which the principle on Side A is most appropriate. Please indicate the letter that matches the principle and write in the space provided on Side A.

Side A		Side B
– Recent failures are recollected more than past successes	A	HRD systems integration
– Excellent past performance is no guarantee for future role performance	B	Potential appraisal
– Behavioural science expertise is essential to specialise in this	C	Performance coaching
– Empowering employees can be done best through this	D	Performance management
– Diagnosis is the first step in this	E	Succession planning
– The best way to develop general management skills and perspectives is through this	F	OD
– Most organisations do not get enough returns on this and yet continue to do it	G	Training
– Most organisations face difficulties in this and yet continue trying	H	Job rotation
– This has to be done with care and sensitiveness	I	Performance appraisals
– This is most useful for building young talent	J	Mentoring

G. Performance Appraisal

1. Performance development systems will be more successful without one of the following:
   -----A. KPAs and KRAs
   -----B. Feedback and coaching
   -----C. Ratings and rewards
   -----D. Linkage with training and other development actions
2. The main difference between KPAs and KRAs is
   -----A. The extent to which they stress results versus efforts
   -----B. The extent to which they stress group and individual performance
   -----C. Extent to which they stress qualitative and quantitative aspects
   -----D. The extent to which they provide role clarity

3. The main reason for the failure of appraisal in India is
   -----A. Normal probability concepts are imposed when there is no normality
   -----B. There are biases in ratings
   -----C. Poor implementation
   -----D. Lack of top management commitment
4. In an open system of appraisal the ratings are
   -----A. Shown to the individual
   -----B. Not shown to the individual
   -----C. Jointly done by the reporting and reviewing officers
   -----D. Based largely on self-appraisal
5. Performance analysis means
   -----A. Analysing the performance for identifying facilitating and inhibiting factors
   -----B. Identifying the causes of poor performance
   -----C. Finding out what differentiates poor performers from good performers
   -----D. Finding our factors behind successful performance
6. In performance appraisals bars are
   -----A. Behaviour descriptions associated with various levels of ratings
   -----B. Behavioural assessment related to specific tasks
   -----C. Graphs drawn to classify performers into different categories
   -----D. Descriptions of KRAs associated with different levels of ratings
7. Complete the performance equation: Performance = Ability × Motivation × ...
   -----A. Extent to which KPAs are achieved
   -----B. Extent to which training needs are fulfilled
   -----C. Extent to which chance factors provided the support
   -----D. Organisational support plus or minus chance factors
8. Hallo effect means
   -----A. The tendency to be strict or lenient on the part of the assessee
   -----B. The impression the appraisee created in the beginning
   -----C. The preconceived notion the assessor carries about the assessee
   -----D. The effect of recent events on ratings
9. A good time to identify development needs as a part of the appraisal process is
   -----A. At the end of the year after completing the assessment
   -----B. In the middle of the year after the appraisee had performed and appraiser had an opportunity to observe his or her performance for six months
   -----C. In the beginning of the year, at the time of identifying KPAs or KRAs
   -----D. Independent of performance appraisals

10. The main task of a 'Performance Manager' (a new role created in some organisations) is to
    -----A. Monitor the performance of line managers
    -----B. Ensure objectivity in ratings
    -----C. Find out what prevented individuals and groups from performing better and initiating corrective action
    -----D. Link rewards with performance

11. A good way to use performance review committees is to
    -----A. Find out and modify biases in ratings
    -----B. Assign rewards on the basis of the quality of assessment
    -----C. Ensure normal probability
    -----D. Educate assessors by giving feedback and assisting in objectivity

12. The following objective in performance appraisals is not easy to achieve and, hence, should not be overstressed
    -----A. Ensuring objectivity in ratings
    -----B. Linking appraisals to development plans
    -----C. Discovering strengths and weaknesses through feedback and counselling
    -----D. Improving planning and executing abilities
    -----E. Integrating individual goals with organisational goals

13. Performance appraisal ratings can be best described as
    -----A. Ordinal scales
    -----B. Nominal scales
    -----C. Approximations of interval scales
    -----D. Ratio scales

14. Performance appraisal system as a part of HRD can be best described as (tick one incorrect response)
    -----A. A central tool for HRD
    -----B. A good OD tool for performance improvements
    -----C. Nuisance value for genuine development
    -----D. A good culture-building tool

15. Rating less appraisals (tick mark one incorrect response)
    -----A. Promote subjectivity
    -----B. Promote healthy relationships
    -----C. Hinder performance planning
    -----D. Hinder achievement of most objectives of performance measurement system (PMS)

16. The main objective of self-appraisal in PMS is to (tick one incorrect response
    -----A. Recapitulate and review the accomplishments and failures of self
    -----B. Remind the boss of one's accomplishments
    -----C. Plan the review and coaching session better and get the best out of it

-----D. Communicate to boss in a subtle way the expectations of ratings and rewards

17. Which of the following is not determined by the annual performance appraisals?
    -----A. Individual KPAs or KRAs
    -----B. Annual departmental goals
    -----C. Annual business plans of the organisation
    -----D. Developmental actions

H. Assessment Centres

1. Assessment centres are not best to be used for
   -----A. Potential appraisal
   -----B. Performance appraisal
   -----C. Recruitment of fresh recruits
   -----D. Succession planning
   -----E. Organisational diagnosis

2. In a well-conducted assessment centre the group of assessors should include (tick two correct answers)
   -----A. The boss and/or the boss's boss
   -----B. Outside experts
   -----C. Seniors at least two levels above the current level of the employee and from other departments
   -----D. Seniors of the employee from the same department or function
   -----E. Seniors from other departments who know the person well and interacted with him or her

3. The normal ratio of assessors to assessees in a good assessment centre is
   -----A. One assessor for each assessee
   -----B. One assessor for two to three assesses
   -----C. Two assessors for each assessee
   -----D. At least three assessors per assessee

4. BEI (Behaviour Event Interviewing) is process of
   -----A. Interview based on situations eliciting behaviour expected of the individual
   -----B. Interview based on the past behaviours of the individual
   -----C. Interview based on the events faced by successful individuals
   -----D. Interviews based on behaviours and events associated with the job

5. In-basket or in-tray methods consists of
   -----A. Comments of the candidates on decisions taken by a role holder as noted in the files
   -----B. Inward mails from a mail box requiring response from the candidate

-----C. Situations from a basket of predetermined success situations encountered by previous role holders to be commented by the candidate

-----D. A basket of situations a candidate can choose from, including the situations he or she likes and dislikes

6. Personality inventories (like MBTI, 16 PF, etc.) in assessment centres meant for promotions suffer from the following:
-----A. Difficult to standardise and make it role focused
-----B. Cultural relevance
-----C. Objectivity in scoring
-----D. Possible to fake

7. Which of the following is not normally given to the candidate at the end of the assessment centre in the following way?
-----A. Feedback on suitability to the position being considered
-----B. Feedback on behaviours or competencies demonstrated in the assessment centre
-----C. Feedback on the limitations of the tests and tools
-----D. Development needs for enhancing potential of the candidate

8. Which of the following is not a precondition for the success of assessment and development centres (ADCs)?
-----A. Trained and competent assessors
-----B. Competency mapping
-----C. Standardised tools and tests for the positions under consideration
-----D. Clearly stated organisational philosophy and policy on ADCs

9. What is the difference between assessment centres (ACs) and development centres (DCs)?
-----A. No difference as it is being practised today
-----B. AC focuses on assessment and DC on development
-----C. AC is for promotions and DC is for development on the current jobs
-----D. AC uses standardised tools well tested out and DC uses any tools for training

10. The first assessment centres in India, as reported in the literature, were used at
-----A. Parishram in Gujarat in 1974 for selection of project leaders
-----B. L&T in 1974
-----C. BILT
-----D. Behavioural Sciences Centre in 1972

11. Assessment centres as we know now were largely initiated in a systematic way by
-----A. AT&T in the USA
-----B. Development Dimensions at Pittsburgh
-----C. Harvard Business school
-----D. Michigan University

12. The following contributed a good deal to our understanding of assessment centres today (tick mark as many as you think):
    -----A. AT&T studies
    -----B. McBer studies
    -----C. DDI studies
    -----D. IOAC by AHRD in India
    -----E. BSC and XLRI in India
    -----F. TVRLS in India
    -----G. IIMA
    -----H. NHRDN
13. Assessment centres normally do not use the following techniques:
    -----A. Classroom lectures
    -----B. Case analysis
    -----C. Simulations
    -----D. Role plays
    -----E. Trend analysis
    -----F. Demonstration sessions
14. Competencies assessed by assessment centres and 360-degree feedback are likely to be
    -----A. The same as competencies remain the same irrespective of who assesses
    -----B. The same as both are objective methods of assessment
    -----C. Different as one deals with assessment by known people and the other involves assessment by unknown people
    -----D. Not the same as the competencies the candidate did not have an opportunity demonstrate get shown in ACs and DCs
15. Competencies assessed by assessment centres and performance appraisals likely to be
    -----E. The same as competencies remain the same irrespective of who assesses and when assessed
    -----F. The same as both are objective methods of assessment
    -----G. Different as one deals with assessment by known people and the other involves assessment by unknown people
    -----H. Not the same as competencies the candidate did not have an opportunity demonstrate on the job get shown in ACs and DCs.

I. 360-Degree Feedback

1. Which of the following is not acceptable practice in 360-degree feedback?
   -----A. Assessor's writing their name
   -----B. Assessee writing his or her name on the forms
   -----C. Assessor indicating his or her relationship with the candidate
   -----D. Indicating the weaknesses the assessor chooses to indicate

2. Which of the categories are normally not included in 360-degree feedback?
   -----A. External customers
   -----B. Juniors who report to his or her direct reports (below two levels of the candidate)
   -----C. All reporting officers
   -----D. Colleagues from other departments who have working relations with the candidate
3. 360-degree feedback in India is largely used for
   -----A. Rewards and increments
   -----B. ESOPs
   -----C. Leadership development
   -----D. Promotions and placements
4. What is now known as 360-degree feedback was initiated in India (tick one as correct):
   -----A. At IIMA in mid-eighties as a leadership-building and organisational effectiveness tool
   -----B. By MNCs in mid-seventies
   -----C. By L&T in the early eighties
   -----D. By HLL in the early nineties
5. Identify the books from the following whose titles are incorrectly stated:
   -----A. *The Power of 360-degree Feedback*
   -----B. *HRD Score Card*
   -----C. *HRD Audit*
   -----D. *The Working HRD Missionary*
   -----E. *HR Champions*
   -----F. *Performance Management*
   -----G. *Managing and Designing HR Systems*
   -----H. *HR Value Score Card*
6. Which of the following objectives cannot be easily addressed by 360-degree feedback (check two most appropriate)?
   -----A. Job rotation
   -----B. Recruitment and selection
   -----C. Top grading
   -----D. Succession planning
   -----E. Career planning and development
   -----F. Change management
   -----G. Culture building
   -----H. Identification of training and developmental needs
   -----I. Leadership development
7. Which of the following names are not used for 360-degree feedback?
   -----A. 360-degree appraisal
   -----B. Multirater feedback

-----C. Full-circle feedback

-----D. Full performance appraisal

8. Which of the following is the most critical pre-requisite for successful impact of 360-degree feedback?

 -----A. The user organisation has an open culture

 -----B. The candidate seeks feedback willingly

 -----C. The 360-degree feedback tool is designed on the basis of the needs of the candidate

 -----D. The organisation provides follow-up support

9. Which of the following is the more likely outcome of 360-degree feedback session by the participant?

 -----A. Increased defensiveness

 -----B. Enhanced knowledge of how to deal with role-set members

 -----C. Enhanced self-awareness

 -----D. Realistic Knowledge of career opportunities

10. RSDQ model of 360 DF means

 -----A. Recruitment, selection, development and quality

 -----B. Roles, styles, delegation and qualities

 -----C. Rights, services, duties and questions

 -----D. Roles, styles, development and qualities

11. Which of the following organisations used 360-degree feedback for career decisions rather than merely for development?

 -----A. NTPC

 -----B. ONGC

 -----C. GE & Infosys

 -----D. Johnson & Johnson

 -----E. Aditya Birla Group

12. Which of the following statements best represents your view on 360-degree feedback in India?

 -----A. Indian organisations are not yet ready for effective use of 360-degree feedback

 -----B. It is a great change tool and has the potential of bringing change at all levels from families to corporates, bureaucrats and politicians

 -----C. It is a good tool for leadership development

 -----D. We need to do a lot more research before we can implement this in India

J. Rewards Systems and PRP

1. Normally the performance-linked pay should be

 -----A. Anything depending on the profits and performance of the company and its divisions

-----B. One-tenth of the employee costs

-----C. Equal to the annual salary

-----D. One half of the annual salary

2. Performance-linked pay means

-----A. A fixed salary given to the employee depending on his or her performance levels

-----B. Variable pay given to every employee depending on his or her and the organisation's performance

-----C. Fixed pay given to all employees as a bonus at the end of the year

-----D. Variable pay depending on the individual performance, irrespective of company performance

3. When promotion decisions are made the common experience in India seem to be

-----A. The promoted candidates outperform others due to high motivation

-----B. Those who could not make it try harder next time to make it

-----C. Those disappointed with promotion decisions seem to outnumber those who are happy

-----D. Those who miss promotion learn from their failures and make it next time

4. Research studies indicate that in the European context performance-linked pay in public sector has

-----A. Worked very well

-----B. Work better if differentiations in pay are made smaller than bigger

-----C. Not worked well at all

-----D. Motivated employees across all levels

5. In order to maintain motivation levels of employees in Indian settings it is better to have

-----A. Highly differentiated performance rewards

-----B. Multiple reward and recognition systems, including team rewards

-----C. No performance-linked pay at all

-----D. Team rewards only rather than individual rewards

12

MEASURING BUSINESS IMPACT AND ESTABLISHING THE HRD SCORE CARD

The HRD Score Card assigns a four-letter rating to grade the maturity level of HRD present in an organisation. The HRD audit is a scientific aid to assign scores. The letters represent the four critical dimensions that contribute to business performance or organisational performance (for non-profit organisations). These four dimensions include:

- HRD systems maturity and HRD strategies
- HRD competencies in the company
- HRD culture and values
- HRD impact and alignment to business goals

The HRD audit described in the earlier sections can be used to assign the scores for the first three parts.

In recent years the concept of intellectual capital has gained momentum. Success of corporations used to be measured earlier by profits achieved annually or, at best, across a few years. However, after the discovery that excellent companies do not remain excellent all the time unless they continuously work for it, the concept of intellectual capital and building sustainable corporations came into existence. Corporations that do not last for 25 years, 50 years and even a 100 years are not called sustainable organisations. In the era of mergers and acquisitions, finding lasting corporations has become important.

The market value of an organisation is the total value of its net tangible assets and the value of its intangible assets. The *tangible assets* include the book value of all assets, shares, land and buildings, machinery and all that

DOI: 10.4324/9781003530534-15

can be seen and accounted for, whereas the *intellectual capital* of the company includes the image of the company; its internal strengths in terms of talent, people, management systems and practices, customers, brands, patents and everything else that comprises its market value.

What constitutes intellectual capital?

- Sound strategy
- Continuing innovation in products and services
- Excellent people
- Loyal and satisfied customers
- Reputation and image in connection with the community that creates the brand
- Synergistic partnerships

Intellectual capital has been found to constitute a high percentage of the market capitalisation of companies. At one time Bill Gates is supposed to have said that 97 per cent of Microsoft's market value cannot be found in their balance sheet implying that it is its intangible intellectual capital. I have argued in my recent writings (see *Hurconomics* by Rao, 2011) that HRD's main contribution should be in forming intellectual capital rather than contributing to tangible assets. In Indian corporations such intellectual capital has been found to vary also up to 90 per cent of the market capitalisation. Therefore, the argument is that HRD function should aim at building long-term intangible assets. Dave Ulrich's 'outside-in' approach also suggests the same and puts high value in customer capital. In doing HRD audit of corporations like BPL and Gati, etc., we have attempted to focus the attention of HR on understanding and servicing customers and even customers' customers.

It is in this context that having knowledgeable and skilled workforce at all levels has been found to be an important contributor to intellectual capital. It is not unusual for corporations to see how their market value changes when they recruit top-level managers or lose some valued talent. The last decade has witnessed the fall of corporations when their talents (values) have been found to be weak. The last decade also has seen stability of organisations at least across a 10- to 20-year period when their talent is good. Birla group focused on getting young talent and changed their strategy to move to professionalism and defined values in the last decade and a half. Tatas always had a stable and competent manpower with its own unique culture. ICICI bank and IT sector corporations like Infosys, Wipro, HCL Technologies, Cognizant, etc., are known to manage their talent well and enhance their market value. Taking into account these two sets of variables the last part of HRD Score Card has been designed to focus on measuring the impact of HRD on intellectual capital and talent management. This aspect is highlighted in the last part of this section while discussing the business impact and alignment of HRD. The score card is not complete without this. HRD function has a great deal to contribute once it is realised that it is not merely helping to manage the present of corporations but build their future as well.

Mechanisms of establishing the score card are presented sequentially as follows, with intellectual capital and talent management as the last cell of the HRD Score Card.

HRD Systems Maturty

The HRD systems maturity assesses the extent to which various HRD subsystems and tools are well designed and are being implemented. There are seven factors that need to be taken into account:

1. The systems should be appropriate and relevant to business goals or organisational goals
2. They should focus on, as well as balance between, the current and future needs of the corporation
3. The HRD strategies and systems should flow from the corporate strategies
4. The systems should be well designed and should have structural maturity
5. They should be implemented well. The employees should be taking them seriously and follow meticulously what has been envisaged in each system. The overheads of implementation should be low; that is, the monitoring requirements should be relatively few, with the employees taking the systems seriously
6. The subsystems should be well integrated and should have internal synergy
7. They should be adequate and should take care of the HRD requirements of the organisation

The following subsystems are assessed on the aforementioned criteria and depending on the extent to which they meet the requirements a score is assigned:

1. Competency mapping
2. Manpower planning
3. Recruitment
4. Induction and integration
5. PMS
6. Coaching and mentoring
7. Training and learning
8. Potential appraisal and assessment or development centres
9. Rewards and recognition
10. Career planning and development, including succession planning

11. Job rotation
12. OD and renewal systems
13. Other subsystems, if any, like HR information system, worker develop-
    ment, etc.

Each of them is assessed on a 10-point rating scale where a score of 10 represents an extremely high level of maturity, 5 represents a moderate level of
maturity and 1 represents an extremely low level of maturity.

The number of systems followed is immaterial. The systems should be
adequate enough and should have no gaps. Table 12.1 can be used for such
an assessment.

A* *Extremely high level of systems.* Maturity score = 90 per cent and
    above. All systems are extremely adequate, relevant to organisational
    goals, well designed, well implemented, highly relevant to organisa-
    tional needs, well linked with corporate plans and well integrated. This
    is the highest maturity level.
A   *Very high maturity level.* Maturity score = 80 to 90 per cent.
B* *High maturity level.* Maturity score = 70 to 80 per cent.
B   *Moderately high maturity level.* Maturity score = 60 to 70 per cent.
    Good on most systems and meets most of the standards to a satisfactory
    level. This is the minimum acceptable grade for a good company. Scores
    below this indicate that the company needs to improve substantially to
    be a world-class company.
C* *Moderate maturity level.* Maturity score = 50 to 60 per cent.
    This is the average score.
C   *Moderately low maturity level.* Maturity score = 40 to 50 per cent.
D* *Low maturity level.* Maturity score = 30 to 40 per cent.
D   *Very low maturity level.* Maturity score = 20 to 30 per cent.
F   *Maturity not at all present.* Maturity score = below 20 per cent. Fails to
    meet the minimum standards on most systems and on most dimensions;
    the organisation has a long way to go.
U   *Ungraded*: Cannot be graded due to lack of data.

Assess below the extent to which your HRD systems are mature.

- What are the various HRD systems you have?
- How clear are their objectives?
- How complete and scientific are they? How comprehensive are they?
- How well are they understood?
- How well are they implemented?
- Are they resulting in any tangible achievement of business goals?

TABLE 12.1 Assessment of HRD Systems Maturity

HR systems	Your rating on a 5-point scale					
	Extent of clarity of objectives (10)	Extent to which well structured (20)	Extent to which it is understood (10)	How well it is implemented (20)	Extent to which it meets organisational needs (10)	Total
1. **Competency mapping:** A system of constantly identifying competency requirements of each job						
2. **Manpower planning:** Systematic planning of manpower requirements both short and long term to suit company requirements						
3. **Recruitment:** Scientific recruitment based on competency requirements and use of appropriate tools						
4. **Induction and integration:** A system on initiating and integrating the individual into the job, role and the organisation						

(Continued)

TABLE 12.1 Assessment of HRD Systems Maturity (*Continued*)

HR systems	Your rating on a 5-point scale					
	Extent of clarity of objectives (10)	Extent to which well structured (20)	Extent to which it is understood (10)	How well it is implemented (20)	Extent to which it meets organisational needs (10)	Total
5. **Performance management:** *A system of performance planning, analysis, development, review and appraisal – includes clarifying role, planning work, identifying development needs, generating and using performance data*						
6. **Training and learning:** *A system of identifying development needs, creating and using development opportunities to multiply talent*						
7. **Coaching and mentoring:** *A system of ensuring continuous motivations and talent utilisation through coaching and mentoring processes*						
8. **Job rotation:** *A system of multiskilling and preparation for future roles*						

(*Continued*)

TABLE 12.1 Assessment of HRD Systems Maturity (Continued)

HR systems	Your rating on a 5-point scale					Total
	Extent of clarity of objectives (10)	Extent to which well structured (20)	Extent to which it is understood (10)	How well it is implemented (20)	Extent to which it meets organisational needs (10)	
9. **Potential appraisal and assessment or development centres:** A system of assessing the competencies for roles not performed and using the data for identification and development of potential talent						
10. **Career planning and development:** A system of planning for succession and future needs of the company and preparing the employees for the future						
11. **OD and renewal exercises:** A system of periodic organisational diagnosis and renewal – includes employee satisfaction surveys and interventions						

(Continued)

TABLE 12.1 Assessment of HRD Systems Maturity (*Continued*)

HR systems	Your rating on a 5-point scale					
	Extent of clarity of objectives (10)	Extent to which well structured (20)	Extent to which it is understood (10)	How well it is implemented (20)	Extent to which it meets organisational needs (10)	Total
12. Recognition and rewards: A system of recognising and rewarding good performance in ways that promotes the performance culture of an organisation – including stock option and other incentives						
Any other						
Any other						
Any Other						
Any other						
Total scores						

1. Please rate each of your HRD systems you have on a 5-point scale:

9–10 = To an extremely great extent

7–8 = To a large extent

5–6 = To some extent

3–4 = To a little extent

0–2 = Totally lacking to a negligible extent

NA = Not applicable

Use the criteria set above for each of the dimensions. Add more systems if you have them and delete systems that you do not have if they are not relevant to you. However, if the system is not there though it is relevant to you please rate the system as it exists today. If nothing exists the points assigned will be zero on each of the five dimensions. Multiply by two for weightage of 20 points.

HRD Strategies

Assess the extent to which the following HRD strategies are used effectively by your organisation. Use the aforementioned rating scale and for each assess on 10 points:

9–10: The strategy is extremely effectively sued by the firm

7–8: The strategy is followed to a large extent in the organisation effectively

5–6: This strategy is used to a satisfactory extent

3–4: This strategy is used somewhat satisfactorily

0–2: This strategy is weak to totally absent

HR strategies dimension	Your assessment
1. **Communication strategy:** Integration with the family and the society as a strategy is included. It has a lot of binding effect on the individual employee and also deals with corporate social responsibility. It also builds a company brand. It is not PR but a communication strategy to integrate the individual with the organisation through his or her family and the society.	

(Continued)

HR strategies dimension	*Your assessment*

2. **Employee engagement (accountability, ownership and commitment):** A heightened emotional connection that an employee feels for his or her organisation that influences him or her to exert greater discretionary effort to his or her work. Eight key drivers: how well managers communicate and 'walk the talk'? Is the job mentally stimulating day to day? Does the employee understand how his or her work contributes to the company's performance? Are there future opportunities for growth? How much self-esteem does the employee feel by being associated with his or her company? Extent to which co-workers/team significantly influence one's level of engagement? Is the company making an effort to develop the employee's skills? Does the employee value his or her relationship with his or her manager?

3. **Quality orientation:** Quality consciousness (in every employee), certification like ISO 9000, HR strategies aiming at total quality and quality-related systems in use. Tolerance level of poor quality of internal customers and feedback from external customers about quality of products and services provided.

4. **Customer orientation:** Regular external customer satisfaction surveys, regular internal customer satisfaction surveys. HR strategies to link employee satisfaction with customer satisfaction.

5. **Efficiency:** Laid down (documented) operational and process efficiency processes, policies and norms – for example, cost reduction, savings, synergy, coordination, etc., and effective implementation of the same. HR strategies linking each and every employee with efficiency and value addition activities and total employee involvement in operational or process efficiency management.

6. **Entrepreneurial spirit:** Full autonomy of tasks to employees and encouragement of risks and initiatives, ROI and cost-effectiveness by all employees – ROI mind-set in all activities; HR systems encourage spotting of opportunities, making business plans and entrepreneurial thinking.

7. **Culture building:** HR policies to address OCTAPACE goals, effective implementation of these policies and use of strategies and systems to encourage culture building.

8. **Talent management:** There is a definite strategy to attract, retain, utilise and develop talent.

Total score out of 80 points

Total score out of 160 points

HRD Competencies in the Corporation

This dimension indicates the extent of development of HRD competencies in the organisation. The competencies include knowledge, attitudes, values and skills. The nature of competencies required for each category of employees is listed and assessed on the basis of the HRD audit. The employee categories that need to be assessed for arriving at a rating on this include the following:

- The HRD staff
- The top management
- Line managers and supervisory staff
- Union and association leaders
- Workmen, operators and grassroots-level employees
- Each of these groups is assessed on the basis of the following:The level of HRD skills they possess
- Their attitudes and support to learning and their own development
- The extent to which they facilitate learning among others in the corporation and those who work with them
- Their attitudes and support to the HRD function and systems

The internal efficiency of the HRD function (HRD department) as a measure of its structure and internal credibility is also assessed for this dimension. The dimensions on which the efficiency is assessed include appropriateness of the systems in operation, operational efficiency (cost-effectiveness), quality of HRD services, speed of delivery and responsiveness (cycle time, speed and quality) and internal customer satisfaction levels. Some insights into these dimensions can be obtained from some parts of the responses to the HRD audit questionnaires and HRD competency surveys.

The following questions need to be answered by the respective groups on a 10-point rating scale.

HRD Staff

TVRLS has evolved a competency list for all HRD professionals on the basis of years of audit and working with HR since mid-seventies. The competency model lists 10 competencies as mentioned in the earlier chapter on HR competencies.

These competencies are assessed using multiple methods:

- Examination of the professional qualification profiles of all HR staff for their functional knowledge and skills
- 360-degree feedback of each individual staff
- Self-assessment

- Assessment centres to test skills
- How professionally qualified are they?
- Are they aware of the business context?
- Do they know about products, customers, markets, competitors, costs, quality, suppliers and other stakeholders adequately?
- Do they seem to demonstrate an adequate knowledge base?
- Are they adequately trained in the appropriate HRD systems?
- Are they sensitive to internal customer requirements?
- How good is their skill base in implementing various systems?
- Do they demonstrate OCTAPACE values?
- Are they quality conscious?
- Are they familiar with the business goals of the corporation?
- Are they cost conscious?
- Are they empathetic?
- Do they spend adequate time trying to understand the requirements of all categories of employees?
- Are they good in administration? Are they changing managers and employee champions?

Table 12.2 gives the list of competencies to be assessed for HR staff and the department.

The professional preparation questionnaire and the TVRLS–HRD–KA test and the TVRLS–HRD–LOC questionnaire can be used for assessing the aforesaid components. The following scoring system can be used for this purpose.

Take your HR staff as a team and assess the percentage of them having this competence in Column 2 below.

---

5 = All (90 to 100 per cent) of the HR staff have this competence

4 = Most (70 to 80 per cent) of them have this competence to an acceptable level

3 = Some (around 50 or 40 to 60 per cent) of them have this competence

2 = Only a few (20 to 30 per cent) of the current staff have this competence

1 = None (0 to 10 per cent) have this competence; those who have it are negligible

Assess in Column 3 the extent to which those who have this competence have this:

4 = An extraordinary level

3 = To a good level

2 = To a satisfactory level

1 = Whoever has it, it is not up to the mark or to satisfactory level

0 = Competency is very negligible or not present

TABLE 12.2 Level of Competency of HRD Staff and the Department

1 *Competence definition*	2 *Percentage of HR staff having this competence*	3 *Level up to which they have this competence*	4 *Score total: Multiply the score in column 2 with the score in column 3*
1. **Business knowledge:** Knowledge of business (products, services, customers, technology, competitors, developments, R&D) and all functions (sales and marketing, production and operations, finance, systems, MIS, logistics, services, etc.), knowledge of business capital (intellectual) and its constituents and methods of building business capital			
2. **Functional excellence:** (*i*) HR knowledge, (*ii*) HR delivery, including culture sensitivity, empathy, coaching and facilitation			
3. **Leadership and change management:** (*i*) communication, (*ii*) initiative, (*iii*) creativity and (*iv*) change management			
4. **Strategic thinking:** Analytical ability, cost and quality sensitivity, ability to spot opportunities, anticipate and find alternate ways of solving problems			
5. **Personal credibility**			
6. **Technology savvy (including HR technology and research methods)**			
7. **Personnel management and administrative skill**			

(Continued)

TABLE 12.2 Level of Competency of HRD Staff and the Department (*Continued*)

1 *Competence definition*	2 *Percentage of HR staff having this competence*	3 *Level up to which they have this competence*	4 *Score total: Multiply the score in column 2 with the score in column 3*
8. Vision of the function and entrepreneurship			
9. Learning attitude and self-management: (*i*) self-awareness and desire to learn, (*ii*) time management, (*iii*) networking and (*iv*) research and analytical skills			
10. Execution skills: (*i*) planning and monitoring skills, (*ii*) cultural sensitivity, (*iii*) persuasive skills, (*iv*) behaviour modification techniques and group dynamics, (*v*) ability to craft interventions for implementation and (*vi*) cost and quality sensitivity			
Overall score	A total of 200 points (10 × 20)		

Professional Preparation of HRD Managers: A Scoring Scheme

As stated in Chapter 8, an HRD manager should have gone through at least about 10 courses equivalent of academic or professional preparation in HRD. Normally, completing a course in an academic institution means about 100 hours of work, including about 30 contact hours with faculty. This makes about 800 hours of professional preparation. TVRLS, a firm specialising in HRD audit, has developed the following scheme to assess the adequacy of the professional preparation using the professional preparation questionnaire for HRD managers given here.

S. No.	*Academic proficiency area*	*Points*	*Implementation proficiency area*	*Points*	*Total points*
1.	Integrated HRD systems (including strategic HR)		HRD business strategy linkages		

(*Continued*)

S. No.	Academic proficiency area	Points	Implementation proficiency area	Points	Total points
2.	Competency mapping and competency-based HR systems		Role of competencies and designing competency-based HR systems		
3.	Performance management systems		Performance appraisals, reward management, performance-linked pay, 360-degree appraisals		
4.	Career planning and development		Career planning, job rotation, succession planning, designing and implementing		
5.	Potential appraisal, development and assessment centres		Potential appraisal exercises, promotion policies, assessment centres		
6.	Organisational diagnosis and OD		OD exercises, self-renewal, quality circles, job redesign and other OD exercises		
7.	Personal growth and counselling		Feedback and counselling, monitoring, research, review		
8.	Training and management of learning systems		Training programmes, identification of training needs, designing, evaluating and monitoring training		
9.	Worker development		Worker development initiatives		
10.	Organisational structure and dynamics		Restructuring, downsizing, new structure designing, role negotiation, role directories		
11.	HR information system and other IT applications		IT applications to HR, skill inventory, scientific recruitment		

(*Continued*)

S. No.	Academic proficiency area	Points	Implementation proficiency area	Points	Total points
12.	Other related areas – leadership, Myers Briggs Type Indicator (MBTI), seven habits, creativity, quality circles, etc.		Continuous learning and networking		

Each candidate is to be assessed on the basis of the form filled in earlier (see Chapter 11). The academic preparation is to be assessed on the basis of educational qualifications, such as diplomas, certificates and degrees. Educational qualifications and training programmes attended indicate this. Items 5, 7 and 9 in the aforesaid questionnaire are useful for this purpose. Items 5 and 9 are useful to assess the implementation experience.

The following guidelines may be used. The proficiency ratings may be based on the 5-point scale given in Item 9 of the questionnaire.

---

5 = very highly proficient; 4 = highly proficient; 3 = somewhat proficient; 2 = only acquainted and not proficient; 1 = needs to learn a lot, long way to go; 0 = not at all proficient and not even familiar with the basics

---

The judgement is to be made by an expert auditor. For an objective evaluation, this format should be supplemented with an individual interview.

Learning Attitudes of Line Managers and Supervisory Staff

- How much do they understand the significance of HRD?
- Are they interested and motivated to develop themselves?
- Are they willing to spend their time and effort in developing their subordinates?
- How supportive are they of HRD efforts?
- Do they have listening and other skills required to facilitate development of their juniors?
- Do they use different sources of learning?

Table 12.3 provides details of the learning attitudes of line managers and supervisory staff.

TABLE 12.3 Attitude of Line Managers to Learn

1 *Weightage points*	2 *Source of learning*	3 *xtent to which line managers use this as a source of learning*
10	Performance planning and review discussions	
10	Departmental meetings, in-house communications	
5	Reading books	
10	Internet	
5	Project reports, including consultancy reports and diagnostic studies	
5	Outside visitors and others	
5	From each other, through presentations, discussions, meetings, etc.	
5	Newspapers and magazines of business	
5	Functional journals and other literature	
10	Training programmes: in-house programmes and seminars	
10	Training programmes, outside programmes	
5	Seniors and mentors from inside the company or outside	
10	Mistakes	
5	Other sources	
Total: Overall learning score (maximum possible: 100 points)		

Given in the following are a number of sources from where line managers learn. The maximum number of sources they use, the higher the learning attitude. Please rate in the following the learning tendency of your line managers on the basis of the information available to you. The scale to be used for a weightage of 10 is given in brackets.

5 = Line mangers use this source very well and effectively (9–10)
4 = Line managers use this source most of the time or quite effectively (7–8)
3 = Line managers use this source sometimes and somewhat effectively (5–6)
2 = Line managers may use this source occasionally or once in a while (3–4)
1 = Line managers do not use this source that effectively (1–2)
0 = Line managers do not use this resource/source (0)

Top Management

- Do they understand the HRD function and its significance in achieving business goals?
- How supportive are they of HRD interventions and values?
- Are their leadership styles facilitative of a learning culture?
- Are they willing to give the time needed for HRD?
- How well do they subscribe to the HRD values like the OCTAPACE values?
- How well do they practice HRD values?
- How committed are they to create a learning culture in the organisation?
- Do they invest their time, effort and energies in employee development?

Table 12.4 is indicative of the assessment to be made of the top management styles that support HRD.

Please rate in the following the extent to which your top-level managers (directors, SBU heads, HODs) and all other senior managers whose styles have an impact on the larger team exhibit a developmental style. Developmental style is defined as a style that encourages learning and development of knowledge, attitudes, skills and values.

Your Assessment

How many of them use the following rating scale?

4 = All or almost all
3 = Most of the top
2 = Some of them; about half
1 = A few
0 = None
NA = This is not applicable

How frequently they use the style? Rate using the following scale:

5 = Almost all the time (90% to 100%)
4 = Most of the time (75%)
3 = Some times (50%)
2 = Occasionally (25%)
1 = Rarely or never (0 to 10%)
NA = Not applicable

TABLE 12.4 Top Management Styles

1 Development style: Area or dimension	Extent of development style by top management		4 Total score 2 × 3
	2 How many?	3 How frequently?	

1. **Decision making:** *Reasons for decisions are given and debated and discussed to promote development among employees.*

2. **Goal setting:** Goal setting is done by learning from each other, and employees are encouraged to discuss and gain from each other.

3. **Managing mistakes:** When mistakes are made they are used as learning experiences.

4. **Managing conflicts:** When conflicts occur, concerned teams and employees are encouraged to sort them out themselves and grow.

5. **Rewards and recognitions** are given to encourage learning and development.

6. **Conducting meetings:** Meetings are used to help employees learn.

7. **Policy formulation:** Employees are communicated and encouraged to learn in policy formulation than keeping the policies as secretive.

8. **Communicationis** open and encourages all employees to learn rather than being secretive.

9. **Top management work as a team** and set role models for others.

10. **:Top management is a reflective and self-renewing team:** They undertake self-renewal exercise and use 360-degree feedback and other mechanisms as learning experiences.

Total score (maximum possible = 200 points)/2 = score for 100 points

Non-Supervisory Staff, Including Workmen and Their Association Leaders and Representatives

- How much of a developmental role are they playing?
- Do they see their own role in HRD?
- Are they committed to create a learning organisation?
- Are they willing to promote employee development?
- Are they positive in their approach and perceive their own roles as supportive of organisation building?
- Do they perceive the significance of employee development for organisation building?

One of the things that can easily be measured is their learning attitude and the sources of learning. Table 12.5 presents a simple way of measuring the learning orientation of non-supervisory staff.

TABLE 12.5 Learning Orientation of Non-Supervisory Categories of Employees, Including Unions Leaders and Representatives (Workmen, Operators, Unionised Categories of Employees, Field Staff, etc.)

S. No.	Activity	Extent to which they take it seriously and learn from the same
1	Training – in-house	
2	Training – outside	
3	Multi-skilling activities	
4	Job rotation, cross-functional teams and work groups	
5	Health-, safety- and environment-related activities, including training	
6	Quality circles, shop floor councils and such other small group activities (not meant for skills upgradation)	
7	Suggestions schemes	
8	Communications from HRD, top management, etc.	
9	Self-initiated activities of the union and other bodies	
10	Other activities unique to your organisation	

Total score: Out of a maximum of 60 points

Please rate the extent to which they take the following activities seriously and are willing to learn from them. Rate the extent to which they exhibit a learning orientation in each of these activities. Use the following scale:

6 = Very great extent
5 = Large extent
4 = Some extent
3 = Little extent
2 = Negligible extent
0–1= Not at all
NA= Not applicable

Your Assessment

HRD Function

The following dimensions need to be assessed:

- Adequacy of manpower
- Appropriateness of the structure
- Cost consciousness of staff
- Quality consciousness of the HRD staff
- Responsiveness of the HRD department to the needs of employees, managers, staff, workmen and union leaders
- Level of internal customer satisfaction
- Internal operational efficiency of the department
- Level of internal synergy among the staff
- Are the staff the first to implement HRD systems? Do they implement them in an exemplary way?

Table 12.6 gives a scoring system for measuring the credibility and competency of HR department:

Please rate in the following the extent to which HRD department and its activities have a credible image in your company. Credibility is the extent to which employees rely, respect and believe in what is said. Credibility includes trust, faith, trustworthiness and a positive image and attitude towards that aspect.
    Use the following scale:

5 = Very much true
4 = Mostly true

3 = Somewhat true
2 = Only a little true
0–1 = Not at all true

Your Assessment

An HRD competency maturity score can be assigned on the basis of the competency levels of each category.

A* All categories of employees (top management, line managers, union leaders and HR staff) have an extremely high competence base in HRD (knowledge, attitudes, values and skills); the HRD department is appropriately structured and has a high internal efficiency and satisfaction levels.

B The competence levels of every group are at an acceptable level, and the internal efficiency of the HRD department and internal customer satisfaction are at acceptable levels.

D The competencies of more than one group are below the acceptable level and/or the HRD department is not internally efficient or is not appropriately structured and does not meet the requirements of the minimum-level internal customer satisfaction.

F There is total failure on almost all the dimensions.

The other scales (A, B*, C, C*, D*) are on similar grounds as given earlier.

TABLE 12.6 Credibility of the HR Department and Its Activities

S. No.	HRD staff and department dimension	Your rating
1	HR staff is relied on for what they say. They are trusted to speak the truth	
2	HR staff is seen as professionally competent	
3	HR department staff is seen as humane and helpful	
4	HR policies are viewed by employees with respect and positively	
5	HR staff is seen as genuine and not indulging in politics	
6	HR policies are seen as unbiased and not favouring any one group or team	
7	HR communications are trusted for what they say	
8	HR systems and practices are viewed with interest and taken seriously	
Total score (maximum 40 points)		

HRD Culture and Values

The extent to which the HRD culture, HRD styles and values are practised and stabilised in the corporation are measured and represented by the third letter in the HRD Score Card. The HRD culture is a culture that promotes the development of human potential. It is also a culture that promotes a learning organisation. The following dimensions are assessed for this purpose:

- *Openness*: The extent to which the employees are open to suggestions of each other, learn from each other and express views, ideas and opinions freely, positively and productively
- *Collaboration*: The extent to which the employees collaborate with each other, are willing to sacrifice individual and personal goals for group, organisational or business goals and priorities; the extent of synergy existing between and within departments or sections, levels, categories of employees, etc.
- *Trust and trustworthiness*: The extent to which employees trust each other and the systems in the organisation and the extent to which they are reliable, keep up their verbal commitments and promises and do not lie
- *Authenticity*: The extent to which employees say things they mean and there is congruence between their intentions and their statements and actions
- *Proaction*: The extent to which employees take initiative; proaction is a culture of the organisation in solving problems and in every other aspect
- *Autonomy*: The extent to which there is an appropriate level of autonomy and at least some amount of freedom available for each role holder in the organisation to exercise some discretion and judgement
- *Confrontation*: The extent to which there is a culture of facing problems and issues squarely and discussing them rather than ignoring them or putting them under the carpet
- *Experimentation*: The extent to which employees are encouraged to take risks and experiment with new ideas and new ways of doing things
- *Learning culture*: The extent to which the organisation uses mistakes and deviations as learning opportunities and the extent to which the top management styles, internal communications, meetings, circulars and other events promote learning
- *Listening*: The extent to which employees listen to each other and have empathy for each other

The culture is assessed using the HRD audit questionnaire. The HRD climate part of the questionnaires gives an idea of the culture. These need to be supplemented by the observations of the auditor.

TABLE 12.7 HRD Culture and Values

OCTAPACE values	Extent professed	Extent of practice	Total
1. **Openness:** Employees are encouraged to express freely their views, opinions and exhibit their talent through the same.			
2. **Collaboration and team work:** Employees at all levels work as a team, help each other and collaborate with each other.			
3. **Trust and trustworthiness:** People trust each other and keep up their promises. People practise what they preach.			
4. **Authenticity:** People speak what they mean and not say things to please each other.			
5. **Proactivity and initiative:** Employees take initiative and do things without having to be directed all the time.			
6. **Autonomy:** Employees have freedom to do things on their own. There is freedom and autonomy in their work.			
7. **Confrontation:** Employees face issues and confront rather than hide issues.			
8. **Experimentation:** Employees are encouraged to experiment and try out new ideas.			
Total score: OCTAPACE			

The system used in *HRD Score Card 2500* is summarised in Table 12.7. This includes both OCTAPACE values and organisational culture for 500 points.

Assess the extent to which the HRD values are professed and practised in this section.

Organisational Culture

From Items 9 to 25 in the following, rate the extent to which the dimension under consideration is a characteristic of your organisation using the following scale:

9–10 = Extremely characteristic
7–8 = Highly characteristic or characterises most of the time and in most parts of the organisation
5–6 = Somewhat characteristic of the organisation or some parts have this culture and others do not

3–4 = This is a little characteristic or in a few sections this is present or practised, but most part of the organisation does not characterise this

0–2 = This is totally absent or present to a small degree

B. *Organisational culture*	*Assessment*

9. *Leadership climate:* Where the leaders manage the mistakes of juniors, manage their conflicts, provide resources and support juniors and respond to their failures.

10. *Motivation:* There are mechanisms to motivate employees, the employees are encouraged to talk about one's responsibilities with enthusiasm and regard, there is a high commitment to work and there is inspiration to work.

11. *Communication:* Where the communication mechanisms are good and meet the needs of employees, and there is adequate upward and downward communication, formal and informal communication and verbal and written communication to meet employee needs and make them feel a part of the organisation.

12. *Decision making:* Where the decision making is participative, logical, analytical, objective and analytical, objective and timely and ensures the interests of the organisation.

13. *Goals:* Where goal setting is objective, follows norms and rules and based on dialogues and SMART.

14. *Control:* Where there is adequate direction and supervision of work, systems are used to ensure checks and there are internal controls.

15. *Shared values:* Where there are well-articulated values of the organisation, they are shared across the organisation, and they are transmitted to new recruits and employees across various levels and departments.

16. *Quality orientation:* Where there is quality consciousness across the organisation and quality systems are used.

17. *Rewards and recognition:* Where there are adequate mechanisms to recognise and reward desired behaviour and efficacy or effectiveness, rewards and recognition systems are administered with objectivity.

18. *Information:* Where information is shared across various levels and departments of the organisation, and people maintain confidentiality where necessary, and there are systems and mechanisms for sharing information.

19. *Empowerment:* Where there are efforts made to empower employees to act with authority, and delegation and autonomy are provided adequately.

20. *Learning orientation:* Where there is support to learning from the top management, organisational efforts are made to stimulate learning and employees have positive attitude towards learning.

(Continued)

B. *Organisational culture*	*Assessment*

21. **Openness to change:** Where the top management and senior managers are open and receptive to change, they are aware of the need to change, they are open to change and have formal mechanisms and facilitators to manage change.
22. **Corporate social responsibility:** Employees are sensitive to their environment and surroundings and exhibit a high degree of social responsibility and citizenship that extends beyond our organisation to the local community and the country where the organisation is located.
23. **Health:** Our climate emphasises health and promotes healthy living. Employees here are health conscious.
24. **Safety:** Employees here are tuned to ensure the safety and security of themselves and each other. Our culture is tuned to ensure safety, and physical and mental security of employees.
25. **Work satisfaction and motivation:** Employees are satisfied and are motivated to work.
Overall score on 17 dimensions out of 340 (add and multiply the total by 2)

HRD Linkage to Business Goals and HRD's Impact

This can measure the extent to which HRD efforts (tools, processes, culture, etc.) are driven to achieve business or organisational goals. The goals include:

- Business excellence, including profitability and other outcomes the organisation is expected to achieve
- Formation of intellectual capital, including customer capital, investor capital, brand, intellectual property, etc.
- Internal operational efficiencies
- Internal customer satisfaction
- External customer satisfaction
- Employee motivation and commitment
- Cost-effectiveness and cost-consciousness among employees
- Quality orientation
- Technology adoption

The HRD system should focus on the aforesaid dimensions and check on the following:

- Are HRD systems aligned towards aforementioned or other important business goals of the corporation?

- Do HRD staff reflects adequate understanding and commitment to the business goals of the organisation?
- Do HRD processes and culture drive the employees and the corporation towards achieving the business goals and address the business concerns?
- Are HRD systems, processes, structure, culture and styles sensitive to the changing needs of the organisation?

Table 12.8 gives the impact measures as envisaged in *HRD Score Card 2500*.

TABLE 12.8 HRD Impact and Business Linkages

Assess the extent to which the following dimensions are impacted by HRD systems, processes and practices in your organisation on the basis of your recent experiences.

Use the following 7-point scale:

5 = To a great extent;

4 = To a significant extent;

3 = To some extent;

2 = To a small extent;

1 = To a very small extent;

0 = Not at all;

−1 = The reverse is perhaps true to a marginal degree (there is a minimal negative impact);

−2 = The reverse is true to a noticeable extent (there has been a significant negative impact).

A. Impact on Talent

Talent management	Your assessment	Final score (assessment × 10)
1. Talent attraction and acquisition		
2. Talent management: induction and integration		
3. Talent management: human resource utilisation and employee engagement (PMS, placements, incentives, performance management, mentoring and coaching, feedback)		
4. Talent management: HR development or competency building and renewal		
5. Retention and separations management		
Total points (maximum = 5 × 50 = 250)		

B. Impact on Intellectual Capital Formation

Assess using the same scale as given previously.

Intellectual capital	Your assessment	Final score (assessment × 2)
6. Intellectual capital formation and structural capital: Customer capital		
7. Intellectual capital: Impact on structural capital formation attributable to HR interventions		
8. Intellectual capital formation: Contributions to human capital formation		
9. Intellectual capital formation: Contributions to social capital		
10: Intellectual capital: Contributions to emotional capital		
11. Intellectual capital: HR contributions to relationship capital		
12. Intellectual capital: Contributions to knowledge capital formation		
13. HRD systems, strategy and structure		
14. HRD competencies		
15. Values and culture		
Total points (maximum points = 10 × 20 = 200)		

C. Impact on Financial Performance

Financial measures	Your assessment	Final score (assessment × 10)
16. Financial performance indicators attributable to HR competencies (cost reductions attributable to departmental or individual competencies). Degree of financial literacy among employees. Increases in sales per employee attributable to HR interventions. Market value to book value attributable to HR (image and brand building due to competent managers and leadership development).		
Total points (out of maximum 50)		

Summary

The HRD Score Card is an assessment of the HRD maturity level of any organisation. It assigns a four-letter rating that represents the four critical dimensions of HRD contributing to organisational performance, namely, HRD systems maturity and strategies, HRD competencies in the company, HRD culture and values and business impact and alignment of HRD (strategies, structure, competencies, systems, culture, styles, etc.). The score obtained indicates the extent to which HRD efforts (tools, processes, culture, etc.) are intrinsically sound (first three) and are driven to achieve business or organisational goals (last one). The score card is resultant of the HRD audit. Using multiple methodologies described in this book, any organisation can be assigned a score. Such scoring is assigned by the external auditors and the HRD audit is the ideal time to assign such scores. The system is intended in due course to become like the ISO certification system. By taking one look at the score card anyone can identify the weak areas and plan corrective action.

13

WRITING THE HRD AUDIT REPORT

The HRD audit report is meant for practitioners. It is not a research report. Its main objective is to highlight areas that need improvement and that need to be acted upon. Its purpose is also to help the top management and the HRD staff recognise and retain the company's strengths. It is likely to be read widely by the line managers and the top management. Since the line managers and top management are not accustomed to reading long research reports, extra care should be taken to make the HRD audit report short and precise. It is useful to prepare it in bullet form highlighting the strengths and weaknesses. A model outline of the report is given as follows.

Model Outline

Executive Summary

Chapter 1   Introduction: Context
Chapter 2   Current Status of the HRD Function; Some Facts
Chapter 3   General Observations
Chapter 4   HRD Systems: Career Systems
Chapter 5   HRD Systems: Work Planning
Chapter 6   HRD Systems: Development System
Chapter 7   HRD Systems: Self-renewal System
Chapter 8   HRD Strategies, Culture and Values
Chapter 9   HRD Function and HRD Competencies
Chapter 10   HRD Impact and Alignment: Intellectual Capital and Talent Management

DOI: 10.4324/9781003530534-16

Tables and Appendices

Chapters 4, 5, 6 and 7 can be condensed into one chapter and called HRD Systems and Strategies. The strategies can be taken as a part of culture and values as the strategies identified are close to culture and values and are long term.

Chapter 1: Introduction

This section can contain the following components briefly:

1.1 An introduction to the company, highlighting its manpower, turnover, locations, products and services, its main concerns and its top management
1.2 A brief description of the dates and reasons for commissioning the audit
1.3 A brief description of the framework and methodology adopted for the study – the methodology should describe details of the sample, audit methods used (questionnaires administered, number of individual interviews, level-wise records and reports examined, group interviews, etc.)
1.4 A brief description of the HRD systems framework (various subsystems of HRD audit, etc.)
1.5 Future plans of the company and competency requirements

Chapter 2: Current Status of the HRD Function

In this chapter the status of HRD function should be presented in detail. This should describe the following:

2.1 Structure and staffing of the HRD function
2.2 HRD department's thrust areas and objectives
2.3 Highlights of the HRD systems and subsystems – a brief description of the existing HRD systems in practice (performance appraisal, potential appraisal, career planning, mentoring, training, job rotation, quality circles, etc.); in describing the factual situation either Rao and Pareek's (Rao and Pareek, 1994) framework can be used, or alternatively, a mere description of the subsystems and main concerns can be highlighted
2.4 Strengths and weaknesses of the HRD function
2.5 HRD needs: An overview – broad highlights of the areas that need attention

Chapter 3: General Observations

This chapter should highlight the salient features of the company that were observed by the auditors in relation to its present competencies and future potential. It may be useful to introduce the importance of the three dimensions of HRD: competence building, culture building and commitment building.

3.1 Business concerns for the present and future: Highlights
3.2 Competencies and competency requirements for the future
3.3 General observations about the competencies found
3.4 General observations about the competency-promoting mechanisms
3.5 Commitment and motivational patterns
3.6 Commitment- and motivation-promoting mechanisms
3.7 Work culture and organisational culture
3.8 Culture-building mechanisms

A brief explanation of the importance of the three components can be given, followed by highlighting the general strengths and weaknesses of the company in relation to the HR areas, which can cover the following:

- Any of the contextual factors that seem to have an impact on the HRD culture of the organisation (e.g., the general situation in the industry posing major opportunities or threats to the organisation, a technological innovation affecting the organisation, profile changes in the customers or changes in their expectations, changes in leadership or management or any recent event or problem having an impact on the HR function)
- Any strikingly excellent or weak parts of the HRD function
- The general strengths and weaknesses of the company

Chapter 4: HRD Systems – Career Systems

This chapter can describe the findings of the audit in relation to competency mapping, manpower planning, recruitment, promotions, career planning and development and succession planning. The general pattern to be followed in this chapter can include:

4.1 Importance
4.2 Manpower planning and utilisation – strengths, weaknesses and recommendations
4.3 Recruitment – strengths, weaknesses and recommendations
4.4 Potential appraisal and fast track – strengths, weaknesses and recommendations

4.5 Career planning and development – strengths, weaknesses and recommendations

4.6 Succession planning – strengths, weaknesses and recommendations

4.7 Competency mapping as a basis for career systems

While describing the strengths, weaknesses and giving recommendations, the auditor should consolidate all sources of data. The auditor should give his or her own observations and then substantiate them, if necessary and wherever possible, by the questionnaire data. Wherever there are discrepancies between the questionnaire data and his or her own observations, it is important for the auditor to point out his or her observations and also highlight the reasons for deviation or difference between the two.

The auditor must bear in mind that the reader is not aware of the technicalities and what is required is an expert opinion. Having studied the organisation for a full week or so and used all different types of methodologies, it is naturally expected that the auditor will give concluding observations rather than tentative ones. Thus, the auditor must reconcile the various data and observations and come to a definite conclusion. Where doubts persist and there are reasons to believe that the issue needs further investigation or observation, the audit report may say so and incorporate a recommendation for further investigation or sensitivity on the part of the top management.

This pattern can be followed in all the following chapters, from Chapters 5 to 9, and, therefore, need not be repeated for the subsequent chapters.

Chapter 5: HRD Systems: Work-Planning Systems

A similar approach can be followed in relation to the work-planning system. The following subsections may be used for reporting. In each of the following subsections, the strengths followed by the weaknesses and recommendations can be highlighted in bullet form.

5.1 Introduction – (introduce the concepts of work planning briefly, followed by the component systems)

5.2 Contextual analysis

5.3 Role clarity through competency mapping

5.4 PMS

Chapter 6: HRD Systems: Development System

This chapter may be presented and organised in the following manner:

6.1 Introduction and components

6.2 Induction training

6.3 Training and learning systems

6.4 Performance guidance and development
6.5 Worker development
6.6 Other mechanisms of development

Chapter 7: HRD Systems: Self-Renewal System

The strengths, weaknesses and recommendations can be highlighted in each of the following sections:

7.1 Introduction
7.2 Role efficacy
7.3 OD interventions and processes
7.4 Action-oriented research

Chapter 8: HRD Culture and Values

8.1 Introduction
8.2 Organisational culture
8.3 OCTAPACE and other values
8.4 HRD Strategies: Quality orientation, communication, empowerment through participation, talent management, etc.

Chapter 9: HRD Function and HRD Competencies

9.1 General observations of HRD Department and its functioning and credibility
9.2 Personnel policies and HRD
9.3 HRD function – structure
9.4 HRD department – competencies
9.5 HRD activities and priorities
9.6 Line managers' attitudes and sources of learning
9.7 Top management styles and empowerment
9.8 Workmen attitudes and development

Chapter 10: Business Impact of HRD and Alignment

10.1 General observations on HR impact
10.2 HR's impact on intellectual capital building: Customers and other forms of capital
10.3 HR's impact on talent management
10.4 HR's impact on financial parameters

Tables and Appendices

14

DESIGNING AND USING HRD AUDIT FOR BUSINESS IMPROVEMENT

This chapter answers a number of issues relating to the design and use of HRD audit. The studies discussed earlier indicate that HRD plays a strategic role in business improvement. In corporations where it has not played a significant role, it has not done so for one or more of the following reasons:

- Top management not recognising the strategic role of the HR function and not paying it the attention it deserves
- Low-level competencies of HRD managers and staff
- Introduction of inappropriate systems and over-focusing on unproductive HR practices
- Failure of the line managers to develop ownership of HRD

HRD audit can point out these or the other reasons for the failure of the HR function. Therefore, HRD audit can become an important intervention to rejuvenate the HR function and align it to business goals.

A good HRD audit should point out the following to the corporation and its top management.

A broad indication of the competency requirements of the future to achieve planned business outcomes

This would need a detailed follow-up to list and develop strategies to develop these competencies. HRD audit does not give any exhaustive list of these competencies but can suggest mechanisms for generating competency lists or profiles. The corporation needs to follow it up and use it as a starting point.

DOI: 10.4324/9781003530534-17

An indication of the value addition, including motivational value, by the current systems and subsystems of HRD, and the areas needing improvement

This may require some redesigning of the existing HRD systems or sharpening their impact. This may also require the elimination of some of the obsolete or unproductive HR systems that have become liabilities for the organisation. Normally, HR audit also indicates the potential of each system relevant to the organisation and the current assets and liabilities in the subsystem. These assets and liabilities may deal with the components or elements of a system; its goals or subclass, mechanisms, the manner of implementation, processes associated with it, including the way the system is managed; the people involved and their roles; historical anomalies; and other bottlenecks. All these require a thorough follow-up by the HR department and other role holders. Usually, the results of an HRD audit tend to give a new life to the HR function and a good opportunity for it to make an impact once again.

An indication of the competency gaps of the HR staff

This can include knowledge gaps, attitudinal gaps and task focus and skill gaps. As indicated by Ulrich (1997b) HRD now is a profession, has its own body of knowledge and requires a good deal of professional preparation. The competency gaps pointed out by the audit should set an agenda for building the competencies of the HRD staff. The follow-up actions may have implications for future recruitment into the HRD department as well as for sponsoring the existing staff for professional programmes, studies, visits, etc. A timetable may need to be prepared and a development plan may emerge on the basis of the audit.

An indication of the current roles being performed by the top management, line managers, union and association leaders and other stake- holders, and the gaps between what they could do and what they are currently doing

These gaps can indicate a course of action to be followed. The course of action can be in terms of redefining roles, time allocations for important tasks, training, appreciation courses, role negotiation exercises and so on. This, therefore, sets an agenda for more involvement or better quality of involvement of some of the stakeholders.

An indication of the alignment of the HR strategies with the business goals

While addressing this issue, the HRD audit may also inadvertently refer to the business goals and processes. Although it is not the job of HRD audit to comment on other systems and processes, no system or process can be totally independent of people. Hence, the HRD audit is likely to indicate the need for aligning the human processes with some of the systems or vice versa. This will throw up a new agenda for further assessment or action.

How to Use HRD Audit

The following are some of the steps that a corporation may undertake after the audit report is presented.

1. *Insist on a written report.* A written document is essential for action. Presentations remain only in the minds of a few and get distorted over a period of time. If there are sensitive issues (business sensitivity and human process sensitivity), the auditor may just give an indication of these rather than writing about them in detail
2. *Insist on making the presentation to the top management.* Normally, without the top management's commitment, not much gets done. In the audits that I conduct, the presentation forms a part of the contract. Sometimes I have insisted on it though the client has not been keen on it for whatever reasons. A presentation gets everyone at the top to become sensitive to the HR issues and the strategic importance of the HR function. Those who are already using the HR function for strategic advantage get reinforced in their beliefs to carry on using it, whereas those who are not using it may get new ideas to focus on the function. In any case, a presentation generates more ownership and the possibility of future action
3. *Appoint a task force or a number of task groups to follow up on the report and its recommendations.* Such task forces can be decided upon during the presentation of the audit report
4. *Finalise the exact membership of the task force subsequently and announce it in appropriate forums.* Being a member of such task forces also builds the capabilities of those involved to become better managers. It gives them a lot of exposure to and experience in HR areas, so vital for success at the top level. Line managers should therefore be encouraged to become members of such task forces
5. *Ask the HRD department to study the report and prepare its own action plan.* This should be made a compulsory requirement. In addition, it is also useful to appoint another independent group to study the report and give its recommendations for prioritising various actions. A group comprising line managers will help in better alignment of the HR function with business concerns

6. *Communicate a summary of the report and the intended follow-up actions in the form of a circular or in-house newsletter.* Those who have provided the data for the audit will feel like giving more in future if they know that their time investments are giving some results. It is useful and even necessary to inform the employees (at least those involved but preferably all) about the relevant recommendations or observations from the audit report. Some judgment has to be exercised while communicating the observations. A group of HR and line managers may be able to decide the content of such communication better. Some of this communication may sound critical of the HR department. The HR staff should set an example of self-criticism and self-renewal. Any HRD audit report will sound critical of the HR function. If it is not critical, then there is no need to change. Any change involves a certain amount of discomfort. The HR staff should realise that the audit itself is a courageous step and the criticism is an invited one to lay the foundations for growth and development

   Disseminating the report and encouraging a critical reflection of the HR processes is the first important step in spreading the influence of the HR function and facilitating business improvement.
7. *Have a review mechanism set up after six months and plan for an internal micro-audit after a year or two.* Review and monitoring mechanisms are important to ensure that the audit results are taken seriously and that improvements are made. The review mechanisms can be in the form of a presentation by the HR department or by an independent task force or a revisit by the external audit team for a quick study

Role of CEOs and Top Management

Getting the best out of HRD audit needs a good deal of involvement of the top management or the CEO and his team. The total time involved may not be more than 10 to 15 hours in a year for the entire exercise, including follow-up. For example, the following (see Table 14.1) will be the time commitments required by the CEO.

Thus, 12 hours is the minimum time that important business issues like aligning the people and their competencies for the business goals and improvements deserve. The returns that a company can achieve from this definitely warrant such an involvement of the CEO. A CEO who cannot give this time may need to examine his or her role as well as his or her time management.

Approximately double this time may be required by line managers to constitute internal task forces for implementing the recommendations of the HRD audit.

TABLE 14.1 Time Commitment Required by the CEO

Activity	Approximate time
• Initial meeting and discussion with the HR chief for initiating an HRD audit	1/2 hour
• First meeting with the consultant to understand the HRD audit and communicate concerns	1 hour
• Second detailed meeting to share business strategies and HR concerns	$11/_2$ hours
• Initiation of the HRD audit and attending the introductory talk by the consultant along with other line managers	1 hour
• Presentation of the HRD audit results and discussions	2–3 hours
• In-house follow-up meeting and plans	1 hour
• Review meeting after three months	1 hour
• Review meeting after six months	1 hour
• Review meeting after one year	1 hour
• Re-audit presentations and discussions	1 hour
Total hours in a year	12 hours

The CEO should play the role of an unbiased participant and should be willing to listen to the external auditor. Of course, he need not accept everything the auditor says. A good CEO can even use the opportunity to generate feedback from the consultant about his or her own role and style and the extent to which they are in tune with what is required by the organisation. The auditors are likely to get a lot of insights about the perceptions of the people about the style of the CEO. What is said of the CEO is also true for the top management team.

The HRD audit can help in aligning human resources with the business plans of various units and departments. This is a good opportunity for all top-level managers to get to know what is happening to the people in their units or divisions or functions. They can set their own departmental agendas for the HRD audit. If they so desire, the auditors can be mandated to give separate division-wise reports. As this may require variations in methodology to some extent (e.g., division-wise meetings and interviews besides questionnaire analysis), the top manager or divisional head should make it a point to provide all the data and set goals from the beginning.

Audit and Other Forms of Evaluation: Role of CEOs

The CEO has a very important role to play in ensuring that a good audit is conducted and that the audit report is used for improvements. If the CEO is looking for only positive feedback about the corporation and expects the audit to compliment his or her accomplishments, he or she may be in for some surprise. This is because there is always scope for improvement even in the best of organisations as every organisation has some weak areas. Some CEOs get an HRD audit done out of curiosity, and once the presentation is made they tend to take a view that they knew most of their weaknesses and the audit has only reinforced their knowledge and that there is nothing new in the report. By saying this they tend to maintain a status quo. This danger of self-justification should be avoided as such CEOs are likely to do more harm than good to their own corporation in the long run. It is recommended that the CEO treat the HRD audit as a serious exercise and do the following:

- Understand what HRD audit means and the potential it has to bring about business improvement. Read some sample HRD audit reports and set a good agenda in addition to focal points for the HRD audit. Some case studies are given in this book to help CEOs set an agenda
- Allocate an appropriate budget for the audit. Inspire and influence the other members of the top management by talking about the potential benefits of the audit and get them mentally prepared to supply information and to use the audit report. They should be enthused to look forward to the audit report
- Enthuse the heads of departments to seek department-wise audit comments as it provides scope for them to improve themselves
- Give time to the auditors in the beginning of the audit and at the end of the audit. In the beginning, time should be given to help them understand the corporate plans and vision, your views of the competency gaps and requirements at various levels, your own efforts to build human competencies and your frustrations and failures
- Give time at the end of the audit to understand the findings. Insist on a draft report. Go through the draft report, circulate it among the HODs, or the top team, or an internal task force, and seek their views or explanations
- Organise a formal presentation along with the draft report, if possible, and see that the data are shared and issues raised and clarified
- Get an implementation team going and monitor the implementation of the recommendations

Role of Line Managers in HRD Audit

The success of the audit also depends on cooperation from line managers. It is the line managers who are the suppliers of information as well as the beneficiaries of a good HRD audit implementation programme. The line managers supply information regarding the HRD needs, their own perceptions of the HRD function, their expectations, etc. The audit reports normally talk about the gaps in the attitudes and behaviour of line managers. These may deal with their attitudes towards HR systems, commitment towards implementation of HR systems, OCTAPACE and other values and their own role in developing their juniors and others. Thus, the audit report provides good avenues for reflection. Line managers will do well by insisting on a department-wise audit and using the data for improvements. They should not use the HRD audit as an opportunity to express their frustrations or as a cribbing session. Line managers should also get involved in seeking feedback from the audit and insisting on the implementation of the recommendations.

Most line managers tend to treat HRD audit as something undertaken for the sake of the HRD department. This attitude partly results from a very inadequate understanding of their HR role. It is by now well established that all forms of resource management constitute the important role of line manager. Among these, managing and developing human resources is the most critical factor for their success. Those who cannot inspire, develop, motivate and manage their own staff cannot do well as top-level managers or CEOs of corporations. Corporations are increasingly judging the potential of their employees to occupy top management positions on the basis of their HR competencies.

Moreover, the compulsions of line managers to compete with other organisations in global economies make it rather imperative for them to acquire HRM skills. HRD audit, therefore, presents a golden opportunity for line managers to set their own HR agenda and realise the same. For a head of a department or a section, the HRD audit data may be indicative of the direction the department needs to take. The following points may be kept in mind by the line managers of corporations that are undertaking an HRD audit:

- Participate in setting the agenda for the HRD audit
- Develop a departmental priority list and pass it on to the auditors so that they pay special attention to the departmental issues
- Ask the auditors to give the HRD audit questionnaire data separately for the department
- Insist on in-house interdepartmental benchmarking on the questionnaire data
- Try to get a department-level presentation of the audit results
- Set up an internal, department-level task force to monitor the changes
- Take the help of HR managers or staff to improve implementation effectiveness

Conducting HRD Audit

Who Should Conduct HRD Audit?

Different organisations may undertake HRD audit at different points of time to fulfil different objectives. Who should conduct the HRD audit depends on the objectives, stage at which the HRD audit is being conducted and availability of experts to conduct the audit.

It is always useful to get HRD audit conducted by an external team. The external team may be of HRD consultants from consulting companies or a group of trained and certified auditors from other organisations. The advantages of using external auditors are as follows:

• They are more objective and are not guided by internal compulsions
• They are likely to bring in newer perspectives
• They are likely to suggest new benchmarks
• They are not influenced by internal politics and familiarities

The disadvantage of having external auditors is mainly in terms of costs. External consultants may be more expensive. Therefore, it is useful to weigh the costs and benefits before taking a decision. A suggested strategy is to get external audit done once in three to five years and get internal audits done more frequently.

We now examine the possible stages of a corporation when an HRD audit can be conducted.

Stage 1: Corporation in the initial years of establishment (one to three years)

For a corporation, which is less than three years old, it is useful to get the audit done by external auditors. The primary purpose of the audit is to set up the HRD systems from the very early stages and align them with the business goals of the company. The first year is the best time to set the organisational culture and get going. The first few employees who join the company matter a lot in terms of setting the organisational culture and values. If the organisation is keen to create a learning culture and a learning organisation, the way various human processes are handled becomes very important. This process can be influenced from the beginning. Normally the first few employees who join the corporation bring with them different cultures and practices from their previous organisations. The first few years, therefore, are a struggle for any organisation to establish its own culture. Thus, the HRD audit can focus on the kind of culture that is evolving and influence it in the right direction.

Stage 2: Corporation after five years of establishment

Normally, by the time an organisation is five years old, most systems get established and patterns set. The organisation will have formed its own culture by then and will be in the process of stabilisation. In such cases, it is useful to get the audit done by an external agency. If an audit has already been done in the third year and the internal capabilities are already developed, then it is useful to get the audit done by an internal team of trained auditors or by a task force trained for this purpose.

Stage 3: Corporation after 8 to 10 years of establishment

For an organisation that has crossed the first five years of age, there is likely to be more stability. By the 8th to 10th year all patterns may have been established and an identity may have been developed. It may also be set to expand or synergise. It is normally in a reflective mood. This is the appropriate time to achieve more stability. Thus, a review and reflection exercise may help. For an organisation that has about 10 years of history, it should have gone through at least three audits. By the third audit, most HRD systems and processes should have been stabilised and the path set.

Stage 4: After diversification or other business expansion decisions

Business decisions, such as diversification, scaling up, new markets, new territories, expansion, new product additions and new technology additions, need a lot of HR support. The effectiveness of most of these decisions depends on the competencies and talent available to execute them. In most cases, such competencies may need to be built. Therefore, it is useful to get an HRD audit done by an external agency. This may help in competency mapping and HRD systems building to ensure that the plans are carried out. While external audit becomes a good tool for such occasions, internal audit has serious limitations in such cases as in-house biases and political issues can bring down the effectiveness of such an exercise. For internal audits, it is useful to associate with some line managers from other corporations or an in-house team to get insights about the competency requirements. On the other hand, a well-trained auditor will be able to further point out to a large number of HR systems and focal areas that the organisation needs to address.

Stage 5: After downsizing, reorganisation and other consolidation or synergy decisions

After downsizing or reorganising a corporation, the competency match becomes a crucial step. In order to ensure that the new and toned-up organisation is managed and led efficiently, it is useful to get an HRD audit done. The focus of such an audit should be on the competency gaps and the new systems needed to build the new competencies among the retained and redeployed employees. However, if such an audit has already been a part of the reorganisation process, it is not necessary to go for an HRD audit again.

Synergy and cost reductions may require revamping of performance appraisal systems and re-establishing accountabilities. Sometimes, such processes may create a low morale in the organisation. In such cases, it is useful to get the audit done after things have begun to settle down rather than in the middle of these exercises. It is useful to undertake an HRD audit after at least six months to a year of the downsizing or other synergy efforts. Such audits can be done by an internal team of trained HRD auditors. It will also be seen as a synergy effort. However, use of external agents for auditing specific systems can be useful.

Stage 6: For restructuring the HR function

HRD audit is a good way to restructure the HR function. Such restructuring can include merging the personnel and HRD departments, revamping the training function, downsizing the HR department, reengineering the HR function to involve or shift the responsibilities to the line managers and cost reductions in the HR function. In such cases it is useful to involve external auditors with the specific mandate of restructuring the HR function. The audit will focus on external and internal customer satisfaction with the HR function and an in-depth study of the HR department. The audit is likely to indicate the desirability of downsizing and the possible ways to reengineer the department.

Stage 7: After the change of the CEO or top management

A change in the top management or the CEO provides the best opportunity for HRD audit. An audit report will provide a good agenda for the new top managers or CEOs for the change process. External auditors can be used for an unbiased view or to guard oneself from being influenced or seen as influenced by a small section of the managers or the HRD department. The HRD audit reports will provide a great deal of insight for the CEO or the top management.

Stage 8: After an HRD audit by an external auditor

The corporation should get an annual audit done by an internal team every year after an external audit is done. It is recommended that the external audit be done once in three to five years and internal audit done every year. The internal audit can be done by task forces and internal teams specially trained for the purpose.

Competencies and Qualifications of Auditors

Auditors require the following competencies:

- Expertise in integrated HRD systems (skills in designing HRD systems)
- Experience in HRD systems implementation as a consultant or as an executive
- Research competencies particularly dealing with survey research
- Skills for identifying developmental needs
- Skills in interviewing, observation, content analysis, etc., and in research methods
- Programme and project evaluation competencies
- Organisational diagnosis and OD skills
- Social science research skills, including data analysis
- Reporting skills (written and oral communication)
- Benchmarking skills
- Networking skills
- Empathy and understanding
- General management competencies – conceptual soundness in general management
- Knowledge of business and HR strategies

The auditor should preferably be trained in auditing or evaluation studies. A certified auditor is better than an untrained and uncertified person. There are not too many agencies involved in training auditors. It may take some more time for professional bodies to establish training facilities for auditors. This may soon become a reality.

Ethics and Values

HRD audit is a serious affair. The audit report is intended to influence the future course of action of an organisation. It can give ideas to the top management for revamping and rejuvenating not merely the HR function or the HR department but also the structure of the entire organisation. It can thus influence the quality of the work life in an organisation as well as the quality of the lives of the employees. Thus, it should be taken seriously by all. Most of all, it should be taken seriously by the auditors themselves. This naturally puts the auditors in several dilemmas. Some of the conflicts and dilemmas faced by auditors are outlined as follows.

1. The auditor should not have his or her own preferences for any particular HRD system. For example, the auditor can be a strong believer in training or quality circles or performance appraisals or job rotation. He

or she should always keep the business interests of the organisation in mind and should see if a particular system or subsystem is likely to assist the organisation than the other system

2. Interviews give data about functions and individuals. The auditor should act like a fly on the wall. He or she should take the data and at the same time not form any opinions about individuals. He or she should act with empathy. He or she should process the information in the context of the HRD needs and business goals of the organisation. The auditor should be constantly aware of his or her own biases

3. If the HRD chief happens to be the first contact who is mainly responsible for initiating the audit, the auditor could unconsciously develop a soft corner for the HRD chief or function. The auditor may not wish to put the HR chief in a bad light, and hence, there is a danger of recommendations getting diluted. The auditor should be aware of this and try to treat the organisation and not the HR chief as the client. However, if the audit is meant for the consumption of the HR chief the auditor should have no hesitation in pointing out the strengths and weaknesses of the HR function. Professional judgement should always prevail and the relations and niceties should have no place in HRD audit. At the same time, the auditor should use an informal approach in obtaining data and sensing the organisation (i.e., understanding the organisation, its dynamics and undercurrents if any). On the whole, the auditor should have a balanced approach

4. The auditor faces a lot of dilemmas while conducting the audit. One of the most frequently asked questions by the respondents is about numerous consultants coming and going and nothing happening in the organisation. Most often managers say that they had given similar data a few months ago and nothing happened after that. While this gives a lead for the auditor to collect information about the nature of suggestions made by them earlier, the intensity of their feelings can be noted. However, the auditor is in no position to guarantee the implementation of any suggestions. Hence, it is only proper to state that he or she is only auditing the HRD function and making suggestions by pointing out areas that do not meet the standard or acceptable processes and practices. It is then left to the management to act on the audit report

5. The auditor should practice the OCTAPACE values normally propagated in HRD. The auditor should be open in answering any questions and also expressing his or her observations. This is the most important value the auditor should have in conducting the audit. The auditor should be trusting and trustworthy. It is better for him or her to be gullible rather than look at the respondents with suspicion. The auditor should have the sensitivity to interpret or reinterpret the data and at the same time trust the respondents. He or she should treat everyone as a

well-wisher of the company. When the auditor comes across highly frustrated individuals he or she should listen to them and try to understand the source and magnitude of their frustration and also gain insights into the implications for the HRD function

Some employees tend to influence the auditor as they see him or her as a powerful person who is close to the top management. They may express their jealousies, antagonism, etc., towards their employees or departments selectively. The auditor should be careful in terms of getting dragged into the internal political issues of the organisation.

Using Audit Data

External agents normally complete the audit in a month's time. They come once a year, or once in three to five years, and do a quick job. They evaluate the corporation in terms of some theory and external standards and benchmarks they carry and then leave. They may not at all times be, and they are not expected to be, sensitive to all the internal dynamics and processes operating in the corporation. Thus, there can be some genuine limitations of the audit report. It is possible for organisations sometimes to feel that the audit report lacks depth. This is because the reader who is an internal person has more insight into the organisation. Auditors normally avoid, as much as possible, getting into the inner dynamics of the corporation. They might give a theoretical explanation for the processes and suggest a systemic or an implementation-based solution to the issue. The audit report, therefore, is a good source to identify and understand the various strengths and weaknesses of the organisation. Also, the audit report is likely to list a large number of weak areas for any organisation. The organisation should have the maturity to understand and treat the weaknesses with respect rather than panicking and blaming itself as a whole, or the HR department, managers or the auditors. The objectives of the audit should not be forgotten and the report should be given its due place.

A very useful way of dealing with or using the audit report is as follows:

1. Presentation of the report to the top management team and preparation of action plans by the top management as a follow-up action: The presentation can be best done as a one-day or half-day workshop. The presentation should be made by the auditors. The auditors can share a lot of 'feeling' data which is normally not put in the report. The report is more intellectual and systems driven rather than feelings driven
2. Appointment of a task force to study and prioritise the areas to be improved and the areas to be maintained: The task force can be cross-functional with the involvement of the HRD department. It can be

mandated to work out an implementation plan. The task force can be given a time frame for action

3. Appointment of a task force by the top management to monitor the implementation of the report, and periodically report to a top management committee or the board

4. Appointment of a number of task forces (one for each sub-system) to ensure the use of the audit findings and to bring system improvements

5. Sharing of data through the in-house newsletter or journal so that employees at all levels are involved, and they do not lose faith in such interventions.

6. Sharing of the findings and action plans through an open house or an open forum

7. Formation of a task force by the HRD department that will then monitor the implementation of the suggestions after prioritising the same

Role of Unions and Associations

HRD audit provides a wonderful opportunity for union and association office bearers to influence the HR function in the company. Rather than looking at the audit with suspicion and concluding that it will be another exercise in futility, they should play an active role. They can insist on meeting the auditors as a group and giving their own views and perceptions of various systems. Due to its comprehensive nature, HRD audit touches on the various measures dealing with the quality of the work life of all the employees. Since this is normally an issue of major concern, the unions and associations may do well by acting like the users and promoters of HRD audit. It is possible for them to conduct informal audit exercises and pass on the data to the consultants. They should also not confuse the audit for a consulting report that could result in changes.

Frequency of HRD Audit

Most organisations treat HRD audit as a one-time affair. It is a good practice to conduct an HRD audit once in two years. Moreover, once in four to five years it should be preferably done by an outside agency. The reason for conducting audits more frequently is to help review and evaluate HRD implementation on a regular basis and ensure its effectiveness.

Preparation of HRD Audit

Organisational Attitudes and Preparation Needed for HRD Audit

If an HRD audit is undertaken without adequate preparation, it can be a waste of effort and money. The following preparation is helpful in getting the best out of an HRD audit:

- Educate all the employees (or at least a large number of them or those who are going to be involved) about the basics of HRD audit. A small note can be circulated for this purpose
- Decide on the appropriate timing for the audit. It is better to avoid the audit when other audits are going on, for example, an ISO 9000 audit, or when the company is facing serious crisis situations. This is because it may draw too many people out and create other issues
- Request all the line managers to be interviewed to cooperate and provide some time for questionnaires and interviews
- Do not expect the HRD audit to solve all or any of the organisational problems. The audit is only an assessment. Problems get solved by action and not by assessment. The assessment may at best provide some directions for action
- Make all the records and secondary data available to the auditors. The HRD department may need to put one or two dedicated employees for assisting the auditors
- Mentally prepare all those to be interviewed to set aside a couple of hours for the same. This can be done by sending out a small note or circular

Developing Internal Auditors and Audit Capabilities

It is a good practice to develop internal auditors. The internal auditors should be trained in HRD audit methods. TVRLS and AHRD conduct HRD audit certification programmes. These programmes are of a short duration, ranging from three to five days for experienced HR managers. The programmes aim at developing audit competencies among the participants. A sample design of the programme is presented in Box 14.1.

BOX 14.1 HRD AUDIT PROGRAMME OUTLINE

The HRD audit programme is meant to develop an internal auditor. The participants admitted to this programme should have the professional background needed to be HRD managers. They should have done at least eight course equivalents of studies in HRD.

Day One

Session 1

- Introductions: Participants introduce themselves to each other and discuss their backgrounds, reasons for joining the programme, expectations (of self and organisation), details of their organisations (size, products, manpower, location, HRD structure, etc.) – 45 minutes

- Faculty introduces the programme – 15 minutes
- What is HRD – conceptual framework for HRD audit – 30 minutes

Session 2

- HRD audit methodology outline – 45 minutes
- HRD audit questionnaire – appreciation (participants will examine different sections of the questionnaire in groups and understand the significance of the variables measured and the significance of the questionnaire methodology) – 45 minutes

Session 3

- Presentation of observations on the questionnaires and discussion – 60 minutes
- Observation methodology – presentation and discussion – 30 minutes

Session 4

- HRD audit case studies, for example, Company X – presentation and discussion – 45 minutes

Session 5

- Interview methodology for HRD audit – concepts – 30 minutes
- Interview methodology – practice sessions (each participant will interview another participant individually to practice HRD audit interviews and report his or her findings) – 15 minutes interview 5 × 3 minutes reporting of experiences of interviewing. Exercise to be repeated for the second set of interviews.

Day Two

Sessions 1 and 2

- Data sharing and benchmarking: Participants share the data they have brought and benchmark their practices, section by section:
  Career systems – 15 minutes
  Work planning systems – 15 minutes
  Development systems – 15 minutes
  Self-renewal systems – 15 minutes
  Culture systems – 15 minutes
  HRD department – 15 minutes

- Effectiveness of HRD audit as an OD intervention: Experiences of four companies – presentation – 45 minutes
- Use of secondary data, reports, etc. (age profiles, personnel manuals, appraisal manuals, qualifications and other employee profiles, annual reports, induction manual, training calendar, worker development pro-grammes and their timetable and evaluation, appraisal form returns, absenteeism data, employee turnover data, leave patterns, employee satisfaction surveys, social development activity reports, exit interviews, appointment letters, resignation letters, circulars and notices, newslet-ters and other formal communications) – 45 minutes

Session 3

Evaluating HRD staff and departmental competencies
HRD profile questionnaire – 30 minutes
HRD competencies checklist – 30 minutes
HRD competencies of departments – 30 minutes

Sessions 4 and 5

The participants will try out the HRD audit on a sample unit. They will be divided into groups of three or four and will do the audit and report their expe-riences – about three hours.

Day Three

Session 1

- Reporting and analysis of data collected the previous day – 90 minutes
- Writing and presenting audit report – dos and don'ts – 60 minutes

Session 2

- Evaluating HRD structure strategy and sharing benchmarking data – 60 minutes
- Empowerment audit and experience sharing of HRD audit – 30 minutes
- Organisational learning audit – 30 minutes

Session 3

- Leadership styles – questionnaire and interpretation – 45 minutes
- HRD styles audit – how to observe, assess, give feedback and report – 45 minutes

- Importance of styles in HRD. Influence of styles on learning culture – 30 minutes.

Session 4

- Planning new instruments – 45 minutes
- Planning follow-up – 30 minutes
- Requirements for certification – 15 minutes
- Course evaluation and feedback – 15 minutes

The participant in an HRD audit certification programme is required to conduct an audit and submit the report before he or she is certified as an auditor. TVRLS has trained a number of auditors by now. However, internal audit has not yet become popular in the country. It is preferable that an internal auditor is certified and has all the competencies to become an auditor, as outlined earlier.

The internal auditor should be given a freehand and should be freed from all other responsibilities during the period of internal audit. He or she should be given all the support like the external auditor. The audit should become a normal and regular part of the organisation's life. It is useful to develop a team of internal auditors rather than one auditor. A single auditor may find it a little complex and difficult to deal with many internal issues that may emerge in the course of the audit or after the audit. Line managers can also be trained in HR audit skills.

Role of the HRD Department

The HRD department has the most crucial role to play in HRD audit. First of all, it requires a lot of courage to get the HRD audit initiated. Any HRD audit is likely to point out the weak areas of the HRD function. Due to a limited understanding of the role of line managers, top management and a number of other factors in the success of HRD, most line managers and sometimes even the top management is likely to put total responsibility for the weak areas on the HR department. It is not quite uncommon to find the successful practice of HRD systems attributed to line managers and the top management, and the unsuccessful ones to the HRD department. It needs a good deal of maturity on the part of the HRD manager and the top management to appreciate the role of all employees in HRD. The HRD function should eventually be owned by everyone, and the line managers should take a higher level of responsibility for the development of their own staff. The HR department should be a facilitator. However, until the time the maturity level of an organisation reaches this stage, the HR department has the tough task of building the HR competencies of the staff and, at the same time, has to be prepared to face criticism. The HRD department can use HRD audit as a step to build the desired awareness among line managers. The following are some useful tips for the HRD department to use HRD audit effectively:

- Do not become defensive. Do not take criticism of the weak areas in the HRD function negatively. You may have initiated the audit, and therefore, you should have the confidence and courage to accept the weaknesses and plan improvements. Weaknesses reflect the status of the HR function, which in turn is determined by the competencies of the staff, the treatment the function is getting in the corporation and also how it was treated in the past, past incumbents, competency gaps in line managers as well as the HR staff, developments or research or knowledge base in the area itself, top management support, role of unions and many other factors
- You cannot ensure everything to be perfect. At the same time you need to ensure that the HR function plays a significant role in giving the right direction to the company

- Use the audit to (*i*) point out to the top management about their role in HRD and the support required from them, (*ii*) educate the line managers about their role in HRD and (*iii*) educate the unions about the opportunities they have to develop their employees and the company
- Create mechanisms to discuss the report and improve the function. The audit provides a great opportunity to improve the effectiveness of the HRD function in the company. It also provides a good opportunity to develop the staff internally, streamline the HRD budget, enhance HRD competencies, rationalise the HRD structure and participate in business strategies and decisions
- Build your own competencies and learn to play a more significant role in making your corporation competitive and world-class

Conclusion

HRD audit can become an important intervention to rejuvenate the whole organisation as it highlights critical issues such as competency requirements, motivational value, competence gaps in that HR staff, roles and areas where more involvement is required and alignment of HR strategies with the business goals.

Several factors are necessary for the success of the audit, the key ones being top management involvement, involvement of line managers and attitude of the HR department and adequate training of employees.

Who should conduct HRD audit depends on the objectives, the stage at which the HRD audit is being conducted, the availability of experts to conduct the audit and the age of the organisation, its diversification/expansion activities, restructuring, change of leadership, etc. The effectiveness of the audit is highly dependent on the competence of the auditors, which includes expertise in HR systems, survey research, OD skills, social science research skills, benchmarking skills, general management competence and ethical soundness. It is also a good idea to train internal people as auditors.

The data generated through the audit should be rightly used by first communicating it across the organisation and forming an implementation task force.

SECTION 4

HRD Audit

The Indian Experience

The earlier sections have presented the various aspects of HRD audit, including the concept and methodologies for conducting it. This section deals with some research observations and case studies. These are meant to give some insights into HRD audit outcomes. This section also presents the results of a study.

The HRD audit itself does not bring change. It is a potential instrument for realigning the HRD function and initiating change. In the hands of an uninterested CEO or HRD chief, the HRD audit can bring discredit to the HR function. People give data for improving their organisation. When an auditor contacts them, interviews them or administers questionnaires to them, they are investing their time. They do it with the hope that it will result in some change. If the change does not take place, or if there is no communication of the consequence of their time investments, the employees may become cynical and may not participate in such studies again. Hence, it is important for the organisation to act on the HRD audit report and also communicate to the participants of the audit the various actions initiated by it. Some organisations take many steps after such an audit, but silently, believing that their actions should speak for themselves and, hence, there is no need to publicise what they have done or intend to do. In such a case it is not necessary that the line managers give credit to the top management or the HRD department for bringing in changes. The choice is left for the top management to make the changes and talk about them or leave it for the employees to experience them.

With a view to finding out the changes resulting from HRD audit, Jomon (1998) studied groups of organisations in different businesses located

DOI: 10.4324/9781003530534-18

in different parts of the country. His study results are very revealing (the research study is presented in the next chapter). Before that, we discuss some case studies of HRD audit to get an overview of HRD outcomes.

15

CASE STUDIES

The role of an HRD auditor can be compared to that of a doctor or an architect. A doctor does not prescribe the same medicine for all his or her patients – he or she first diagnoses the ailment and then suggests an appropriate cure.

An architect does not design all his or her buildings identically; he or she has to keep the requirements of the builder, including his or her future needs, in mind and then visualise and design an appropriate structure.

Similarly, an HRD auditor has to first diagnose the opportunities and problems; identify deficiencies in the strategy, structure, staff and systems of the HRD process in an organisation; and then recommend steps for improvement. He or she also has to base his or her recommendations on the future responsibilities of the HRD department as derived from the business plans of the organisation.

HRD audits of different organisations can reveal different things. The case studies of four HRD audited organisations presented in this chapter amply illustrate this.

The audit process is like an operation where the strengths and the weaknesses of the organisation are brought to the fore. It takes a lot of courage and maturity for an organisation to face the unpleasantness of undergoing an audit, acknowledging the deficiencies and seeing them in the proper light and undertaking measures for improvement and change.

It is understandable that no organisation would want its strong and weak points to be exposed to the world. Thus, the names of the organisations, whose cases we discuss in this chapter, have been kept confidential.

As one goes through these cases, a common feature that stands out is the absolute support given to all HRD activities by the top-level management. In most cases, the HRD audit process itself was initiated by either the CEO

DOI: 10.4324/9781003530534-19

or the HRD chief. It only goes to prove that for any HRD intervention to be a success, the total commitment of the top-level management and its undivided support is a prerequisite.

Case Study 1: Company Z

Background

Company Z belongs to the manufacturing sector. It has set itself a goal of becoming an organisation that delights its customers and makes high-quality products at competitive prices, in other words, a world-class organisation, by the year 2010. It has already initiated changes in its manufacturing technology, marketing and R&D. It has also started a change management process through cultural programmes and various quality and HR interventions.

The president and the senior-level managers of Company Z wanted to know how the HRD function could assist them in attaining their goals. To get an answer to this question they approached a consultant to conduct an HRD audit.

Considering the future plans of the Company Z, the audit consultant listed the following as the primary tasks of the HRD department at that point in time:

1. Continuous competency building at the individual, team and organisational levels
2. Keeping up the motivation and commitment levels of all employees, enhancing employee satisfaction and tuning their energies towards the future challenges
3. Nurturing a culture that reflects a world-class organisation

Methodology

The following methodology was used by the auditor:

*   Forty senior managers were interviewed individually
*   Hundred managers from a cross-section of departments were interviewed in small groups
*   Various forms and documents were studied and analysed
*   Training data available on the computers were observed and studied
*   HRD audit questionnaires were administered to 120 line managers
*   The professional preparation and competencies of the HRD staff were evaluated on the basis of their bio-data
*   Workplace and physical facilities were also observed. The HRD competencies checklist was also administered to the HRD staff to assess their professional preparedness for performing their jobs effectively

HRD Structure at Company Z

The HRD department in Company Z is decentralised. The 20 members of the HRD department are assigned to various departments (marketing, R&D, etc.) to look into the needs of these departments. For example, the HRD staff assigned to the R&D department had plans of introducing team appraisal and a reward system based on team performance, whereas the HRD staff in the marketing department had plans of conducting dealer training, manpower planning, assessment of training needs, etc.

The auditor felt that though the decentralised structure was a step in the right direction, the HRD managers in various departments were facing problems of dual reporting. They were accountable to both the HRD department at the headquarters and to their own line departments.

HRD Staff at Company Z

The average age of the employees in the HRD department is 45 years. The analysis of their bio-data revealed that none of the officers had any HRD-related qualifications. Some members were ISTD diploma holders and a few had qualifications in personnel management. Most officers had work experience in training and some had work experience in quality circles, ISO 9000 and personnel administration. It was also found that out of a total of 700 training man-days attended by the HRD staff, only 10 per cent of the time was directly related to the subject of HRD. The self-assessment of the officers in the competencies checklist revealed that the HRD department as a whole was not adequately prepared to handle the following: potential appraisals, OD and culture building, career planning and development, job evaluation, HR information systems and strategic planning. It was concluded that the qualifications and the experience of the HRD department as a whole was inadequate to plan, organise and monitor some critical interventions required to become a world-class organisation.

The consultant recommended that the HRD department undergo a series of HRD competency-building workshops. A modular training programme consisting of seven modules covering various topics right from integrating HRD systems for business improvement to HR information systems was designed by the auditor for the Company Z.

HRD Systems at Company Z

Recruitment

There is adequate participation from the line managers in the recruitment and selection process in Company Z. The qualification and experience of the candidate is given due weightage. There are three rounds of panel interviews that a candidate has to face before selection; this ensures considerable objectivity in the selection process.

Induction

Induction in Company Z extends over two weeks. New recruits are taken around and given an overview of the company, its activities, the various departments, etc. Some departments such as marketing conduct their own induction programmes.

Performance Appraisals

The performance appraisal system at Company Z has been introduced only recently and some short orientation programmes have been conducted. Plans are on to introduce quarterly review discussions.

Career Planning and Succession Planning

There is no system in place at Company Z for career planning and succession planning. It is done in an ad hoc manner and is at the discretion of the senior officers.

Training

Training is given a lot of importance by the top management as well as by the HRD department in Company Z. There are no budgetary limitations for training. Technical training as well as training related to cultural change are considered relevant and practical by the line managers. A large number of persons have also been sent abroad for training.

Job Rotation

Job rotation is done intermittently and is need based. As such there is no formal system of job rotation at Company Z.

HR Information System

Apart from using the information stored in the computers, the HRD department does not make use of information technology in its day-to-day operations.

Organisational Culture, Culture Building and Top Management Commitment

The top management at Company Z is committed towards organisational development and believes in the empowerment of employees.

Findings of the HRD audit

Recruitment

It was found that the recruitment process at Company Z was not systematic. It was not based on job descriptions or on manpower plans. Line managers were not happy with the speed and responsiveness of the HRD department in matters related to recruitment. They were not happy with the quality of the recruitment process and the candidates selected. It was also found that softer dimensions, such as values, attitudes and corruptibility of the candidate with the organisation's culture, were not adequately tested. Candidates were not given complete information regarding their jobs at the time of the interview. Promises made at the time of recruitment were not translated into action later. There was no uniform policy regarding emoluments and appointment levels. This led to a lot of frustration. To add to this, applicants were treated badly, appointment letters were delayed and sometimes misplaced. The company also lost out on some good candidates when recruitment offers were delayed. All this gave the company a bad image.

Induction

The audit revealed that the induction programme at Company Z was not well structured. The two-week-long induction that was in operation did not acquaint a new recruit with some very important functions such as quality assurance, product planning and control. There was no induction manual either. Senior managers did not take any interest in the induction process. In fact many inductees after being sent to the departments were left unattended. All this led to a considerable amount of dissatisfaction among the new recruits.

Performance Appraisals

The auditor felt that it was too early for the impact of the recently introduced performance appraisal system to be felt by the employees. However, some lacunae in the system were already showing up. The objectives of the system were not clearly stated; hence, its implementation varied from person to person. Furthermore, the promises made during the performance review discussions were not kept, nobody knew what happened after the appraisal ratings, the data generated were not put to any use, there was no transparency in the system and personal biases influenced the ratings. The line managers were not adequately trained to conduct performance review discussions. Another stumbling block was the general perception that the performance appraisal system was the baby of the corporate HRD department, as the local HRD department did not take up the responsibility for it.

Job Rotation

The auditor pointed out that job rotation in Company Z was considered synonymous with transfers. It was not linked to career planning or career growth as the case should be. Employees were not informed in advance about job rotation plans resulting in a disruption of their schedules.

Training

Though Company Z gives a lot of importance to training, this has proved to be more of an expenditure than an investment. The reasons are given as follows:

- Individual requests for training are not entertained. More often, the HRD department finalises training programme based on the brochures received from training institutes
- There is no system of sharing the knowledge acquired from training
- There is no systematic effort made to utilise the competence developed through training. There is no post-training follow-up or evaluation of training. Action plans made in the training programmes are not followed up
- The company does not have an annual training schedule or calendar. Training, according to the employees, happens in hiccups: sometimes there is an overdose and sometimes there is no training for months
- Apart from this, it was also found that training in soft areas, such as communication, personality development and public speaking, was inadequate

Organisational Culture and Culture Building

The audit revealed a high level of bureaucracy at Company Z. Furthermore, there were no social gatherings held in the company. And most often the seniors were too busy to guide the juniors.

Recommendations by the Auditor

Manpower Planning and Recruitment

The auditor gave the following recommendations to the company:

- Develop proper manpower plans with inputs from department heads

- Prepare a recruitment system specifying the recruitment process for the yearly (budgeted) manpower requirements and for recruitment needs arising out of transfers, retirement, resignations and so on
- Develop a recruitment policy manual
- Train line managers in recruitment and selection techniques
- Re-examine the level fixations for employees with different work experience and qualifications and develop some norms for the fixation of grades
- Improve the facilities and seating arrangements for candidates visiting the company for recruitment. First impressions matter
- Computerisation of the recruitment process can also save a lot of time for the HRD department that already feels overburdened

Induction

The auditor recommended setting up a systematic induction programme that covered the following:

- Induction to the company, its products, market share, mission, vision, values, norms, current endeavours, future plans, current structure, technology, manufacturing process and other details
- Introduction to different functions – marketing, manufacturing, R&D, etc.
- Information about personnel policies, facilities, guidelines, leaves and so on

This should be followed by a detailed induction to the department where the person is expected to work

A new recruit should be also given the details about his or her job responsibilities, work station and other such details that will help him or her start work

Performance Appraisals

The auditor made the following suggestions:

- A complete review of the performance appraisal system with respect to the mission of the company; a shift in emphasis from mere appraisals to employee development
- The inclusion of parameters such as quality consciousness, cost consciousness, proaction, change orientation, customer orientation, utilisation of training inputs received, efforts to develop juniors through the performance appraisal system; apart from these, division-specific critical parameters of performance should also be incorporated

- Training of all the line managers in the use of performance appraisals
- Designing a performance appraisal manual

The auditor also pointed out that the success of the system depended on the seriousness of the HRD department; it should take charge of the system and treat it as its own.

Training

The auditor made the following recommendations to facilitate better utilisation of training at Company Z:

- Develop a training policy in accordance with the business plans of the company and make it known to every employee in the organisation
- Work closely with the line managers to determine training needs
- All training sponsorships should be entirely need based
- Evaluate the impact of training
- Make it mandatory for every person attending a training programme to give a presentation and submit an action plan on how inputs from training can be implemented. Make the person accountable for his or her action plans and conduct periodic reviews to evaluate the progress made

Job Rotation

The auditor pointed out that first and foremost it was important to develop a job rotation policy in tune with the business goals of the organisation. This would lead to the enhancement of the human resources in the organisation in the form of multiskilling and increase the commitment level of the employees, resulting in better production. The auditors also recommended that the departments should be given the freedom to develop their own job rotation plans and be assisted by the HRD department.

Career Planning and Succession Planning

The consultant pointed out the need for the following:

- Identification of broad career paths for employees
- Providing career-related information
- Career counselling
- Succession planning for all strategic roles

Organisational Culture, Culture Building and Top Management Commitment

It was recommended that the senior-level managers should articulate the culture that they want to build. They should promote interdepartmental benchmarking and learning.

For an organisation like Company Z, which was all set to enter into a fast-growth phase, the complete support of the top management in all HRD-related activities was a must. Hence, the importance given to the HRD function by the top management at Company Z was examined. It was found that though the president and senior general managers at Company Z were committed to the HRD function, many general managers and deputy general managers did not comprehend the significance of the function. The HRD officials were not involved in the process of vision building and strategy formulation.

The auditor pointed out that the company needs to evolve an HR strategy to assist the organisation in attaining its business goals. Senior executives need to be oriented towards the significance of the HRD function and how it can become an instrument to attain business goals. The auditor also suggested a presentation of the HRD audit findings in a one-day workshop, followed by a series of sessions on the role of the top management in HRD.

Case Study 2: Company X

Background

Company X belongs to the manufacturing sector. It has a sleek organisation structure and employs 200 staff and officers (managers, supervisors, assistants) and 200 workers. The senior-level managers have identified the following main concerns of Company X in the coming years:

- Expansion in capacity
- Improvement in the quality of products and services
- Developing good labour relations
- Reduction in costs and increase in efficiency
- New product development
- Managerial effectiveness

The company has also been looking at export opportunities and has plans of setting up another unit within a year or two. Since this unit will be equipped with the latest technology, only a marginal increase in manpower requirements is expected.

To determine the role its HRD department could play to help the organisation attain its long-term goals, the senior managers of Company X invited audit consultants to conduct an HRD audit in their organisation.

Considering the business plans of the organisation, it was decided that the agenda for the HRD function consisted of the following:

- Human resource utilisation (particularly at the worker level)

- upgradation of skills (both technical and managerial)
- Creation of a healthy and productive organisational culture

Methodology

The auditors camped at Company X for over three days during which time the interviews were held. The entire audit process was completed over a period of two months. The methodology used by the auditors to conduct the HRD audit consisted of the following:

- Twenty-five senior managers were interviewed individually to determine the direction in which the company wanted to move, the future plans and the role that the HRD department was expected to play
- Five group interviews were conducted to enable a participative and diagnostic evaluation of the individual HR systems and the HRD function as a whole. In all 25 officers, 20 staff members and 20 workers participated in these group interviews
- The HRD Audit Questionnaire was administered to 20 managers for an in-depth assessment of the HRD systems in the company
- An open-ended questionnaire on the strengths and weaknesses of HRD was administered to the staff and the officers
- Various reports and forms were also scrutinised

HRD Department at Company X

The HRD function at Company X is part of the Personnel and General Administration Department. The major accomplishments of this department in the last few years have been in the areas of training, job rotation and performance appraisal. The HRD department has put in a lot of effort towards the utilisation of the existing competencies of the employees. In fact, a few years earlier, the company was able to increase its production with no addition to its manpower. The president of Company X has been a constant source of encouragement for all the HRD activities undertaken by the HRD department.

HRD systems at Company X

The following systems were in operation at the time of the audit.

Career System

Manpower Planning

Whenever a person leaves, the need for a substitute is reviewed. Departmental heads propose manpower requirements every year. It is reviewed by the respective divisional head and again by the president along with the deputy general manager – HRD and the divisional head. The final sanction is given by the president. There is a Central Technical Cell that also reviews the manpower needs periodically. Surplus manpower is transferred to other units after consultation with the employee concerned.

Potential Appraisal and Development

The identification of employees with a high potential is done by the heads of departments (HODs) and the divisional heads. The qualifications of the candidates and their contribution on the job are also given due importance. This information is used for taking decisions related to promotions. The appraisal form provides ample scope for identifying persons with high potential.

Career Planning and Development

In the present system, successors are identified for the top 12 posts by the HODs, the divisional heads and the president. The successors know that they have been identified and are groomed accordingly. They are also given the chance to act on behalf of their boss. Considering the fact that not many people were expected to retire in the next five years, no retirement planning was done.

Work-Planning System

Role Clarity

Employees at Company X are quite clear about the tasks they are expected to perform. They are also given proper feedback on their performance. This is an indicator of effective human resource utilisation.

Contextual Analysis

The employees have gained a good deal of understanding about their company through communication meetings held periodically. They are also highly aware of the business parameters – long- and short-term plans.

Performance Appraisal

Company X has a highly participative system of performance appraisals. Adequate importance is given to the developmental component of the system. In the present system, each appraisee is required to state the major responsibilities handled by him or her, his or her accomplishments, the factors that affected the achievement of his or her goals, the help that he or she requires to improve his or her performance, training needs, etc. Recommendations for job rotation, promotions and increments are also made on the basis of performance appraisals.

Development System

Training

Training at Company X is given top priority by the management. A training calendar is prepared every year, outlining the programmes to be held, the target group, the faculty and the duration of training. Training needs are identified from the performance appraisal, the annual (technical) training needs assessment and through individual requests for training. Employees attending training programmes outside the company are required to give a presentation and submit a report on their return. Worker training has also been started in this company.

Job Rotation

Though job rotation is quite common at Company X; there is no formal policy on it. The HOD's recommendations in the performance appraisal are normally used for deciding the finalisation of candidates for job rotation.

Delegation and Participation

Delegation is propagated by all top-level managers in the company. There are 30 different types of meetings conducted in the company, which are meant to serve as participative forums.

Inter-Unit Visits

Many employees are sent for inter-unit visits so that they can learn how various functions are performed in other units.

Personnel Policy Manuals

The HRD department has prepared a manual of personnel policies that is given to all the managers. It is an open document, which is accessible to all employees. Concise manual providing information about salaries and perks is also under preparation.

Findings of the HRD audit

Career System

Manpower Planning

On the whole the manpower planning system at Company X was found to be satisfactory.

Potential Appraisal and Promotions

The audit revealed that the employees were not aware of the criteria for promotions. There was no promotion policy. Decisions on promotions were considered to be highly subjective and were at the discretion of senior-level managers.

Career Planning and Development

There was no career planning policy in Company X. It was also felt that the successors were not groomed sufficiently.

Work-Planning System

Performance Appraisal

It was found that the weaknesses in the performance appraisal mainly stemmed from its implementation. Appraisers were not trained in performance review discussion skills. Most employees had still not understood the objectives behind the introduction of the system and most linked performance appraisals to increments.

Development System

Training

The company does not have a training policy. It was also found that the training provided in relation to managerial subjects was inadequate. The lower-level staff were not given sufficient opportunities for attending training programmes. Post-training presentations had become more of a formality in some departments. Sometimes the training programmes were organised only to meet the annual training programme targets. This affected both the quality of the training received and the image of the HRD department.

Job Rotation

Job rotation at this company was instrumental in developing a high level of motivation and enhancing the human resource base (via multiskilling).

Delegation and Participation

The auditors found that 'delegation' was not really practised in the right sense of the word. Many employees complained that even leave was not sanctioned without involving the assistant vice-president. Most meetings were task oriented, and there was little employee participation in improving the softer dimensions, such as culture, welfare, social events, teamwork, etc.

Inter-Unit Visits

It was found that inter-unit visits were limited to technical areas only. Moreover, employees were not given adequate time to observe and study the unit they visited. It was also felt that the same group was being sent to most of the places.

Personnel Policy Manual

It was discovered that most HODs had not yet shared the manual with others in their department. The manual was also not updated periodically. In the absence of information on the personnel policies, most employees felt that there was a lot of favouritism and adhocism in the way the organisation functioned.

Living Conditions and Other Motivational Factors

There are many factors that affect work, demotivate employees and discourage them from giving their best. These include:

- Lack of transportation and communication facilities, even in the case of emergencies
- Lack of proper drinking water
- Even when employees were sick they were not granted leave and in some cases employees were called back from home after their leave was sanctioned
- Medical facilities were inadequate
- Some employees felt that there was no freedom of expression, good work was not recognised and mistakes were ridiculed in public; all this was causing a lot of frustration

Perception of the Workers and Staff

Since the first item on the HR agenda at Company X was increasing in human resource utilisation, particularly at the lower levels, the auditors spent some time interacting with the workers and the staff to find their opinion about the company and the functioning of HRD department. Their findings are briefly presented as follows:

- Most workers were educated and had prior work experience before joining Company X. For them, the quality of the products that they manufactured was of utmost importance, which they would not sacrifice at any cost. They felt that if the quality of the raw material was improved and adequate emphasis laid on quality control, the product quality could be improved further. The production output could also be improved with some technical training and exposure to other units
- The staff felt that they had learnt a lot while working for the organisation. Most of them had acquired computer and communication skills, including drafting of letters
- Both the workers and the staff felt that quality circles were not effective since many meetings were postponed because the higher authorities were too busy to attend
- They felt that the HRD department only catered to the higher levels. Many times training needs had been identified, but no action had been taken
- Interpersonal trust between the management and the workers was very low since the workers felt that they were being manipulated by the management when it came to issuing a medical certificate. The workers felt that the management failed to give them adequate support when they did something in good faith for the company
- Information related to the job, technology, rules and other related matters were not being shared with the workers and staff
- There were similar grievances with respect to leave sanctions, inadequate communication facilities, transportation facilities and drinking water

Recommendations

Career System

Manpower Planning

The auditors recommended that considerable attention to long-term skill requirements should also be given while determining the manpower needs of the company.

Potential Appraisal and Promotions

The formulation of a promotion policy was recommended by the auditors. It was also important to make it accessible to everyone in the company so that the general perception that promotion decisions are totally at the discretion of the HOD and the divisional head can be changed.

Career Planning and Development

The recommendations included the formulation of a career planning policy that ought to be shared with the employees. The career planning policy and the promotion policy should also be linked.

Work-Planning System

Performance Appraisal

The auditors recommended the following:

- The preparation of a comprehensive manual of guidelines giving the objectives of the system, the process, the roles of the appraiser, apprai-see, HRD department and reviewing officer; it should also spell out the guidelines for conducting an effective performance review discussion
- Educating the appraisers and the appraisees about the new appraisal system with an emphasis on sharpening their listening and counselling skills
- Every item in the appraisal form should be analysed, tabulated and used for performance improvements (identification of training needs, job rotation, etc.)
- The factors affecting the performance as mentioned by each appraisee should be tabulated department-wise and presented by the HRD department to the each HOD
- The top management should attempt to introduce 360-degree appraisal to improve their own performance

Development System

Training

The recommendations given by the auditors include the following:

- Develop a training policy
- Monitor the utilisation of training inputs

- The department should not be overconcerned about meeting training targets; the targets should be taken as notional and desirable, not something that has to be met at any cost whatsoever
- Data available from appraisal forms of the last two to three years should be analysed for determining the training needs of each individual, which, if still relevant, should be attended to as soon as possible
- Training programmes (of more than one-day duration) should be evaluated more actively by the HRD department through a dialogue with the trainees after the programme rather than just asking them to fill an evaluation form
- Briefing sessions should be held by the HOD or the HRD department before every external or long-duration internal programme to ensure that the employees take the programme seriously and make good use of the opportunity

Job Rotation

It was recommended that job rotation be carried out in a more planned manner. The formulation of a job-rotation policy, it was suggested, would also prove quite useful.

Inter-Unit Visits

It was recommended that inter-unit visits be extended to other areas also so that employees can learn about quality circles, HRD practices, management practices, human relations, leadership, etc. Apart from providing adequate time to the employees to gain knowledge about the systems in other units, it was suggested that the teams or individuals returning from such visits should share their experiences with their colleagues through a formal presentation and discussion.

Personnel Policy Manual

One of the most important recommendations made was to update the Personnel Policy Manual and to make it available to all employees.

Living Conditions and Other Motivational Factors

The views of the employees on matters related to their living conditions were conveyed to the senior managers so that appropriate remedial actions could be taken. The importance of improving the living conditions of the employees in order to create a motivating organisational climate was emphasised. This could be done via empathising and solving problems related to the minor irritants in the living conditions of the lower-level officers, staff and workers.

On the whole the auditors felt that the HRD department should focus on delegation, quality circles and small group activities, the use of appraisals as a tool for development, enhancing the effectiveness and relevance of training, career planning, the implementation of personnel and welfare policies and, most importantly, improving the living conditions of the lower-level staff.

Case Study 3: Company B Background

Background

This 10-year-old company belongs to the service sector. It employs 530 people at three locations. The company banks heavily on its employees and the strengths it has built in terms of developing a learning attitude, service orientation and a proactive and informal culture. In the last three years, several HRD interventions, such as the introduction of a Performance Planning Review and Development System (PPRDS), establishing an in-house training facility, periodic stock-taking surveys, etc., have been completed successfully. In all these activities the CEO and the chief of HRD have played a highly facilitating role. A considerable number of line managers have also internalised the philosophy of HRD and treat it as a part of their job. The company is presently diversifying into various other fields.

The Senior Manager, HRD, of Company B approached the audit consultants for assistance in the following areas:

- To help articulate an HRD policy for Company B
- To measure the efficacy of HRD interventions and benchmark the HRD practices through an HRD audit
- Role analysis of the senior management committee
- Institutionalising the PPRDS through skill workshops
- Initiating potential appraisal for the managerial cadre
- Integrating the HRD function with the personnel and administration functions and the line managers by imparting HRD skills through an HRD facilitation programme for a select group of individuals

Subsequently, the audit team visited the three units of Company B. Based on the needs expressed by the Senior Manager of HRD, they set the following objectives for the HRD audit at Company B:

- To examine the HRD needs of Company B in the context of the current and future strategic plans of the company

- To examine the efficacy of various HRD interventions made so far and outline the direction in which new interventions need to be made, keeping in view the experiences available from other Indian organisations
- To examine the appropriateness of the structure, strategy and processes being used to implement and institutionalise HRD and recommend future directions
- To examine the implementation of the various HRD systems and HRD culture and make recommendations for the future structure of the HRD department

Methodology

The HRD audit methodology included the following:

- Interviews were held with 80 managers, 80 supervisory cadre officers and 75 staff at all three units of the company
- A detailed diagnostic workshop with the HRD and personnel and administration group was held where the managers presented a critical review of various HRD systems in operation; about 15 officers and managers attended this workshop
- Various documents such as the personnel policies manual, PPRD forms and manual, HRD budgets, training documents, etc., were examined
- A comprehensive HRD audit questionnaire was administered to 75 managers and officers from all three locations
- Besides these, some important workplaces, such as the training centre, were also visited to observe the facilities
- Discussions were also held with inductees and management trainees

HRD Department at Company B

The HRD department was set up in 1991 to establish a culture of development in the organisation. It consists of a senior manager, an assistant manager and a senior officer besides four other officers in the training centre. The personnel department is manned by a total of eight employees. A new complementary department that has recently come into existence is that of management services with a new manager and a new assistant manager. The new department is well equipped to look after TQM, job evaluation and manpower audit.

HRD Staff at Company B

The department has eight members. All of them have acquired their professional knowledge and skills on the job and through short-term training programmes. Most have undergone the basic human processes personal growth laboratories. The HRD department has played a very proactive, productive and integrating role in the past and has done an excellent job in the last four years.

Strengths

A high level of competence of the HRD chief, a sleek organisational structure, a desire to learn and implement the various subsystems of HRD and participation and interest in all business activities of the company, particularly in the strategic planning process, form the strengths of the HRD department at Company B.

Weaknesses

The audit revealed that the HRD department suffers from an inadequate skill base. There is no well-trained second-level person with similar capabilities of the CEO in terms of leadership, dynamism and acceptability. Considering the future needs of the organisation, the HRD department has inadequate staff strength.

HRD System at Company B

A study of the HRD budget indicated that almost 60 per cent of it is allocated to training activities. Besides this, only two direct HRD activities, namely, role empowerment and climate survey, seem to be given prominence. There is considerable stress on TQM, manpower audit and strategic planning. The audit revealed the following strengths and weaknesses of individual HRD systems.

Career System

Strengths

The audit identified the following strengths of the HRD system:

- Manpower requirements are worked out by the department and divisions well in advance
- Recruitment has been made more systematic and uniform through centralisation and is carried out by the concerned divisions
- Top managers have demonstrated their commitment to search talent for the company and allot adequate time for this purpose
- There is increasing stress on developing internal talent to take on new responsibilities

- This company's staff may ideally be characterised as young in age, energetic, dynamic, adaptive and customer sensitive; this type of employee profile is ensured by the recruitment strategies

Weaknesses

The following lacunae were seen in relation to this system:

- The company has not carried out any long-term manpower-planning exercise
- Recruitment is done mainly on the basis of interviews; psychological tests and other devices are not used
- Career planning and succession planning have not been given the much-needed attention
- There is no system for potential appraisals either

Recommendations

The following were the recommendations to improve the HRD function:

- The recruitment system can be improved by training the interviewers on how to look for the right attributes during interviews and rate them. The candidates should be assessed for a service orientation
- The company should also undertake career planning for the 'high-fliers' as well as for those who do not show potential beyond their present roles
- Succession planning is urgently needed for some key roles in the company. With more expansion and diversification, both succession planning and identification of potential people to fill newly created positions will require priority attention
- The company has done an admirable job in reducing the 20 levels in the company to 12. The organisation may further be de-layered by reducing the 12 layers to four only. Each layer may have several grades. However, the designations may be restricted to only one of the following four: general manager, manager, executives and operators
- A potential appraisal system should also be introduced

Work-Planning System

The company has introduced a performance-planning review and development system for supervisory and managerial staff. It is divided into three modules: performance planning, performance review and performance development. The planning part aims at role clarity through communication of job responsibility and key result areas to the appraisee, integrating individual performance with that of the organisation and making planning participatory to get increased involvement of employees. The performance review module aims at increased communication between the appraisee and the appraiser. The development module aims at identifying the training and development needs of the employees for performing well their present as well as future roles.

Strengths

The PPRDS is well designed in response to a survey result that pointed out the need for increased communication. It was rightly assumed that PPRDS will serve as a tool for increased communication. The HRD department has put in considerable effort in introducing the system through a series of education and skill development programmes, particularly for the reporting and reviewing officers. The department also conducted a survey about the effectiveness of the system at the end of the first year and introduced appropriate changes. Its flexibility and desire to improve continuously is its strength.

Weaknesses

The following weaknesses were identified:

- Performance planning at the individual level needs a lot more skill and positive attitude on the part of the employees, particularly the reporting officers. The training presently given to the appraisers is not adequate to identify the key result areas and to conduct performance review discussions
- There is still some degree of confidentiality and lack of openness due to its linkage with rewards. Employees perceive biases in the rating process

Recommendations

The auditors made the following recommendations:

- The system should not be linked to rewards. The rating scale should be eliminated and instead the emphasis should be shifted to the processes of planning, analysis, communication and development
- The 16 factors included in the form should be reduced to a few critical factors. Every appraiser–appraisee pair should be given the freedom to identify the factors they consider as critical to the job being performed by the employee
- The managers should be trained in PPRDS skills and this training should be followed up annually with one-day renewal programmes until the system stabilises

• A much simplified version of the PPRDS can be extended to the staff

Development System

In Company B, training is one of the core activities of the HRD function. There is a Training and Development Centre (T&D Centre) that conducts technical training and managerial and skill development programmes.

Strengths

The T&D Centre is very well equipped with a good library and other facilities. It is headed by a highly motivated group of individuals. A large number of programmes are conducted and training is considered an important function in the company.

Weaknesses

The company does not have a long-term training strategy. It seems to be oriented towards quantity and not the quality of training programmes. Training needs are based solely on the data collected from the PPRD system. There is very little follow-up after the training, either by the department head or by the head of the training centre.

Recommendations

The auditors recommended the following:

• Adoption of a planned approach to training in terms of need analysis, faculty selection, organisation of programmes and follow-up
• Training of more competent internal faculty to be assigned to the T&D Centre for the technical skills development programme
• Provision of more training material, aids and equipment in the training centre
• To take care of expansions, careful consideration of future training needs in terms of location of the T&D Centre in a bigger campus, appointment of professional people to run the centre, expansion of the centre's scope of operations to include consultancy services, diagnostic services, research, etc.

Self-renewal System

Strengths

The company has demonstrated its commitment to the development of the self-renewal function by sending a large number of employees to programmes conducted by the Indian Society for Applied Behavioural Sciences (ISABS). Periodical surveys on organisational culture and climate have also been undertaken.

Weaknesses

The following weaknesses were identified:

- No work has been done on OD although the company recognised the need for it
- The results of surveys done so far have not been used for designing relevant interventions
- Attention has not been given to the development of OD competencies of the HRD staff

Recommendations

The auditors made the following recommendations:

- The HRD staff needs to be trained in various HRD competencies, including those required for designing self-renewal interventions
- Periodical survey results should be analysed and communicated to all the departments along with clear recommendations and action plans for improvement
- Special attention may be given to the socialisation of the new recruits in other divisions about the culture and values of the company

With increasing diversification and expansion of operations, a balance between decentralisation (due to various divisions) and coordination (integration into the company's culture) needs to be maintained

Culture System

The company has a healthy culture and a developmental climate.

Strengths

The company has a high level of trust and openness, family spirit, learning culture, quality service orientation, excellent crisis management, emphasis on initiative and creativity.

Weaknesses

The following are the weaknesses in the culture system at Company B:

- Low internal cooperation and collaboration
- Very low empowerment of the staff
- Inadequate reward system
- Inadequate dissemination and differing interpretation of personnel policies, though they are intrinsically sound

Recommendations

The auditors recommended the following action points:

- An abstract of the personnel policies should be given to all employees at the time of appointment
- Team rewards in addition to individual rewards for excellent performance can be considered

The auditors also observed that there were presently two units under one general manager to facilitate their integration. Though attempts have been made to achieve the objective of integration, such as visits of supervisors and operators from one site to the other, the exercise has not been successful. The auditors recommended that the general manager may be located at the corporate office to plan the future expansion and improvements in the present operations. The two sites may have deputy general manager-level persons to manage them. These can operate as two independent profit centres with some healthy competition. Task forces for various purposes may have members from both sides and staff-level inter-location visits may also be planned.

The Agenda for HRD

Considering the future plans of the company, the auditors foresee the following agenda for the HRD department.

The company has already set up another unit in Northern India. Since it has not been in this field earlier, it has to develop employee competencies afresh. Hence, as a part of its strategic plans, the company must be aware of the employee competencies required for setting up and running its new plant. The auditors suggested the recruitment of an HRD specialist with a technical orientation.

In another diversification plan, the company plans to set up 25 manufacturing and distribution plants in the next two years. With an estimated requirement of 50 persons per plant, the manpower requirements in the near future are estimated at about 1,250 persons. This will pose several challenges for HRD, such as recruitment, compensation and reward systems, retention, training, career planning, organisation self-renewal, etc.

Being a new business area with its own consequent industry culture, HRD faces the challenge of balancing the special identity and autonomy of the group with its integration into the main Company B.

HRD Audit as OD Intervention

A great deal of work has been done in India regarding the use of HRD audit as an OD intervention and is a unique feature of Indian organisations. The author's experience in initiating OD with the aid of HRD audit has shown the following results:

- The audit in several organisations resulted in establishing several organisational systems and processes such as potential and performance appraisal, career planning, training, mentoring. Performance appraisal and job rotation are the two most frequently affected changes
- In a few companies, it has resulted in the formulation of clear-cut policies, including promotion policy, communication policy, reward and recognition policy, etc.
- In other organisations, it seemed to have drawn their attention to issues like developing trust, collaboration, teamwork, quality orientation, etc.
- In a few others, it has resulted in more role clarity and direction to the employees in terms of their work leading to higher level of role efficacy
- In one of the organisations, when the audit started exploring future strategies, the top management team could not identify the future plans. They stated that the plans came from the multinational head office and they had no freedom in influencing the same. The revenue turnover from Indian operations was negligible, and therefore, the parent office paid little attention to the corporation. As a result, the top management could not communicate the future of the organisation clearly to the employees. This resulted in morale and motivation issues among employees, though of not a significant magnitude. The corporation has good practices and the employees were proud. On the basis of the HRD audit report, which indicated the difficulties in ensuring employee commitment without an appreciation of the future plans of the company, the top management team made it a point to negotiate and plan the future strategy and plans for the company

- In another company, the HRD audit indicated the need for developing locals as HRD managers and the need for reorienting the HRD systems to local culture. The company recruited an HRD manager on a short-term basis who designed a number of HR systems and also trained the local line managers in HRD. These systems were later integrated into TPM, ISO 9000 and similar practices

The above discussion indicates that HRD audit can provide valuable insights into a company's performance and is cost-effective in initiating improvements. While various methods like individual and group interviews, workshop, questionnaires and observation can be used as diagnostic tools, the success of the audit as an intervention depends on the efficiency of implementation in the post-audit phase.

HRD Audit Failures

There are at least two cases of HRD audit not resulting in anything. The HRD manager was very enthusiastic in getting the HRD audited. The audit report indicated a very poor state of HRD in the company. The staff competencies were rated as poor, the practices questioned and improvements suggested. The benchmarking data also indicated this company to be one of the poor performers in terms of HRD, though in terms of the profits, etc., the company was in the forefront and was facing competition. Although the audit started with an interview with the CEO, no opportunity was provided to the auditors to make a presentation to the CEO. As a result, the audit report did not receive any attention and the auditors considered the effort a waste.

In another company, the top management commissioned the audit but got busy with reorganisation of one of their critical marketing functions. In the process and due to market competition, all the energies of the top management and their HR staff got diverted to the new organisational structure, and they did not even have an opportunity to know the findings of the audit. The auditors felt that some of the audit findings directly relate to business improvements in terms of the very reorganisation they were planning. However, the auditors were not in a position to draw the attention of the top management. The effort did not result in any thing.

These two events make it clear that the success and the ROI on HRD audit depend heavily on the following in initiating and managing change:

- Genuineness of the interest of the top management in change and particularly their openness to criticism. If they only want to hear good things then HRD audit may not always help
- The power base of the HR chief. If the HR chief is operating from an 'Expert Power Base' than 'Political Power Base' of being close to the CEO and being seen as a 'nice person', HRD audit may not work
- Timing of the HRD audit. It should be done when the organisation is free of other preoccupations

- Presentation by the auditors at the end of the audit. The report itself and the way the report is handled. If the concern is only with getting the audit done and not with using the audit, the presentation of the audit report plays a critical role. If the presentation to top management does not take place for some reason, it probably signals the first step to failure. Then comes the presentation of the report itself. If it is too threatening and derogatory then the top management or the HR managers may not be interested in change

It is this consideration that has led to the formation of a new emphasis to HRD audit–strength-based HRD audit (SBHRD-A).

Strength-Based HRD Audit

Given this potential of HRD audit, how do we make it strength based. The following is a conceptualisation for SBHRD-A:

Assumptions

1. Every organisation has some form of HRD or the other; organisations are reasonably sensible enough to initiate and promote systems and practices that are appropriate for them at a given point of time
2. Most HRD interventions have evolved on the basis of the thinking and the necessity of the owners, promoters or trustees
3. The current HRD interventions are the bare minimum that are required and have been appropriate for the current situation
4. The current practices have enough strength that enabled them to sustain and improve the organisation
5. Any change has to be built on the existing strengths
6. It is the job of the auditor to find out the strengths of the current systems and practices and build the future on the basis of the same
7. By focusing on the weaknesses, the auditor may induct defences that may be not so functional in change management
8. All employees contribute to the audit in some form or the other
9. Seeing weaknesses in the current practices and bringing them out is seen as a strength and not a weakness

Methodology for SBHRD-A

The methodology of SBHRD-A is similar to the HRD audit described earlier. The principal difference is in underplaying the weaknesses and playing on the strengths. This means that all evaluations aim at looking for what exists and taking what exists as positive strengths. The objective is to use the positive strengths in deciding the next step so as to create more strength in a shorter period of time. Rather than making ambitious long-term plans, it devises action steps for changes to occur in the next few weeks or months. The following are the thoughts of the author on designing and implementing SBHRD-A. These could be treated as the proposed tenets of the SBHRD-A.

- SBHRD-A also focuses on line managers as change agents rather than HRD department as the change agent
- It shifts the ownership of the audit intervention to the line managers. The HRD manager works closely with the auditors. The auditors can be an internal team or an external consultant or a combination of both
- The SBHRD-A starts with first building on the strengths of the auditors
- The auditors place on table their own strengths and articulate the same
- The strengths of auditors are then enhanced if necessary through study and benchmarking visits
- It is only after the audit team is ready to audit they start the audit. The strengths of the auditors are circulated to all the members. The participation of all employees is ensured in the audit process
- The reports are presented in stages to groups of employees as the auditors gather the data, and feedback is used as a means of evolving implementable plans
- SBHRD-A starts with the systems that are strong in the company and builds on them rather than focusing on what is lacking. For example, any form of PMS could be taken as a strength, including the lack of system. The auditors extensively debate and discuss the strong points in the current state and build to improve rather than criticise the current state for improvement

Effectiveness of HRD Audit: An Empirical Study

Jomon (1998) conducted a research study to identify the factors influencing the use of audit as a change tool. He studied four organisations where HRD audit was conducted. These organisations were studied about three years after the first audit. This gave an understanding of the benefits accrued from HRD audit by evaluating the post-audit scenario. The aim of the research was to assess the influence of the following variables in the effective use of HRD audit:

- Organisational characteristics
- Profile of the HRD Department
- Competency levels of HRD department
- CEO's commitment towards HRD
- HRD chief's commitment towards HRD

Post-Audit Scenario: Organisation 1

Soon after the audit, the management held a number of meetings, and a final action plan was formulated. Although the action plan covered HRD at the policy-making level, at the operational and departmental level it contained a joint action plan for the HRD–training department. The reports as well as the plan were kept confidential. The following changes were brought about as a result of the audit exercise:

1. A well-established system to assess the potential of higher-level people based on key competencies
2. Promotion policy is now shared with everyone
3. Each employee is aware of his or her career path
4. Mechanisms to help employees plan their work efficiently have been set up; for example, employees are helped by their supervising officers in planning their work
5. Employees now go for training with a clear understanding of the knowledge and skills they are expected to acquire from training
6. Regular circulars and notices and bulletins give adequate information to the employees about the company, the market situation, the changes in the environment, etc.

Post-Audit Scenario: Organisation 2

This company has come a long way since the time when the audit was conducted. The situation three years after the audit exercise can be described in the following way:

1. Clear personnel policies, including promotions policy, communication policy, reward and recognition policy and many more
2. Team spirit at this company is of a high order as conveyed by the employees themselves
3. PPRD (prevention, preparedness and response to natural disaster) systems have been revamped. A well-structured feedback mechanism is in place now
4. KPAs provide role clarity and direction to the employees in terms of their work and role clarity is very high among employees
5. External training programmes are chosen carefully after collecting enough information about their quality and suitability
6. Action-oriented research is very well established and taken seriously and acted on

Post-Audit Scenario: Organisation 3

The first audit was conducted in 1993. A management council meeting was organised to discuss the strengths, weaknesses and the recommendations of the audit. Strategic issues related to HRD were also considered at this juncture. The status in 1997 (four years after audit) is presented as follows:

1. Manpower requirements for each department are identified well in advance
2. Key competencies have been identified and a system is in place for assessing the potential of people for higher-level responsibilities
3. Employees also participate and contribute to annual performance plans
4. KPAs provide role clarity and direction to the employees in terms of their work
5. A very high level of role efficacy exists as stated by the employees themselves
6. OD initiatives, research orientation, communication, empowerment and reward systems are yet to be established
7. The HRD staff, though inadequate in number, was considered highly competent

Post-Audit Scenario: Organisation 4

In this company some of the weaknesses highlighted by the HRD audit were as follows:

1. No potential appraisal system and an ad hoc performance appraisal system
2. No career-planning system
3. Lack of role clarity
4. Poor induction procedure
5. Absence of mentoring
6. High confusion and friction in values and approach
7. Lack of initiative and a mechanical approach to work
8. Human orientation was missing
9. Operators were treated badly
10. Personnel policies were not development oriented but discipline oriented

Once the HRD audit report was submitted, the HR chief called all the managerial staff for dinner and presented the findings. Based on the discussions, an action plan was drawn up, which after implementation brought about the following changes:

1. A well-established potential appraisal system and a systematic performance appraisal system
2. Career planning is done up to the executive level
3. Role clarity brought about through identification of KPAs
4. Systematic induction and training programme have been established
5. Initiation of mentoring
6. An increase in the level of trust among employees
7. High involvement of employees at all levels
8. Human orientation injected into the business process with opportunities for growth and development provided to all employees
9. Empowerment of operators through various mechanisms, and efforts made towards improving management–operator relationship
10. Integration of all HR-related activities, which now support developmental activities

The findings of a research study have been summarised as follows:

- There is a direct relationship between the CEO's commitment towards HRD and the effectiveness of the HRD function
- An interesting revelation was that in all four organisations, the CEO was rated higher than the HRD chief in commitment towards HRD. The reason for this could be that many communications announcing new ideas were signed by the CEO in order to convert them into practices and systems to be put into effect. This also ensured a greater acceptability by the members of the organisation
- There is also a direct relationship between the ratings of the HRD chief in commitment towards HRD and the effectiveness of the HR function
- The organisations with a highly competent HRD staff were able to derive much more benefit from the audit process resulting in a higher impact on the effectiveness of the HR function. In fact, in one company, though the HRD department was small and inadequately staffed, the utilisation of HRD audit and its effectiveness on HRD practices were high mainly due to the high competency level of the HRD staff

Summary and Conclusions

HRD audit was originally not intended to be an OD tool. By virtue of its diagnostic and participative methodology, it seems to work like an OD intervention. The interview methodology, its comprehensiveness, the audit methodology insisting on starting and ending with top management involvement – all have high potential for initiating change processes. It could be further refined as an OD tool. It involves all the HRD staff and a large number of managers in the audit process and makes them conscious of the areas needing improvements. HRD audit is needed for realigning and rejuvenating the HR function in any company. In the times to come, this is likely to gain momentum and become a good self-renewal tool for the HR function. Thus, it is congruent with the prime objectives of OD, that is, to foster the self-renewal capability of the organisation and enhance organisational effectiveness.

Effectiveness of HRD Audit: An Update

A large number of organisations got themselves audited for their HRD in some form or the other. While most of them have gone for comprehensive HRD audit, some of them have got only some of their subsystems audited. The following is a illustrative list of organisations that have gone for HRD audit or its subsystems in the last two decades and more. TVRLS has been conducting certified HRD Auditors programs in Malaysia and Sri Lanka and trained over 150 auditors in these countries.

Aditya Birla group	Gujarat Gas
Afprint, Nigeria, Chanrai Group	Gujarat State Petronet Ltd.
Aga Khan Foundation	Gujarat Gold Coin Ceramics
Alexandria Carbon Black	Gujarat Venture Finance Limited (GVFL)
AMP	Hindalco
Apollo Tyres	HPCL
Astra Zeneca	IBM
Bajaj Auto	IDBI Bank
BEL Bangalore	IFFCO
BFL Software	IL & FS
Bosch Rexroth	Indian Oil Corporation
BPCL	Indo Rama, Indonesia
BPL Ltd.	Interra IT
C-DOT	Kumaran Software Systems
Central Bank of India	Life Insurance Corporation of India
Centre for Environmental Education	Madras Refineries
ColorChem	Mafatlal Industries
Dr. Reddy's Laboratories	Mahindra & Mahindra
EID Parry (India) Ltd.	National Stock Exchange
FAG Bearings	National Stock Exchange-IT
Federal Bank	NDDB
Fluent India Ltd.	NIIT
Gati Cargo Management Services	NMDC
GMR	NOCIL
Godrej Hi-care	NTPC
Godrej Soaps	OIL India
Grasim Industries	Operational Research Group
Gujarat Cancer Hospitals	Reserve Bank of India (RBI)

(Continued)

State Bank of India
Swiss Development Corporation
Titan Industries Ltd
UniAbex Alloys
Uni Dendrite
UniDeritend

Uni Klinger
Vardhman Group
Waghbakri
Wockhardt Heart Care Institute
Wockhardt Pharmaceuticals

USE OF THE BOOK FOR AUDIT PROGRAMS AND APPRECIATION IN RECENT TIMES

A large number of Certified Auditors programs and Train the Trainer programs in HRD Audit are being conducted by T V Rao Learning Systems Pvt. Ltd. (TVRLS). Besides undertaking HRD audit themselves (among the organizations illustrated earlier) TVRLS is actively promoting *training of certified auditors*. Over eighteen such programs have been conducted in Asian countries: three in Malaysia, Five in Sri Lanka besides over a dozen in India in the last couple of decades. In order to give the advantage of training internal auditors including the non- HR managers, corporations are increasingly exposing their senior management of these organizations to HR Audit.

The author (Prof. T V Rao) taught HRD Audit as OD Intervention and Action Learning for two batches of Ph. D. Scholars of Assumption University, Thailand, Bangkok.

TVRLS conducted a Certified HRD auditors program for *Taylor's University in Malaysia*. Over 30 academic administrators participated in the same and used the methodology to reorient and rejuvenate their departments.

Two certified auditors programs were conducted in KualaLumpur. They are all equipped to HRD audit and facilitated by Malaysian Open University.

DOI: 10.4324/9781003530534-20

Some illustrative comments are given below:

"In HRD Audit, Rao Delivers both a broad description and intricate aspects of HRD and also brings specific examples of how audit fits the Indian organizations. This is a real how to guide for organizations, human resource professionals and front line managers seeking to improve broader business practices analysis"

(South Asian Journal of Human Resource Management
Journal Review, Amy Warren)

We are pleased that the very first certified HRD Auditors program conducted in Sri Lanka was able to attract very high profile HR practitioners. Going by the feedback we got from the participants, the program was an absolute success.

Rohita Amarapala, President IPM Sri Lanka.

"The Certified HR Auditor program is an important and valuable asset. It also helps to build capacity in our human capital which is an essential ingredient in managing growth and expansion," said CIPM Sri Lanka Chairman Standing Committee on Consultancy, Training and HR Services, Sarah Jayasinghe.

"CIPM Certified HRD Auditors program conducted with the help of TVRLS has produced 125 certified auditors. Those trained are making good impact"

Sri Lanka Mirror, 19 April 2019

This was the best program organised on HR Audit. This provides knowledge to develop audit with methodologies to audit our firms.

John Filler, Ceylon Electricity Board.

REFERENCES

Abdullah, Z., N. Ahsan and S.S. Alam. (2009). The effect of human resource management practices on business performance among private Universities in Malaysia. *International Journal of Business and Management*, 4(6), 65–72.

Abraham, E. (1989). *A Study of Human Resource Development Practices in Indian Organisations* (Unpublished doctoral dissertation). Ahmedabad: Gujarat University.

Agrawal, A. and T.V. Rao. (2022). *Leaders in the Making.* New delhi: Penguin Random House.

Agusioma, N.L., H.P. Gommans and M.K. Kihiko. (2014). A critical analysis of human resource management practices influencing performance in public universities *International Journal of Economics, Commerce and Management*, United Kingdom, 2(9), September, 1–25.

Arab, A.M. and M.O.S. Mahdi. (2018). Human resources management practices and organizational excellence in public orgnizations. *Polish Journal of Management Studies*, 9, 1–21

Arthur, J. (1994). Effects of human resource systems on manufacturing performance and turnover. *Academy of Management Journal*, 37, 670–687.

Atanu, T. (2016). Human resource policy, organizational culture and organizational effectiveness: A conceptual study. *International Journal of Business Management*, 4(10), October, 216–223

Bilmes, L., K. Wetzker and P. Xhonneux. (1997). Value in human resources. *Financial Times*, 9 February, 10.

Buller, P.F. and G.M. McEvoy. (2012). Strategy, human resource management and performance: Sharpening line of sight. *Human Resource Management Review*, 22, 43–56.

Caliskan, N.E. (2010). The impact of strategic human resource management on organizational performance. *Journal of Naval Sciences and Engineering*, 6(2), 100–116.

Chadwick, C., J.-Y. Ahn and K. Kwon. (2012). Human resource management's effects on firm-level relative efficiency. *Industrial Relations: A Journal of Economy and Society*, 51, 704–730.

Chand, M. and A.A. Katou. (2007). The impact of HRM practices on organ- isational performance in the Indian hotel industry. *Employee Relations*, 29(6), 576–594.

CIPD (2021). https://www.coursesonline.co.uk/everything-you-need-to-know -about-cipds-new-2021-qualifications/

Colakoglu, S., D.P. Lepak and Hong Ying. (2006). Measuring HRM effectiveness: Considering multiple stakeholders in a global context. *Human Resource Management Review*, 16, 209–218.

Delery, J.E. and D.H. Doty. (1996). Models of theorising in strategic human resource management: Tests of universalistic, contingency and configurational performance predictions. *Academy of Management Journal*, 39, 821.

Delery, J.E. and N. Gupta. (2016). Human resource management practices and organizational effectiveness: Internal fit matters. *Journal of Organizational Effectiveness: People and Performance*, 3(2), 6 June, 139–163.

Dr. Sundari, D. and P. Mounika. (2018). A study on HRD climate and its impact on employee engagement in Andhra Bank. *International Journal of Mechanical Engineering and Technology*, 9(5), 692–702. http://iaeme.com/Home/issue/IJMET?Volume=9&Issue=5.

Durlav, S. and S.M. Hussain. (2015). HRD climate survey at Bokaro steel plant, India using OCTAPAC factors: An empirical evidence. Management Today, 5(4), October–December, 165–168.

Friedman, B., J. Hatch and D.M. Walker. (1998). *Delivering on the Promise: How to Attract, Manage, and Retain Human Capital*. New York: Free Press.

Ganesh, S. (2004). *Competency-based HRM*. New Delhi: Tata McGraw-Hill.

Guest, D. and N. Conway. (2011). The impact of HR practices, HR effectiveness and a 'strong HR system' on organisational outcomes: A stakeholder perspective. *The International Journal of Human Resource Management*, 22(8), 1686–1702. http://dx.doi.org/10.1080/09585192.2011.565657.

Guthrie, J. (2001). High involvement work practices, turnover, and productivity: Evidence from New Zealand. *Academy of Management Journal*, 44, 180–192.

Huselid, M.A. (1995). The impact of human resource management practices on turnover, productivity and corporate financial performance. *Academy of Management Journal*, 38, 645.

Huselid, M.A. and B.E. Becker. (1997). *The Impact of High Performance Work Systems, Implementation Effectiveness, and Alignment with Strategy on Shareholder Wealth* (Unpublished paper; 18–19). New Brunswick, NJ: Rutgers University.

———. (2000). Comment on measurement error in research on human resources and firm performance: How much error is there and how does it influence effect size estimates? *Personnel Psychology*, 53, 835–854.

Ichniowski, C. (1992). Human resource practices and productive labour management relations. In D. Lewin, O. Mitchell and P. Sherer (eds), *Research Frontiers in Industrial Relations and Human Resources* (239–271). Madison, WI: Industrial Relations Research Association.

Johnson, R.H., A.M. Ryan and M.J. Schmit. (1994). *Employee Attitudes and Branch Performance at Ford Motor Credit*. Paper presented at the Ninth Annual Conference of the Society of Industrial and Organisational Psychology, Nashville, TN.

Jomon, M.G. (1998). *The Effectiveness of HRD Audit as an OD Intervention* (Thesis report submitted to the XLRI–AHRD doctoral-level fellow programme in HRD). Jamshedpur: XLRI.

Kaplan, R.S. and D.P. Norton. (1992). The balanced score card measures that drive performance. *Harvard Business Review*, January–February, 71–79.

————. (1993). Putting the balanced score card to work. *Harvard Business Review*, September–October, 134–147.

————. (1996). *The Balanced Score Card*. Boston, MA: Harvard Business School Press.

Katou, A.A. and P.S. Budhwar. (2007). The effect of human resource management policies on organizational performance in Greek manufacturing firms. *Thunderbird International Business Review*, 49(1), 1–35.

————. (2010). Causal relationship between HRM policies and organisational performance: Evidence from the Greek manufacturing sector. *European Management Journal*, 28(1), 25–39.

Khalid, G. and M.Z. Rehman. (2010). Impact of HRM practices on organizational performance. *NUML Journal of Management and Technology*, 16–27.

Khan, M.A. (2010). Effects of human resource management practices on performance optimization – an empirical study of oil and gas industry in Nigeria. *European Journal of Economics, Finance and Administrative Sciences*, 157–175.

Khandwalla, P.N. (1992). *Organisational Designs for Excellence*. New Delhi: Tata McGraw-Hill.

————. (1994). *Notes Circulated for the Workshop on Managing Excellence* (Mimeo). Ahmedabad: Indian Institute of Management.

Kim, J. (2010). Strategic human resource practices: Introducing alternatives for organizational performance improvement in the public sector. *Public Administration Review*, 70(1), 38–49. http://www. jstor.org/ stable/40469109. Accessed: 13–03–2016 11:04 UTC.

Koys, D. (2001). The effects of employee satisfaction, organizational citizenship behaviour, and turnover on organizational effectiveness: A unit-level, longitudinal study. *Personnel Psychology*, 54, 1101–1114.

Macduffie, J.P. (1995). Human resource bundles and manufacturing performance: Organisational logic and flexible production systems in the world auto industry. *Industrial and Labour Relations Review*, 48, 199.

Macduffie, J.P. and J.F. Krafcik. (1992). Integrating technology and human resources for high-performance manufacturing: Evidence from the high performance auto-industry. In T. Kochan and M. Useem (eds), *Transforming Organisations* (209–226). New York: Oxford University Press.

Masood, T. (2010). *Impact of Human Resource Management (HRM) Practices on Organizational Performance: A Mediating Role of Employee Performance* (Thesis submitted to the Department of Management Sciences, in partial fulfilment of the requirements for the degree of doctor of philosophy in management sciences). Islamabad, Pakistan: Mohammad Ali Jinnah University.

McClelland, D.C. and D.H. Burnham. (1976). Power is the great motivator. *Harvard Business Review*, 54(2), 100–101.

Moeller, A. and B. Schneider. (1986). Climate for service and the bottom line. In M. Venkatesan, D.M. Schmalansee and C. Marshall (eds), *Creativity in Services Marketing* (68–70). Chicago, IL: American Marketing Association.

Mohamad, A.A., May-Chiun Lo and Maw King La. (2009). Human resource practices and organizational performance. Incentives as moderator. *Journal of Academic Research in Economics*, 1(2), 229–244.

Mukhtar, U., S. Siengthai and S. Ramzan. (2011). Mediating role of HRM in organizational conflict and impact on organizational effectiveness: Empirical evidence of Pakistan public universities. *International Journal of Business Management and Economic Research*, 2(6), 391–403, ISSN 2229–6247.

Nagabrahmam, D. (1980). *Adoption of Management Systems in Indian Organisations* (Fellow programme dissertation in management). Ahmedabad: Indian Institute of Management.

Nair, N., N. Vohra, T.V. Rao and A. Srivastava. (2010). *HR Best Practices*. New Delhi: Steel Authority of India.

Ostroff, C. (1995). Human resource management: Ideas and trends in personnel. *CCH Incorporated*, 21 June, 356.

Pareek, U. and T.V. Rao. (1975). *Human Resources Function in Larsen & Toubro: A Consultancy Report* (Unpublished Consultancy Report 2). Ahmedabad: Indian Institute of Management.

———. (1981). *Designing and Managing Human Resource Systems*. New Delhi: Oxford & IBH.

———. (1992a). *Designing and Managing Human Resource Systems* (2nd ed.). New Delhi: Oxford & IBH.

———. (1992b). *HRD Audit of Indo-Gulf Fertilisers* (Unpublished Consultancy Report). Ahmedabad: Indian Institute of Management.

———. (1998). *Pioneering Human Resources Development: The L&T System*. Hyderabad: Academy of Human Resources Development.

Pfeffer, J. (1994). *Competitive Advantage through People: Unleashing the Power of the Work Force*. Boston, MA: Harvard Business School Press.

———. (1998). *The Human Equation: Building Profits by Putting People First*. Boston, MA: Harvard Business School Press.

Prahalad, C.K. (1999). The power of imagination: India's legacy and the path to the future. *Business Today*, 22 February, 115–119.

Quah, Jon S.T. (1993). *Human Resources Development of Four Asian Countries: Some Lessons for the Commonwealth Countries*. London: Commonwealth Secretariat.

Qureshi, T.M., A. Akbar, M.A. Khan and S.T. Hijazi. (2010). Do human resource management practices have an impact on financial performance of banks? *African Journal of Business Management*, 4(7), 1281–1288.

Rao, T.V. (1985). Integrated human resources development systems. In L.G. Goodstein and J.W. Pfeiffer (eds), *The 1985 Annual: Developing Human Resources (227–238)*. San Diego, CA: University Associates.

———. (1986). The supervisory and leadership beliefs questionnaire. In J.W. Pfeiffer and L.D. Goodstein (eds), *The 1986 Annual: Developing Human Resources* (111–116). San Diego, CA: University Associates.

Rao, T.V. (1990). *The HRD Missionary*. New Delhi: Oxford & IBH.

———. (1996). *Human Resources Development: Experiences, Interventions and Strategies*. New Delhi: SAGE Publications.

———. (2002). *Assimilation and Integration* (Unpublished Paper; Seminar on Assimilation and Integration). Ahmedabad: TVRLS (Cited in Rao, T.V. (2011). *Hurconomic*. New Delhi: Pearson Education).

———. (2008a). Lessons of experience: A new look at performance management systems. *Vikalpa*, 33(3), 1–15.

———. (2008b). *HRD Score Card 2500 Based on HRD Audit*. New Delhi: SAGE Response.

———. (2010). *A New Look at Performance Management systems for Organization Development*. Taipei: Summit on Globalisation of Human Capital.

———. (2011). *Hurconomics*. New Delhi: Pearson Education.

Rao, T.V. and U. Pareek. (1994). *HRD Audit Questionnaire*. Ahmedabad: Academy of Human Resources Development.

———. (1998). *HRD Audit Questionnaire* (Rev. ver.). Ahmedabad: T.V. Rao Learning Systems.

Rao, T.V. and R. Rao. (2000). *360 Degree Feedback and Performance Management Systems* (Vol. 1). New Delhi: Excel Publications.

Rawashdeh, A.M. and I.K. Al-Adwan. (2012). The impact of human resource management practices on corporate performance: Empirical study in Jordanian commercial banks. *African Journal of Business Management*, 6(41), 10591–10595.

Rotea, C.C., A.-N. Ploscaru, C.G. Bocean, A.A. Vărzaru, M.G. Mangra and G.I. Mangra. (2023). The link between HRM practices and performance in healthcare: The mediating role of the organizational change process healthcare, 11(1236). https://www.mdpi.com/2227-9032/11/9/1236.

Schmit, M.J. and S. Allscheid. (1995). Employee attitudes and customer satisfaction: Making theoretical and empirical connections. *Personnel Psychology*, 48, 521–536.

Schneider, B. (1991). Service quality and profits: Can you have your cake and eat it too? *Human Resource Planning*, 14, 151.

Schneider, B. and D.E. Bowen. (1985). Employee and customer perceptions of service in banks: Replication and extension. *Journal of Applied Psychology*, 70, 431.

Shabbir, M.S. (2014). The impact of human resource practices on employee perceived performance in pharmaceutical sector of Pakistan. *African Journal of Business Management*, 8(15), 626–632.

Sharma, C.K. and D. Basha. (1994). Public service providers—the challenge for HRD. In T.V. Rao, D.M. Silveira, R. Vidyasagar and C.M. Srivastava (eds), *HRD in the New Economic Environment* (163–169). New Delhi: Tata McGraw-Hill.

Singh, K. (2004). Impact of HR practices on perceived firm performance in India. *Asia Pacific Journal of Human Resources*, 42(3), 301–317.

Som, A. (2002). Professionalised HRD and sustainable performance in the context of economic liberalisation in India. In U. Pareek, A.M. Osman Gani, S. Ramnarayan and T.V. Rao (eds), *Human Resource Development in Asia: Trends and Challenges* (373–378). New Delhi: Oxford and IBH.

Teclemichael Tessema, M. and J.L. Soeters. (2006). Challenges and prospects of HRM in developing countries: Testing the HRM–performance link in the Eritrean civil service. *The International Journal of Human Resource Management*, 17(1), 86–105.

Thang, N.N. and T. Quang. (2007). Training and development in Vietnam. *International Journal of Training and Development*, 11(2), 139–149.

Tzafrir, S.S. (2006). A universalistic perspective for explaining the relationship between HRM practices and firm performance at different points in time. *Journal of Managerial Psychology*, 21(2), 109–130.

Ulrich, D. (1997b). *The Human Resource Champions: The Next Agenda for Adding Value and Delivering Results*. Boston, MA: Harvard Business School.

Ulrich, D. and D. Lake. (1990). *Organisational Capability: Competing from the Inside/Out*. New York: Wiley.

Ulrich, D., J. Younger, W. Brockbank and M. Ulrich. (2013a). *HR from the Outside In: Six Competencies for the Future of Human Resources*. New Delhi: Tata McGraw-Hill.

———. (2013b). *Global HR Competencies: Mastering Competitive Value from the Outside In*. New Delhi: Tata McGraw-Hill.

Welbourne, T. and A. Andrews (1996). Predicting performance of initial public offering firms: Should HRM be the equation? *Academy of Management Journal*, 39, 839–919.

Wright, P.M., T.M. Gardner and L.M. Moynihan. (2003). The impact of HR practices on the performance of business units. *Human Resource Management Journal*, 13, 21–36.

Wright, P.M., T.M. Gardner, L.M. Moynihan and M.R. Allen. (2005). The relationship between HR practices and firm performance: Examining causal order. *Personnel Psychology*, 58, 409–446.

Yeung, A.K. and B. Berman. (1997). Adding value through human resources: Reorienting human resource measurement to drive business performance. *Human Resource Management*, 36(3), 321–335.

INDEX

Printed in the United States
by Baker & Taylor Publisher Services